Doc

To Frank Huber M.D.
Best Wishes

[signature] M.D.

Doc

Memories from a Life in Public Service

OTIS R. BOWEN, M.D.

with William Du Bois, Jr.

Indiana
University
Press

BLOOMINGTON & INDIANAPOLIS

This book is a publication of

Indiana University Press
601 North Morton Street
Bloomington, IN 47404-3797 USA

http://www.indiana.edu/~iupress

Telephone orders 800-842-6796
Fax orders 812-855-7931
Orders by e-mail iuporder@indiana.edu

*The paper used in this publication meets the minimum
requirements of American National Standard for Information
Sciences—Permanence of Paper for Printed Library Materials,
ANSI Z39.48-1984.*

MANUFACTURED IN THE UNITED STATES OF AMERICA

Library of Congress Cataloging-in-Publication Data
Bowen, Otis R.
Doc : memories from a life in public service / Otis R. Bowen ; with William Du Bois, Jr.
p. cm.
Includes index.
ISBN 0-253-33767-4 (alk. paper)
1. Bowen, Otis R. 2. Politicians—Indiana—Biography. 3. Governors—Indiana—Biography.
4. Physicians—Indiana—Biography. 5. Indiana—Politics and government—20th century. 6.
Cabinet officers—United States—Biography.   I. Du Bois, William.   II. Title.

F530.22.B68 B69 2000
977.2'043'092—dc21
[B]
00-024321

2 3 4 5 05 04 03 02 01 00

*This book is dedicated to my own family and
to my working families in Indiana state government
and the U.S. Department of Health & Human Services.
Each of my families occupies a special niche
in my heart.*

ORB

Contents

Preface

Lurking in the back of my mind, I've had thoughts about writing my memoirs. However, I've been busy being retired. I'm also a bit wary of the idea, because I'm not certain that my life merits such treatment. Realizing how unusual it is for a physician to be involved in politics, government, and non-medical public service, I've now decided that I ought to share my experiences. Only my children, grandchildren, and great-grandchildren may be interested in the final result, but leaving a record for them is in itself a worthwhile endeavor. Since I'm 82 and had a cancerous kidney removed just before reaching 80, it's also obvious to me that I had better get with it.

These pages are not a last ego trip or an attempt to set the record straight or to expose, tattle on, or "get" anyone. (There are only a few people I will even politely criticize.) I have tried to record the moments in history through which I lived, make observations about governmental processes, remember those with whom I served or who impacted my life, and do that in a way that is a bit philosophical and humorous. What's here is my best effort to write a truthful account of what happened to a Hoosier who loved being a small-town physician, but saw politics and public service become his incurable disease.

This is an informal book, a personal account drawn from memory. For that reason, it has no bibliography or footnotes.

This book would have been impossible without the help of others. They include:

• Bill Du Bois of Greenwood. Bill did the necessary research to develop questions that would prod my memory, took me through a year-long series of interviews, and edited the transcripts of the interviews into this volume. He also checked my recollections against the facts when I was uncertain of them or could not recall the details.

• Becky Feldman, a retired Bremen teacher, who transcribed our interviews.

• Gordon Englehart of Indianapolis, who before retiring was the very able Statehouse correspondent for the Louisville *Courier-Journal*, and Fred McCarthy of Indianapolis, who before retiring headed the Indiana Manufacturers Association. Both read the draft manuscript and made many helpful suggestions.

• Those who helped with research for this book. These include Bowen Museum curator Dr. Stanley M. Taylor, a Bethel College professor emeritus of education and one of the college's original faculty members when it opened in 1947; Bethel College archivist Timothy Paul Erdel, a theological librarian and an assistant professor of religion and philosophy who maintains the Bowen Archives; Star Jarvis, Educational Resources Center coordinator at the Bowen Library; State Librarian C. Raymond Ewick; Andrea B. Hough of the State Library and her staff; and Dr. Gerald (Jerry) Handfield, Commission on Public Records director, and his Archives Division staff.

Otis R. Bowen, M.D.
Bremen, Indiana
June 1998

Doc

❧ I ❧

Family, Friends, and School

I WAS BORN on February 26, 1918, to Vernie and Pearl Irene (Wright) Bowen at the farm home of my paternal grandparents, John Pierce and Rebecca Jane (Hartman) Bowen, who lived north of the Tippecanoe River between Richland Center and Leiters Ford in Richland Township, Fulton County, Indiana. My understanding is that I weighed between seven and seven and a half pounds at birth.

When a few months old, I'm told, I had a severe case of whooping cough that raised questions about my survival. We now know that I lived, and I have concluded that there were no permanent ill effects.

My first childhood memory is the birth of my sister, Evelyn. I was two years old. I don't recall where my mother was, but I remember Dad shepherding my older sister and me around. When he made breakfast, I didn't like the boiled egg he prepared. I'm reputed to have been a "mama's baby," so that probably accounts for my protest.

Another early memory involves crocks of apple butter we were taking home from my Uncle Leo and Aunt Alice Norris's place. We were in our family car's back seat, the crocks on the floor in front of us. My father says I fell asleep, awoke with a start, and put one of my new red shoes through the paper covering on a crock. Forever after, Aunt Alice teased me for saying, "I stepped in the apple butter."

My light-colored hair and freckles may be why my great-uncle, Daurcy S. Smith, husband of Berdelia (Della) Rush, my Grandma Wright's sister, called me "towhead."

I can't explain why I recall these isolated episodes and facts but remember nothing else until I started school at age five.

The Bowens are a typically American mixture of Welsh, English, Irish, German, and other nationalities. My roots run deep in Fulton County. Constant Bowen (1781–1843) and his wife, Sarah (Hill) Bowen (1799–1849), my paternal great-great-grandparents, came to Fulton County at least two years before the Potawatomi Indians were removed west. Two sets of maternal great-great-great-grandparents, Jeremiah and Achsah Ormsbee and Joseph and Mary (Horn) Robbins, came to Fulton County in the 1830s. Many other ancestors came there before 1850.

Dad was just plain Vernie. He had no middle name. I always thought Grandma and Grandpa Bowen ran out of names or lost interest when they got to Dad, who was their fifteenth child. After graduating from high school in 1915 at age 17, Dad attended a six-week Valparaiso University summer course. That fall, he taught all eight grades in a one-room school for $2.50 a day. He was the janitor and nurse and carried in wood for the stove and water for drinking. For that extra work, he received another 10 cents a day.

To keep his teaching permit, Dad attended "summer school" at Manchester College and Valparaiso University for seventeen straight years and took courses by correspondence. His studies took him away for six weeks each summer. We lived on a small farm most of that time. In his absence, Mom and I (and, to a lesser degree, my older sister) tended our big garden and did the chores. As a high school sophomore, I attended Dad's college graduation. He later worked on his master's degree.

Dad started teaching in one-room rural Fulton County schools, including Germany Station, District 11, and "Dead Man's College," so called because it was on the site of an old cemetery. He later taught at Kewanna (1920–24) and Fulton (1924–34) in Fulton County; Francesville in Pulaski County (1934–36); Crown Point in Lake County (1936–41); and McKinley, Roosevelt, Washington, and Riley schools in East Chicago, Lake County (1941–51). In 1952, he bought the Village Hardware in Leiters Ford in Fulton County, intending to retire from teaching. Local officials needed a math and shop teacher and persuaded him to return to the classroom at Leiters Ford, where he taught until 1958. In forty-three years of teaching, Dad touched thousands of lives in a positive way as a teacher, coach, and counselor, and through his involvement in the communities where he lived.

Back then, teaching was no easy job. At Fulton, Dad taught five subjects and coached the school's basketball teams—the boys' varsity, second team, and seventh- and eighth-grade teams and the girls' teams. In the spring, he coached baseball. He even swept out the gym. When players had no way home, Dad took them. (While doing that once, Dad ran over a skunk. His player trapped animals for fur and insisted on retrieving the dead animal. He smelled of skunk for a week. Dad had a tinge of skunk odor, too.)

Dad was firm and strict but fair. I don't recall spankings, but probably got a few taps. (Dad said that if I ever got a spanking at school, I could expect a second one at home. Luckily, I never did.) Dad was the family disciplinarian and Mom the balm who kept us children at peace with each other. Dad was indulgent to a point, then "explained" what he expected. My lasting images of him are of a beloved and admired teacher. He loved sports but was too busy for fishing or other diversions. Totally honest himself, he instilled that value and those of hard work and thrift in us.

To augment his meager teaching income so he could feed and clothe us, Dad took the toughest farm jobs, stacking straw from the threshing machine and mowing back hay at a time when it wasn't baled. The hardest-working farmers gladly paid someone else to do these dusty, dirty, choking jobs.

A master carpenter, cabinetmaker, and woodworker, Dad made a pulpit, lectern, and communion table, all with fancy carving, for a Crown Point church. He created beautiful candlestick holders for his children and grandchildren, a masterpiece cradle for a grandson's newborn child, end tables, and wooden bowls.

My mother was the daughter of George Wright and his wife, Sarah Eleria Rush, of near Tiosa, a crossroads village near Talma, Richland Center, and Leiters Ford in Fulton County. My youngest sister, Sarah Jane, got her first name from Grandma Wright and her middle name from Grandma Bowen. Mom was a quiet, hard-working, uncomplaining, always encouraging, and ever-protecting angel. She appreciated it when we helped with dishes or yard work without being asked. An excellent cook, she made tasty dishes from vegetables we grew and the strawberries, cherries, and peaches we picked. Except for chicken and side meat or fish I caught, meat dishes were not plentiful.

An excellent seamstress, Mom made her own and many of my sisters' dresses. Her housecleaning was as good as any. I didn't like such work, but I helped her with spring cleaning, when rugs had to be hung on a clothesline and whipped with a rug beater and curtains had to come down to be laundered, ironed, and re-hung.

Our life had its routine. Sundays were for church and visiting grandparents. Mondays were wash days. We used washboards and a hand-cranked wringer and hung the clothes outside. On Tuesday, we dampened and rolled up the clothes for ironing on Wednesday. I don't recall special Thursday or Friday duties except garden or yard work.

Saturdays were for baths, haircuts, and baking. Mom saw that we took weekly baths in a wash tub filled with water heated by the sun in a woodshed. She cut our hair—my dad's, my brother's, and mine. Using only egg whites, keeping the yolks for noodles, she baked angel food cake from scratch. When she baked devil's food cakes, she warned us not to roughhouse because her cake would fall. Inevitably, with our encouragement, some did. Then we got thicker fudge icing—sometimes a half-inch thick, like a good piece of candy.

Like Dad, Mom taught us thrift, honesty, and the value of work. She added a certain gentleness and consideration for others. She gave us tender, loving care, sacrificing things she needed so that her kids could be better dressed or more content.

My oldest sister was Esther. Then I came along. Next were Evelyn, my brother, Dick, and my baby sister, Sarah Jane. Dick passed away in 1991 from colon cancer. Esther (Bowen) Plain, Evelyn (Bowen) Amacher, and Sarah Jane (Bowen) Scandling are in pretty good health. Esther lives in Munster. Sarah Jane, a retired nurse whose husband, Lee, passed away in 1998, lives in South Bend. Evelyn, who has lived by herself for forty-five or fifty years, resides in Kouts.

My brother and sisters were the best. I had no favorite, but I probably neglected Evelyn, the "in-between" child. Our relationships were no different than those of other groups of siblings. We had spats and quarrels, but defended each other against outsiders.

I recall sitting in an easy chair, feverish, with warm cloths on my neck and cheeks because they were swollen from the mumps. Dick, about two then, looked up at me and said, "Oleo, how you are?" His question showed his concern, but for the rest of his life he was reminded about how he had phrased it and how he had mispronounced my name.

We worked together a lot—especially in the pickle patches, which provided needed income for the family. We planted, hoed, weeded, and dusted for pickle bugs, then did the backbreaking work of picking. Every other day, we were in the patch at dawn, picking pickles until we left for school at 7:30. After school, we went back to finish.

The top pickle grades were small and just a little larger. A first-class pickle had to be perfectly straight. Other grades were nubbins ("nubs"), crooked pickles ("crooks"), pickles that had grown beyond first-class size after we missed them two days earlier, and cucumbers, the largest size. Dad sorted and separately sacked each grade. We filled our Model T's back seat with sacks and stacked them on both fenders and over the hood. We must have looked like Okies or the Beverly Hillbillies chugging along to the Heinz Pickle Company's receiving station at Fulton. There, sharp-eyed graders invariably found fault with Dad's sort. Pickles with a slight crook, one end a bit bigger than the other, or a fraction of an inch longer than allowed got a lower grade—and we got a lower price.

We first lived at Kewanna. As Dad accepted new teaching positions, we moved to Fulton and then to Francesville. After I went to college, my parents moved to Crown Point and East Chicago. In Kewanna, we lived in two rented homes. In Fulton, we lived in four different rented homes, two on farms and two in town. We loved and wanted to stay on the farms, but the owners needed their places. Our last Fulton home had indoor plumbing. So did the one at Francesville, the best house in which we lived in my youth.

When we lived out of Fulton, we kids slept upstairs. About five o'clock one morning, I smelled smoke and roused my parents. In the center of the room, fire was coming up around a big register. Dad ran across the fire to the phone and dialed the operator. (Everyone was on a party line then, and an operator handled all calls.) The fire was spreading fast enough that Dad broke the bedroom window so we could get out.

The town's sidewalks came to the other farm. My sisters and I used a coaster wagon to deliver milk to a few customers at five cents a quart.

One year I had a 4-H hog, the next a calf. The hog was a beautiful, spoiled, tame Chester White. I named the Hereford steer Ted. At the fair, I won second with the hog, third with Ted. Dad let me raise five more Chester Whites. I kept track of feed and other expenses. When the hogs weighed about two hundred pounds, we sold them for $10 each. Feed for each had cost about $11. Dad absorbed the loss. I learned about the risks of farming and came face to face with the fact that we were in a depression.

In my early years, I don't remember anything remarkably mischievous. When I was 2 or 3, I'm told, my older sister boosted me up onto a woodshed roof, then got up herself. Our mother got us down safely. I once wandered out of our yard and down a railroad track. A neighbor brought me back. These escapades occurred at Loyal, called Germany Station until World War I. Loyal no longer exists.

When I was 10 or 11, I fell out of our haymow, breaking my arm. I went to Dr. Frank C. Dielman alone. His son held my upper arm while the doctor pulled on my hand and manipulated the bone. He then put it in a yucca board splint.

Blessed with compatible, understanding, caring, and loving parents, we had a very good home. Mom and Dad didn't show their love and caring publicly, or even much at home, but it was there and we knew it. Although poor, we were content and happy and not really envious of better-fixed families. We didn't want or need much. There was nothing complicated about my parents' way of life. They survived the Depression without panic, by hard work and careful monitoring of their means.

Despite his life of unrelenting hard work, serving, and giving, or because of it, Dad lived to age 85 and was in good health until his last six weeks. He spent those weeks in Rochester's Woodlawn Hospital after a stroke involving the medulla, the lower part of the brainstem, left him unable to move or speak. A feeding tube down his throat caused fluids to accumulate, necessitating a suction tube that irritated him immensely. He understood us, but could communicate only by blinking his eyes. Mom stayed with him in the daytime. She had to rest at night, so we sat with him then. Occasionally Rose sang softly to him, and that had a soothing effect.

When we were alone one night, I said to him, "Dad, I'm so thankful for you and so grateful for all you taught and showed me. I would never have been able to accomplish the things I have without you." I know I didn't imagine the way his eyes lighted up and the faint but very visible smile that came to his face. His response told me that he understood what I said and knew that I meant every word of it.

Dad passed away on July 13, 1983. This reflection on my father's life, written by editor William Freyburg, appeared in the Rochester *News-Sentinel* of July 22, 1983:

> After 43 years on the job, a man could look forward to a slower pace and the good life of retirement. And if those four decades had been spent as a public school teacher, as was the case with Vernie Bowen, the man could feel he had left his mark in having touched the lives of countless people over the years. But Bowen, who died last week at the age of 85, did not retire

when he left his teaching career. And his influence over others did not cease, either. For another 25 years, Vernie Bowen continued to take an active part in the world about him—and to make a difference.

When he gave up teaching in 1958, he chose to remain in the tiny town of Leiters Ford, where he had taught for six years. For the next 13 years, he devoted full time to the Village Hardware Store which he had purchased seven years previously. But that was not all he did in his "retirement." Bowen was a trustee of Aubbeenaubbee Township for four years. He was an active member of the Leiters Ford Merchants Association, a variation of a chamber of commerce. He was a Sunday School teacher at the Leiters Ford United Methodist Church for several years. Truly, Vernie Bowen was a person of consequence long before he became known statewide as the father of one of the most popular political figures in Indiana history.

It was the father who administered the oath of office when his son, Otis R. Bowen, became the first Indiana governor since 1851 to be elected to a consecutive four-year term. It was because of Vernie Bowen and his wife Pearl that the little town of Leiters Ford managed to have the governor of Indiana crown its Strawberry Festival queen five consecutive years.

But the difference that Vernie Bowen made extended beyond his hometown. Fulton County's modern hospital exists today partly because of this unassuming, quiet man with a reputation for integrity and good sense. For 14 years, he was a member of the Woodlawn Hospital board of trustees. He was in the forefront of the effort to upgrade this county's health care facilities. It was not an easy task to bring the dream of a new hospital to fruition. Indeed, the first attempt failed. But Bowen and other members of the hospital board were determined that this county should have adequate facilities for the care of the ill and the injured. And the ultimate success of this determination was due in no small part to the fact that some people felt that "if Vernie thinks it's a good idea, it must be the thing to do."

For this, as well as for all the other contributions made to improving the quality of life wherever he resided, we say, "Thanks, Vernie."

Mom remained home in Leiters Ford after Dad's death. My sisters stayed with her for a few weeks. She was her old sweet self except for her deep grief over the death of her husband, to whom she was married almost sixty-eight years.

In the fall of 1984, she went to a doctor with abdominal pain, but got no relief. After a trip to Leiters Ford, I convinced her to come to Indianapolis and stay with my wife Rose and me. As a professor at the IU Medical Center, I had access to specialists.

A gastroenterologist, Dr. Philip A. Christiansen, admitted her to University Hospital. Her problem was diagnosed as an abdominal abscess from a perforated diverticulus. Dr. Jay L. Grosfeld, University's chief surgeon, removed a segment of her colon and put her on antibiotics. She soon was sitting up, taking steps, and doing so well that Rose and I felt we could go to a dinner theater.

When we got back, I returned a call from Dr. William L. Hilde-brand, a Department of Family Medicine colleague, and learned that Mom had suffered a cardiac arrest. A code blue—an emergency call for all doctors and nurses—brought them to her room. They revived her, got her lungs working and her heart beating with defibrillators, and took her to an intensive care unit.

When I went there, I found her aware of her surroundings but "tethered" to a tube, about the circumference of a thumb and anchored in her trachea. It was necessary to prevent anything from blocking her breathing and to keep her from aspirating food or anything in her mouth. In great misery in her throat, she couldn't talk. It was several days before the pulmonologist removed the tube.

Mom survived, but it would have been better had she not. During her cardiac arrest, she was without oxygen for a critical three to five minutes, causing major brain damage that left her mentally like an in-fant. Soon transferred to a Plymouth nursing home, she was placed at my request under the care of Dr. Kent Guild. She remained there until her death three years later.

It was a miserable time for her. She talked as if her husband were alive. She thought her kids were small or babies. She begged Rose and me to take her home, telling us she would be a good girl and stay in the corner of the room. She got out of bed, went to other patients' rooms, and took things, swearing they were hers. She fought restraints and struck at other patients. She fell out of bed and broke her arm. On walks, we had to watch every step because she would walk away. This was a far cry from my sweet, gentle mother, and it was devastat-ing to see her that way. We were tempted to take her home, but bet-ter judgment told us we just couldn't watch her every minute of ev-ery day.

Later she developed what—because of bleeding from the bowels—I felt was cancer. She passed away peacefully on November 20, 1987. We all were saddened and yet relieved.

My sisters and brother never hinted that I should have stayed at her side, but for me the question remains: If I had been in her room that evening, could I have seen the emergency and gained a vital minute or two to protect her brain?

Losing my parents was hard. Before letting go, it's human to revisit what happened and, with the advantage of hindsight, review what we did or did not do. That changes nothing. In the end, we realize that we should celebrate the fact that our parents lived long and useful lives and gave so much to us and others.

To return to my childhood years, I was blessed by the fact that my two sets of grandparents lived near us. They also were very special.

Grandpa and Grandma Bowen were simple, salt of the earth, deeply religious people. They were very poor, but didn't know it. Both were up in years when I was growing up. I probably was their favorite grandson because I was the oldest son of their youngest son, was born in their home, and stayed with them more often than the other grandchildren.

There was no electricity in rural areas then. For morning chores, Grandma and Grandpa Bowen used lanterns. At night they used Coleman lamps. They used a windmill to pump water when the wind was up. When it was not, they pumped water by hand for the livestock and to use in the house. They had no indoor plumbing. They kept a little chamber pot under their bed to use at night. A wind-up Victrola was their only "luxury." They had only five or six records, but I played and replayed them.

I stayed with Grandma and Grandpa Bowen often and at least two to three weeks each summer. I learned to milk cows, gather eggs, and run the cream separator. In my early years, I got in their way more than I helped, but they were patient and tolerant. Grandma usually bought me candy when the huckster came along. I fished in a nearby creek, using a bent pin on a string tied to a long stick. I drove old Maude, their only horse, an old gray mare we hitched to a spring-seat wagon. Grandma and Grandpa Bowen also had a collie dog with which I played continually.

In my mind's eye, I still see Grandpa Bowen, sitting on the porch of their old clapboard house, chewing tobacco and hitting a spittoon from at least six feet away. (Grandma didn't let him chew in the house.) I also have images of Grandpa singing "In the Garden," "The Old Rugged Cross," and "Amazing Grace." At their small church, about a mile from their home, he was the Sunday school superintendent and song leader. When I stayed with them, we walked there on Sundays.

Grandpa's sixty-acre farm was all hills and low-ground muck. The hills eroded all the time. When it rained, the muck was too deep to drive Maude and the wagon through. Grandpa rented the farm for a meager amount. The rest of my grandparents' small income came from hand-milking eight to ten cows twice a day and separating and selling the cream. A truck picked up the cream every other day, so it was kept in milk cans in cold water to prevent souring. Skim milk was fed to the pigs, but Grandma made great cottage cheese from some of it. Cream was kept back to churn butter, which took thirty to forty-five minutes of pulling up and down on the paddle in a deep wooden churn. I helped with that.

Grandma was a short lady, and her hands were so deformed with arthritis that I never understood how she could milk cows, but she did. Helping her wean calves was fun. She wrapped a rag tightly around her finger (or just used the finger), put two inches of skim milk in a bucket, put the calf's mouth in the milk, and put the rag or her finger in the calf's mouth. The calf sucked up the milk, and in a few days it started drinking from a pail.

She often served us corn mush and milk, not because that was all they could afford, but because they liked it and, I thought, because they couldn't chew well with their ill-fitting false teeth. You don't have to chew mush much!

Grandpa and Grandma Bowen had a big garden, but Grandma did most of the work. We enjoyed being there because something was always in season—tomatoes, sweet corn, strawberries, raspberries, or melons. While staying with them, I recall a snow on May 7th, just after the garden was up and doing well.

We always spent Thanksgiving and New Year's Day there. Since my grandparents were up in years, my aunts and uncles gathered on Thanksgiving to do their butchering and on New Year's Day to cut firewood so they had meat and firewood for the worst months of winter. It was interesting to watch hams being salted and put in the smokehouse and to see sausage, lard, and chitlings made.

Held annually at the home of one of the Bowen children, our family reunions featured mountains of food and occasional entertainment, usually a little corny. When I was 9 or 10, my older sister, Esther, and I played a piano duet at the reunion. It was scary, but Mom and Dad urged us to do it. The Bowens also pitched horseshoes and played ball games. Cousin John Bowen, who was my age, and I explored haymows and haystacks and checked out the livestock.

At the reunions, I saw lots of cousins, aunts, and uncles. Of Grandpa and Grandma Bowen's fifteen children, thirteen lived to be adults. Each reproduced heavily except my Uncle Ray, from whom I got my middle name. The fourteenth child, Uncle Ray was overseas in the Army in World War I when I was born. My Dad, the fifteenth child, had nieces and nephews older than he was. There were so many aunts, uncles, and cousins that I never knew many of them well. We were closest to my father's brothers and sisters nearest his age—Uncle Clem Bowen, who married Marie Bayless; Aunt Rose Bowen, who married Clem Miller; and Uncle Sam Bowen, who married Lena Perkins.

Married nearly sixty-three years, Grandma and Grandpa Bowen died nine days apart. Ill with heart problems, Grandma stayed her last few weeks with Aunt Lena, a practical nurse, and Uncle Sam. She died on a Thursday evening. The funeral was on Sunday. We took Grandpa home to Francesville. He went to bed and soon died. We believe he decided he didn't want to live with his wife gone. Then a high school senior, I was a pallbearer with several cousins for both funerals.

Grandma and Grandpa Wright also were wonderful grandparents. Grandpa Wright was a country mail carrier. His steady job meant that they were a little better off than our other grandparents. Because of that, they could buy Christmas presents for each of us. We always had Christmas at their house.

A gentle and quiet man, Grandpa Wright played cards and dominos with us. In addition to a card game called Casini or Casino, he loved croquet so much that he had a section of yard plowed up, smoothed, and planted with a special variety of grass. It was the best croquet lawn I've ever seen.

He purposely allowed a small horse tank to get low every time we were coming, then always gave me a quarter for pumping it full of water. He used his two horses and a buggy to deliver mail. I played a lot with my grandparents' dog, Nib.

Grandpa Wright always had a watermelon patch. One summer, I picked one of his biggest melons. It was still green. Grandpa then taught me how to tell when a melon is ripe. You thump it and then thump the toe of a shoe. When the two thumps sound the same, that melon is ripe. Grandpa also taught me that once the stem attaching a melon to the vine begins to curl and separate, the melon is plenty ripe.

Grandpa Wright smoked heavily and died far too early, at about 67, I believe.

Grandma Wright was a cheerleader type who made the best fried chicken dinners and homemade ice cream I ever ate. My older sister, Esther, was her favorite, probably because she was the oldest daughter of Grandma Wright's only living daughter. Grandma wanted each grandchild to have one thing special. When I was about 12, she took me to a Rochester jewelry store and bought me a gold ring with a beautiful big ruby. It cost $10. Today, it's probably worth $300 or more. I still have it and still wear it.

In Fulton, one of my closest friends was Paul Waltz, the child of divorced parents who lived across the street with his grandparents. His grandfather had a farm a mile out of Fulton. We spent days there, riding a horse, playing in the horse tank, and helping with chores. We stood on a rafter in the haymow, turned somersaults, and landed in the hay several feet down. One time I didn't get over far enough, and I landed on my head and neck. My neck was so stiff and sore that I had to turn my whole body to look to the side or back. Luckily, I had no spinal cord injury.

We rode to and from the farm in Grandfather Waltz's small pickup truck. Chugging up a hill into town, we jumped off the back and ran, holding the tailgate. One time when I couldn't keep up, I held on and finally managed to pull myself back into the truck bed. Cars coming from the rear made this a dangerous thing to do.

Another best friend was Bobby Louderback. His dad was a fast and reckless driver. The father's driving took Bobby's life when he was about 6 or 7, and I lost a friend.

Reflecting on my childhood, I realize I was born at a good time, under circumstances that made me a better person. I feel fortunate that I lived in and near small towns. There was a feeling of stability there that would have been missing in bigger cities.

I began school at age 5. My older sister Esther escorted me the first day. My father claimed that when a neighbor asked me, "are you starting school?" Esther quickly answered, "Yes, if the teacher can handle him."

School was easy and pleasant. Final exams determined if we were to be promoted. In the fourth, fifth, and sixth grades, I made such good grades all year that I didn't have to take finals. I used this extra day to roller-skate. A crabby neighbor named Hiram Rouch, sitting on his front porch, growled so loudly as I skated up and down the sidewalk that I went elsewhere.

Playing ball one day with Wilbur Rouch (no relation to Hiram), I accidentally threw a ball through a window of his home. His parents had several children and were poorer than the Bowens, which made them pretty poor. I confessed to Mom and Dad, went to my iron elephant piggy bank, took all I had ($1.50), and gave it to Mrs. Rouch. She reluctantly took it. In grade school, I took piano lessons, a bore when there were ballgames to be played or fish to be caught. I'm grateful for the lessons, because what I learned remains with me, and I still play, strictly for my own enjoyment.

I walked to school most of the time. The distance was short except in the ninth and tenth grades, when we lived a mile and a half from school and usually rode the bus.

The school year began in early September and ended in mid-April, a calendar that recognized that farm boys were needed in the fields.

School days lasted from 8 A.M. to 3:30 P.M. We brown-bagged lunches. In the early years, we gulped them down so we could go to the playground. In ninth to eleventh grades, those of us on the basketball team practiced free throws. I hit eight of ten regularly, with an occasional ten of ten. On rainy days, we crowded into the gym at lunch. We even boxed for entertainment. Small for my age and short, I got cuffed around by boys who were my age but much bigger.

The Kewanna, Fulton, and Francesville schools were small brick buildings with wooden floors, cracker-box gyms, and small playgrounds. In September and April of some years, they were as hot as could be. The gyms seated 150 to 200 and were jammed for games. Schools were the center of small-town social activities. Consolidation meant that towns like Grass Creek, Metea, Twelve Mile, Lucerne, and Kewanna later lost schools and population and seemed to decline.

Desks were the usual—all in a row, with seat and desk in one piece. If one was so inclined, it was easy to pull the hair of a girl sitting in front of you. We had no projectors, computers or calculators then—just pens, pencils, chalk, and blackboards.

My fifth-grade teacher, Harold Clevenger, a fun-loving, caring teacher, had a great impact on me. Only five feet, two inches tall, he was the basketball scorekeeper and close to Dad, who was the coach. I got to go to all the games, even away ones, with Dad and the team in the school bus. Mr. Clevenger also rode with the team, so I got to know him well. In the summer after fifth grade, he hired me to work on his folks' farm, hand-replanting field corn that hadn't germinated the first time. Probably because I never knew them, I can't remember the first names of most of my elementary teachers. However, I remain grateful to:

• Mrs. Kline Reed, my second grade teacher, who drilled and drilled us on phonics. It was boring then but very helpful in future years.

• Frank Graham, my stern but good sixth-grade teacher. He lived on a small farm at the edge of Fulton and had cattle. At a young age, I helped him do chores. When his daughter Virginia, then about two or three, fell into a horse tank, I pulled her out, and Mr. Graham was grateful. Another time, however, I left a cornfield gate open. His cattle went through it and would have foundered on green corn had my carelessness not been quickly rectified. Mr. Graham was not pleased, and he let me know it.

In the third grade, the high school needed someone to play Peter Rabbit in an operetta. Chosen for the "role," I got to sing a couple of songs. Surprisingly, it went well.

Dad was my most influential high school teacher. He taught me algebra, geometry, manual training (later called shop), mechanical drawing, and physical education, and he coached the basketball and baseball teams on which I played. He was a tough teacher. Any student had to earn an "A" to get one from him, but it was tougher if you were his son. He wanted no one to claim that he had pets. Dad never pushed me to get high grades, but he always encouraged me to work hard as a student.

Dad didn't put up with classroom foolishness. He believed in discipline. His move back to Leiters Ford came after students began carrying switchblade knives and other weapons to class in East Chicago. Wanting no part of that, he decided to retire, although—as noted—he taught several more years at Leiters Ford.

The Crown Point school board did not rehire teachers eligible for tenure. When Dad got to that point, the board let him go. Students marched through town and demonstrated in Dad's behalf. I heard about the situation on the radio while in medical school. Dad's students often thanked him at commencements for guiding them in the right direction and teaching them well.

Charlie Cline, our class sponsor, was a favorite teacher (or perhaps I should say a favorite among favorites). Each morning, we had a twenty-minute homeroom with him. He was a futurist. I remember his prediction that we would one day sit in our living rooms and watch events taking place thousands of miles away. Many years later, TV made that possible. Charlie taught Latin. I didn't like the subject, but I needed a foreign language for college. Latin was all that was available. I'm glad I took it and a college course, "Greek and Latin Derivatives," because many medical terms come from these languages.

On his farm five miles out of town, Charlie let us have a couple acres for our truck patch. We planted half in pickles and half in potatoes and other vegetables. Knowing about our family's meager income, I'm certain that Mr. Cline charged us no rent. He even plowed the ground. We tried to repay him with work like hauling manure, pitching the stuff onto a wagon and pitching it off in the fields. Once, when I was going to the pickle patch, Charlie's cantankerous ram butted me.

Mrs. Cleo Teeter, my high school English teacher, was an excellent instructor. She was strict, but never showed anger, and she truly wanted us to learn.

My scariest time involving a teacher came in a physical education class when Dad collapsed on the gym floor. Dr. Dielman was called and arrived in minutes. By that time, Dad was sitting up, although in a cold sweat. Later, he told me the reason. He had been hit in his privates by an errantly served volleyball.

I don't think I had any bad teachers. Some were stern and I feared them, but all were fair, kind, patient, heavy on praise, and lightly and constructively critical. They taught me, or I taught myself, rapid addition—adding two or three numbers at a time. They taught me to excel in spelling, reading, and pronunciation, something I think was an outgrowth of good phonics teaching in my early years. They instilled a desire in me to do my best, and they taught me that whatever needs doing should be done right.

Considering a word I once misspelled, it may be hard to believe that I was a good speller. I represented the fifth grade in a PTA spelling contest. Allene Buckingham, a sixth grader, and I were the last two standing. My word was "quail." I spelled it "quayle," and Allene got it right. Perhaps I had a premonition about Dan Quayle.

Our teachers also were our counselors. Dad did the most counseling, but others also encouraged me—Mr. Cline; Mr. Truman Ward, a math teacher; and Mrs. Teeter. Fulton was a small school in a small town, so their counseling may have come outside school.

One of my best high school chums was Roger Kent, a veterinarian's son. We fished and played with his BB gun. His parents were much better off than mine, and they gave him a larger allowance than my nickel a week, so he occasionally treated me. Robert Dielman, the doctor's son, had a bigger allowance and treated me to candy. I never asked either one to do so, but I guess I never refused, either.

Another was Donald Sutton, whose dad hauled livestock to Chicago, made trips to Michigan to bring back peaches, and moved furniture—in the same truck. (He moved us from Fulton to Francesville.) Don's motorcycle with a sidecar was great fun to ride. In high school, we double dated with our "temporary steadies."

L. V. Teeter, son of my high school English teacher, was a good friend. He was more of an intellectual than the rest of us. We played basketball in his barn and talked of life to come and going to college. A pilot, he was shot down in the Pacific in World War II and is numbered among the missing and presumed dead.

L. V.'s sister Helen was a friend and classmate who competed with me academically. She could not overexert herself because her heart had been damaged by rheumatic fever. She died too young at 43. Charlie Runkle and Cleon Gilbert were special friends. Charlie and I vied with Helen Teeter for top grades. He and Cleon were basketball yell leaders. This was unusual then, because girls usually dominated the cheerleading squad.

As junior class president, I was master of ceremonies at the junior-senior prom, one of my first public speaking efforts. I took speech as a senior and almost withdrew. My mother's gentle persuasion kept me in the class.

In small towns like Fulton and Francesville, activities were either school- or church-related. The only Fulton churches were a United Brethren Church we attended, a Baptist church, and a very small emotional congregation whose denomination I don't recall.

I attended Epworth League meetings at our church and was the group's president. The group included kids from eighth grade age to young people two or three years out of high school. In one period, we had to recite a Bible verse that began with a different letter of the alphabet at each meeting. I don't recall a verse beginning with "Q" or "X," but it took nearly six months. I played the pump organ at Sunday school. One summer, I spent a week at Oakwood Park on Lake Wawasee with boys and girls from our church.

At Fulton and Francesville, the only competitive sports were basketball and baseball, but we had volleyball and track-type races in physical education classes. There was no girls' basketball at Francesville, and its female athletes were limited to cheerleading.

I played basketball and baseball throughout high school. We practiced after the evening meal every other day. If we budgeted our time, plenty was left for homework. My interest in basketball began in grade school, when I attended all of Dad's practices.

Somewhat facetiously, Dad always said that all the tall Fulton boys came from farm families who wanted them home doing chores. The tallest boy in school, six-foot, four-inch Everett Rentschler, was the only son of a big farmer. He played noon basketball and was good. To no avail, Dad urged the father to let Everett play on the school team. The father's decision made economic sense, but it wasn't good for his son.

I played two years on the second team and was on the varsity in my third and fourth years. Probably because Dad worried about being accused of favoritism, I did not start until my senior year. As a substitute, I was the first player off the bench. As floor guard, I was the playmaker who brought the ball up the floor and the shooting guard. The back guard stayed in the backcourt to ensure that the other team got no easy shots or baskets. Teams jumped center after every basket. There was no ten-second line. We took "set" or two-handed shots. One-handed jump shots were unknown. There was no three-point shot.

I had good legs and jumped well due to Dad's technique for improving his players' leaping ability. He hung a ball or object beyond our reach and had us try to touch it at every opportunity. When we could do so regularly, he raised the ball higher, and we started over again. This approach helped me overcome being short, enabled me to out-jump taller players, and paid off with many "held balls."

Back then, basketball was not a contact sport. A three-point lead was a pretty good one. The leading team usually stalled near the end of the game. Keeping possession of the ball was all that was required to stall successfully. That wasn't hard. Fouls were called then when a player touched an opponent, a far cry from today, when players use their elbows and butt everyone around.

At Fulton, our parents took turns serving a post-game dinner. One occurred on my birthday at the home of Lawrence and Arnold Norris, two of my teammates. The day before, teammate Virgil (Bud) Johnson had also observed his birthday. Our teammates were not indifferent about these anniversaries. After we ate, they picked up Bud, took him outside, and dumped him in a horse tank. Before I got the same treatment, I slipped out the back door and hid in the haymow until they went home.

In my junior year, we finished the season with a 17-4 record, then won the sectional for the first time in school history. (Fulton won again after I was out of school and several times after consolidating.) We defeated Francesville, 37-18, on a Friday afternoon; took out Akron, a much larger school and a big rival, 25-18, on a Saturday morning; and edged Winamac, a much larger school, 22-19, on a Saturday afternoon. In the Saturday night title game, we defeated Rochester in overtime, 21-19. We lost our first regional game, but finished with a very respectable 21-5 record.

School and work kept me busy, and I had little money, so my dating was limited. Mildred Dubuque at Fulton and Mary Tillett at Francesville tolerated my attention. I played trumpet in the high school band. Since I played basketball, I couldn't blow my horn at the best place—a gym full of fans. I had minor roles in junior and senior class plays.

Throughout school, we were taught honesty, hard work, thrift, and persistence. I learned that Mark Twain was right—if you always tell the truth, you don't have to remember what you said. That lesson served me well as House speaker, governor, and Health & Human Services secretary. I also learned the importance of being dependable and keeping one's word, and I never admired anyone who said they would do something and didn't.

I also learned persistence, determination, sticking to a project, and never giving up on a goal. Those close to me in government later saw these traits as stubbornness. I admit their point, but Shakespeare wrote in *King Lear* that "our doubts are traitors and make us lose the good we oft might gain by fearing to attempt." I first read that passage in a crude tent library on Okinawa. It came back to me many times, especially as governor when I was trying to get a property tax relief program passed, and as H&HS secretary when I was trying to get a Medicare catastrophic insurance bill passed. It's hard to allay people's fears about trying something for the first time, but persistence pays off.

From my childhood, Dad never talked about any goal but college. He told us that "education is the only thing I'll ever be able to leave you," but he never dictated what we should become or what college we should attend.

The Rector Scholarship at DePauw University was about the only one available then. I applied, but came in second. Dr. Virgil Miller, son of my Uncle Clem and Aunt Rose Miller, was a Delta Chi member, so I even attended the fraternity's rush day at DePauw and pledged. Because of the expense and lack of a scholarship, I eventually went to Indiana University, where I still became a Delta Chi.

I decided to become a doctor early on and don't remember wanting to be anything else. Our family doctor, Frank Dielman, whom I saw only twice as a patient, influenced me a bit. Dr. Dielman let his son and me ride along on house calls. For me, it was mostly a chance to ride in one of the biggest, fanciest cars in town, a decided contrast to our old Model T.

By high school, I was determined that the only things that could prevent me from becoming a doctor were the time it took and the cost. Being determined (stubborn, some might say), I didn't allow myself to dwell on other choices. Being practical, and knowing that medicine was a long course of study, that our family's income was meager, that no scholarships were available, and that I had no ability to borrow, I had plans B and C.

Plan B was to become a farmer. I loved the outdoors, animals, gardens, shrubs, trees, and flowers, and I was unafraid of hard physical work. Plan C was to teach, because I saw how Dad influenced kids as a teacher. In retrospect, I doubt that I would have made a good teacher. Teachers have to talk a lot. My tendency is to be quiet. I think I would have been a good farmer, but doubt that I would have been satisfied in that occupation.

I made the honor roll in every grade—first to twelfth. I studied very hard in high school. I knew I had to prepare myself for three tough years of pre-med studies in college, in which my grades would determine whether I was admitted to medical school. I started school at 5, and I was only 17 when I began college. I now realize how immature I was.

Knowing that I needed money to get through medical school, I took every odd job that came my way. I did farm chores, hoed potatoes (10 cents an hour), milked a cow morning and night for an elderly lady (10 cents a day), and built her a chicken coop ($5 for the week's work it took). I helped Dad mow hay and stack straw from the threshing machine blower. For these hot, dirty, dusty jobs, we tied wet handkerchiefs over our noses and mouths for protection. That filtered out the big particles, but we "ate" most of the dust. I took a team of horses through the threshing ring and shocked oats and wheat ($1 a day). I had to harness and hitch the team, be in the field loading sheaves by 7:30 a.m., and work until 5 or 6 p.m. In this cooperative effort, area farmers worked each other's fields and used the only threshing machine available.

Using a push mower that Dad kept sharpened with a hand file, I mowed about five lawns a week, usually for elderly people (15 cents for small yards, 25 cents for the rest). One summer, I shined shoes in the barbershop on Saturday nights (5 cents a pair), earning 50 cents a night if I was lucky. For a time, I opened up a gas station at 6:30 a.m. and stayed until the owner arrived at 9 a.m. My commission was a penny a gallon. Occasionally I made nothing. Usually, I picked up 35 to 40 cents. I always hoped that Hall's feed grinder truck would drive up. It usually took twenty-five to thirty gallons to fill its tank.

Always, 75 percent of what I earned went in the bank, and I kept 25 percent for use for my own needs.

There was time for mild mischief. While visiting one summer at my Uncle Sam and Aunt Lena Bowen's home, my cousin John and I decided to hitchhike to Burlington, Wisconsin. My Uncle Ray Bowen, from whom I got my middle name, and his wife, Jennie, lived there. With an okay from Uncle Sam and Aunt Lena, we started hitchhiking. When we didn't get a ride, we hopped a freight car and rode it to Chicago. A railroad detective intercepted us in the yards there. After a stern lecture, he directed us to a road where he said we could get a ride. We did, and we arrived safely in Burlington, stayed three or four days, and hitchhiked back. I don't think I ever told my parents about the trip. John later did, and they laughed, but I know they would never have given their okay at the time.

The Bowen family often discussed politics. The township trustee–based school systems in which my father taught were political. My Uncle Clem Miller was the elected Fulton County surveyor. (Dad and I worked as summer help for him.) For me, however, involvement in politics and public service was not in my life's plan.

George B. and Sarah Eleria (Rush) Wright, parents of Pearl Irene (Wright) Bowen, mother of Otis R. Bowen.

John Pierce and Rebecca Jane (Hartman) Bowen, parents of Vernie Bowen, father of Otis R. Bowen

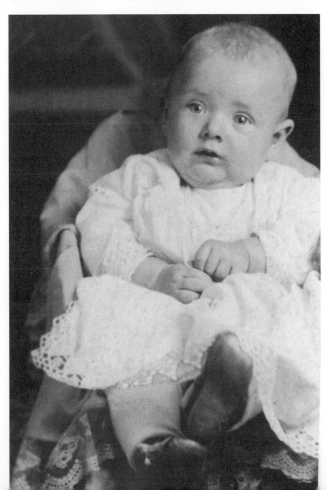

Otis R. Bowen at six months of age.

Otis Bowen and his 4-H steer, a Hereford he named Ted.

Otis R. Bowen at graduation from Francesville High School in 1935.

Otis R. Bowen and Elizabeth Anna Agnes (Beth) Steinmann after their marriage on February 25, 1939. Best man Harry Steinmann, brother of the bride, and bridesmaid Florence Ruffman are with them.

Otis R. Bowen in 1943 as a first lieutenant. He later was promoted to captain.

Captain Otis R. Bowen inspects a mess used by Japanese soldiers on one of the Ryukyu Islands.

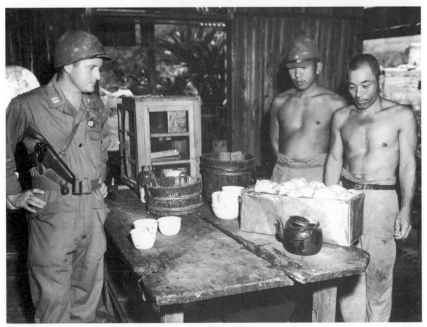

Dr. Otis R. Bowen about 1947, a year
after starting practice in Bremen.

Otis R. Bowen checks a bill in 1967,
his first session as House speaker.

Bridgett Lees was the last of the approximately 3,000 babies that Dr. Otis R. Bowen delivered before becoming governor.

A billboard on the side of a barn promotes Otis R. Bowen for governor in 1972.

Beth Bowen, seated with Dr. Bowen, holds Nicole McGrew, her first grand-daughter. In back are Rob Bowen, Rick and Sandy Bowen, Tim Bowen, and Judy and David McGrew.

Vernie Bowen adjusts a campaign hat for his wife, Pearl, at the hospitality room of their son, Dr. Otis R. Bowen, who was nominated for governor the next day (June 23, 1972).

President Richard M. Nixon and gubernatorial candidate Otis R. Bowen shake hands in a campaign photo, taken in the White House on September 7, 1972.

Josie and Bob Orr and Otis and Beth Bowen celebrate their victory in 1972.

Joseph Kotso of Munster swears in Otis R. Bowen as the forty-fourth governor of Indiana on January 8, 1973. Beth Bowen is barely visible behind Kotso.

Governor Otis R. Bowen hams it up with the 1975 State Fair senior citizens queen.

Dr. J. O. Ritchey of the Indiana University School of Medicine receives a Sagamore of the Wabash from Governor Otis R. Bowen in 1975.

Governor Otis R. Bowen speaks at a 1976 groundbreaking at New Haven, Indiana. Holding the umbrella is Congressman Dan Quayle, later a U.S. senator and vice president.

President Gerald R. Ford and Governor Otis R. Bowen in the Oval Office in 1976.

Vernie Bowen swears in his son, Otis R. Bowen, for a second term as Indiana's governor on January 10, 1977. Beth Bowen holds the family Bible.

Governor Otis R. Bowen arrives at Lafayette by Guard helicopter after the 1978 blizzard, the worst ever to hit Indiana. Others shown are UPI Statehouse reporter Hortense Myers (*left*), Adjutant General Al Ahner, and executive aide Jim Smith.

Governor Otis R. Bowen in fatigues at the Indiana National Guard's summer encampment at Camp Grayling, Michigan.

Dr. Otis R. Bowen at his desk in the Department of Family Medicine of the IU School of Medicine.

Senator Dan Quayle sits beside Dr. Otis R. Bowen as the Senate Finance Committee begins hearings in late 1985 on Dr. Bowen's nomination as secretary of the U.S. Department of Health & Human Services.

President Ronald W. Reagan and H&HS Secretary Otis R. Bowen in a Cabinet meeting.

Coach Bob Knight presents H&HS Secretary Otis R. Bowen with a basketball autographed by the Indiana University team that won the 1987 NCAA championship.

H&HS Secretary Otis R. Bowen delivers his "mean, underhanded" softball pitch at an H&HS outing.

President Ronald W. Reagan watches as Vice President George Bush administers the oath of office to H&HS Secretary Otis R. Bowen. Rose Bowen holds the Bible during the White House ceremony.

H&HS Secretary Otis R. Bowen with Vice President and Mrs. George Bush in 1988. In the background are Senator and Mrs. Dan Quayle. Later that year, Mr. Bush was elected president and Mr. Quayle was elected vice president.

Unveiling the official portrait of H&HS Secretary Otis R. Bowen are Vice President Dan Quayle, Mrs. Louis Sullivan, H&HS Secretary Louis Sullivan, Rose Bowen, artist Everett Raymond Kintsler, and Dr. Bowen.

Dr. Otis Bowen mows the lawn at the Lodge at Donnybrook, near Bremen, where he lives in retirement. Photo was taken in June 1990.

Dr. Otis R. Bowen and Carol Lynn (Hahn) Flosenzier Mikesell at their wedding on February 5, 1993.

⇒ 2 ⇐

IU, Medical School, and Beth

I CAME TO Indiana University for the first time two days before classes started in the fall of 1935. It now takes a U-Haul trailer to take a child to college, but I arrived with a small suitcase and a laundry case. My wardrobe was limited—a suit, a couple sweaters, two pairs of trousers, and the other usual things. My raincoat doubled as a topcoat.

In the rooming house where I first stayed, my roommate came in drunk the first night. Homesick, not feeling well, and disgusted by his behavior, I moved to a rooming house a block away. My roommate there was a Jewish fellow named Feingold from Worcester, Massachusetts. Our bare room had two desks but only one bed, so we slept together. Rent was $3 a week. Our landlady made our bed, but we cleaned the room. In the first semester of my sophomore year, my roommate was Victor Hoehne, son of the principal at Francesville High School, from which I had graduated in 1935.

As a second-semester sophomore, I pledged Delta Chi fraternity and moved to its house. In my senior year, the first year of medical school, I moved closer to campus, to an East Eighth Street home that was owned by a sweet old widow lady, Mrs. Ella R. Springer. I fired her furnace, kept her sidewalks clean, and washed her windows to earn my rent. My roommate was Frank Whitlock of Fairbanks, Indiana, another medical student.

As I began college, my major concerns were money and grades, but I quickly became homesick. I remember being in the football area, probably looking down at the mouth, when Chris Del Sasso of South Bend (later to be an assistant IU football coach) engaged me in conversation. He probably would have done the same for anyone looking so sad, but I never forgot his thoughtfulness. The first time I went home, I talked to Dad about getting a job in a Monticello factory. I am grateful that he insisted that I return to campus.

I was poor, but because I was frugal and I earned some income, I was in pretty good shape for my first year. I limited food expenses to 50 cents a day—10 cents for a roll and a glass of milk at breakfast, and 20 cents at noon and in the evening. Occasionally I went over my dinner limit and had a blue-plate special costing 25 or 30 cents.

To make ends meet, I was a substitute waiter for a sorority, usually on weekends. My "pay" was the food I could eat. For Dr. Henry Holland Carter, the English Department head, I searched specific books for special words, making a card file on them. I do not know the purpose for this National Youth Administration (NYA) job, but the $10 a month that I earned covered my food costs for half a month.

I sent dirty clothes home in the laundry case. Mom returned clean clothes and a batch of cookies. My uncle Dorsey Wright, my mother's brother, who worked for National Biscuit Company (Nabisco), also sent me broken cookies that couldn't be sold.

My class was the first to take three years—rather than two—of premedical school. We then faced four years in medical school and a year of internship. Students now do a four-year pre-med program, four years of medical school, and three years of residency.

To get into medical school, I needed good grades. I studied hard. In my first year, my only relaxation was listening to "Moon River," a radio show that came on at 11 o'clock and featured great songs that put you in the mood for sleep, sort of like a sedative.

Those first-year studies were difficult. I got a "smoke-up," a pink warning slip, on the mid-term in zoology, a required class for pre-med students. I rectified my deficiencies, did well on the final, and ended up with a B. In other courses, I made A's and B's. (I received one C in college—in physics, a tough subject for me.) My grade point average (GPA) was about 3.5. Those freshman grades were good enough to get me into medical school if my MCAT score and interview were satisfactory, so I felt good about them.

I did well in the classes of Mrs. Grace Nealy Martin, my pleasant and patient German and medical German professor. I'm glad I chose

German, because many medical terms derive from German. The language also was to come in handy with my wife-to-be, Beth.

My most notable first-year professor was Herman Briscoe, a renowned chemist who later was vice president and dean of faculties. He did all the lecturing. Will Scott, my zoology professor, probably was the toughest.

Walking to campus, I became acquainted with Clarence ("Shorty") Long, a Blackford County farm boy who lived in a rooming house a couple of doors down. We had things in common, including a love of sports, and enjoyed each other's company. A studious and brilliant individual, Clarence intended to become a CPA. He was as determined about reaching his goal as I was about mine. After I pledged Delta Chi, I convinced Clarence to pledge, and we became roommates. He and his future wife Mildred, also an IU student, became lifelong friends. Upon graduating from IU, Clarence joined Ernst & Ernst, now Ernst & Young, eventually becoming the senior partner at the Indianapolis office.

Joe Dumas Howell from Illinois and I almost always were lab partners. He didn't get into IU Medical School, but was admitted to Washington University Medical School in St. Louis. Later he became one of Indianapolis's foremost allergy specialists.

Since my Dad coached and I was raised with a basketball in my hand, sports were an intense interest. I attended basketball and football games and track meets, even scraping up $3 for basketball season tickets. By helping direct game-day traffic or working as a spotter for a radio announcer, I got into some football games free. Under Coach Everett Dean, Hoosier basketball teams were a perennial threat to win the Big Ten title. The Hoosiers had excellent track and swimming teams. The football teams were mediocre.

With fifty walk-ons, I tried out for basketball, but survived only the first cut. Vic Hoehne, who was six-foot-two, made the freshman team but not the varsity.

In retrospect, my first year was a good one, but it didn't seem that way then.

Between my freshman and sophomore years, I lived and worked on a Pulaski County dairy farm. Up at 3:45 a.m., I helped milk twelve cows by hand, then cooled the milk and bottled and delivered it. I then helped make hay or plow corn until evening milking time. By night, exhausted, we were ready for bed. The owner, a man named Wuetrich, was stern, but he worked as long and as hard as his hired men did.

As a sophomore, I still had the NYA job. By the second semester, I was at the Delta Chi house and covered my food costs and room by working as a waiter and dishwasher. The food was great for someone unaccustomed to variety or quantity.

Many of my second-year professors were ones I had had in my first year. I took a full load—sixteen hours—each semester. There were few electives in the pre-med program, so most classes related to my field of study. I took Reserve Officer Training Corps (ROTC) classes because we were told that if war came and we had to go, we were more likely to become Army officers. As a sophomore, I posted a B+ average. My move to the Delta Chi house brought me a host of new friends, including Glenn Beams from Fort Wayne, later one of Indiana's finest attorneys, and Bob Trenner, a tall, handsome, friendly young man from Fort Wayne who died in World War II. Ralph Bentle was a lot like Glenn, an advisor and a common, good, friendly upperclassman.

George (Dizzy) Miller became such a good friend that he was godfather to our daughter, Judy. A member of the Marching Hundred, IU's marching band, Dizzy played at age 81 in an alumni band at a 1997 IU football game. Another good friend was Ted Jones, the Marching Hundred's drum major, a fine musician and an excellent piano player. He molded the Delta Chis into a singing group that did well in competition with other fraternities. Whether for practice or for fun, we had good times around the piano, with Ted playing and leading the singing. I also played basketball and swam on fraternity teams.

Others friends from the fraternity were John Hurt (later Governor Matthew E. Welsh's man Friday) and Tom Gillam, with whom I renewed acquaintances while governor and while attending the Rose Bowl in Los Angeles with IU president John Ryan.

I was in total awe of Sparky Miller of Pennsylvania, the center and place-kicker on IU's football team; Corby Davis of Lowell, the Hoosiers' All-American fullback; and Don Lash of Bluffton, world record holder in the two-mile run and a member of the U.S. team for the 1936 Olympics in Berlin. All were upper-class Delta Chis. Lash became a real friend and served in the Indiana House while I was governor.

As a pledge, I slept in a fourth-floor dormitory with bunk beds and plenty of fresh air. Clarence Long and I later shared a room that was large enough for comfort, but not fancy. We had closet space, a couple of chairs, and two study tables. Clarence had a popper and plenty of popcorn, so our room became popular.

In the Delta Chi house, I mostly worked or studied. At work, I learned to carry four plates at one time—two in one hand, one resting in the crook of that arm, and one in the other hand. Upperclassmen often brought university bigwigs, parents, or guests to the house. On some nights, the house hosted a sorority for dinner. These events required our best behavior. (We were apprehensive about spilling something.)

I remember "hell week" well. We wore scratchy gunnysack underwear. The actives built a fire in a first-floor fireplace that the pledges had to put out. That sounds innocuous, but we had to fill our mouths with bitter, nasty-tasting stuff, crawl down the stairwell from the second floor to the fireplace, and spew that concoction on the fire. It took us a long time to extinguish the blaze.

The actives paddled us, for no reason or an insignificant one, usually no more than a claim that we weren't courteous enough. After telling us to bend over and grab our ankles, they applied the paddle forcefully. It's good that this activity now is banned. Every pledge was a "fetch-it stooge," and we had to wax and clean floors and hallways, usually on Saturday mornings. Freshmen pledges wore green beanie caps. By pledging as a sophomore, I escaped that "privilege."

Told that Delta Chi was going broke, the pledges at one point agreed to eat "charity" type meals for a week. At week's end, the upperclassmen kept us out of the dining room until a banquet—complete with a roast pig with an apple in its mouth—was ready for us to eat. As happy as we were to eat a good meal, and as relieved as we were to learn that the frat was solvent, we wondered how we were so easily taken in by that charade.

It was too far and too much of an expense for my parents to come to campus in their old car. One year, they did attend the fraternity's annual Mother's Day program.

I was reputed to look like Spencer Tracy, who was not handsome but was one of my favorite actors. Someone from Delta Chi reported my resemblance to some campus bigwigs looking for student lookalikes to play movie actors in a stage show. I was drafted as the Spencer Tracy lookalike. A bit embarrassed and a little scared, I delivered my two or three lines and paraded onstage without incident.

Fraternity life was a broadening experience. I learned table manners, how to meet people, how to dance, and other social niceties that a Fulton County farm boy needed to know. We wore coats and ties at least three nights a week. Perhaps the most important lesson we learned was tolerance for others.

By this time, my folks were living in Crown Point. At home for the summer, work was hard to find for a new boy in town. I earned too little, a fact that was to haunt me in the next school year. I don't like high places and wasn't anxious to get on a ladder, but I desperately needed money for school. Dad let me help him paint a couple houses.

Harold Clevenger, Dad's close friend, had moved to Crown Point to be the elementary principal a year before Dad came there to teach and coach. Harold and Priscilla Clevenger's apartment was above the Steinmann Meat Market on the east side of the courthouse square in Crown Point. Mrs. Bertha Steinmann owned the market and the building where it was located and lived with her daughter, Elizabeth, in a second apartment across the hall from the Clevengers.

Elizabeth Anna Agnes Steinmann was the daughter of Alwin Hans Steinmann (1890–1926) and his wife, Bertha Louise Luhmann (1888–1978). A butcher, Steinmann came to America from Germany, found a job, and saved until he had enough to send for his fiancée and sister. On Bertha Luhmann's arrival in 1914, they were married. Elizabeth and her brother Harry were born in Chicago. The Steinmanns later moved to Crown Point, where Alwin opened the meat market. He died before his daughter's ninth birthday. His widow then operated the meat market, and his son later ran it.

The Clevengers had Elizabeth and me for dinner. This was the first time I met the young woman who was to be my wife for nearly forty-three years. I had never been really serious about a girl, but my interest in this one immediately was serious. For the rest of the summer, we dated two or three times weekly.

She was reserved, meek, friendly, and very religious. I was the first person to call her Beth. Her mother and brother called her Elizabeth or "Lieschen," a German word of endearment. Beth spoke only German until she started school at age six. I especially liked her enthusiasm for my objective of becoming a physician.

Mrs. Steinmann belonged to a Lutheran church affiliated with the Missouri Synod. That meant she was strict and rigid. I felt that she preferred keeping her daughter as a companion and seemed upset that Beth was receiving serious attention from a boy. However, I enjoyed Mrs. Steinmann's good German food and her heavy German accent. In fact, I was pleased about everything except Mrs. Steinmann's ill-concealed indecision about her daughter's boyfriend.

I soon proposed to Beth (exactly five weeks after we met, Beth said) and gave her a small diamond. She had finished business school but had not yet found a job. Worried that a prospective employer might not hire someone about to get married, we kept the engagement quiet. Our quickly developing relationship made it difficult to go back to Bloomington, but Beth was as determined that I stay in school as I was.

That school year, I saw her only a few times—at Thanksgiving and Christmas vacations and the time or two I hitchhiked home each semester. We wrote each other regularly—two or three times a week. Our separations deepened our feelings for each other. Patient and tolerant when I was moody and overly quiet, Beth understood the pressure of medical school studies and my financial difficulties.

My organic chemistry class stands out in my junior year. Clarence May, a walking encyclopedia on organic chemistry and one of IU's toughest, grouchiest professors, was the instructor. Organic chemistry was the course that more or less determined a student's capability of doing medical studies and medical work. Since almost everyone in his class was a pre-med student, he shocked us by bluntly saying on the first day that few of us would do well enough to get into medical school.

Professor May did the lecturing, writing on the blackboard with one hand and erasing what he wrote with the other so quickly that we had to scribble fast to make notes. We learned formulas for all kinds of compounds, most of them organic materials used in medicines and other chemicals. We memorized a tremendous number of these compounds. There are a lot more now than there were then. I earned an A. (Throughout college, I made straight A's in chemistry—general, quantitative, qualitative, and organic chemistry and biochemistry. Even so, I'm sure I couldn't now make a living in that field.)

Although not difficult, my course on Greek and Latin derivatives was interesting and important to me. A delightful old gentleman named Guido H. Stempel, probably in his seventies, was our professor. While in India as secretary of the U.S. Department of Health & Human Services, I met Dr. Stempel's grandson, John Dallas Stempel, a career diplomat and U.S. consul general for South India. He was the son of John E. Stempel, who for many years headed IU's department of journalism.

When I came home for Christmas vacation, I was broke but kept it to myself. Noting that I still was there when I should have been back on campus, Beth forced me to "fess up." When I told her what the problem was, she quickly said that we would use her small inheritance to keep me in school. Determined to earn my own way, I resisted. Finally, but still reluctantly, I accepted her help and returned to IU.

I kept looking for ways to make money for school. *Gray's Anatomy*, a huge, heavy book, was a burden to carry. I devised a denim cover with handles to make it easier. After seeing my "invention," most of the medical students in my class wanted one. Mom bought denim and thread and made more. I sold them for $1.50 each, accumulating a tidy sum toward my next year's tuition and board. I needed to do that, because medical school fees were more than $200 a semester, compared to $35 a semester for university classes.

I took the MCAT exam in April 1938, and soon learned that I had been accepted for medical school. I couldn't afford the call, but telephoned Beth to give her the good news. My GPA must have been between 3.5 and 3.7. My straight A average in chemistry probably was a principal factor in getting me into medical school.

Late in my junior year, Dr. Burton D. Myers, medical school dean at Bloomington, chose me as cadaver boy for my senior year. This last undergraduate year was the first year of medical school. A short, heavy, stern man, Dr. Myers had a tremor in his voice and hands that I now would recognize as an early symptom of Parkinson's disease. Everyone, me included, was scared of Dean Myers. In my interview, I learned that he was all bark and no bite. Financial need determined which of several applicants got the job. The fact that I was chosen illustrates how financially strapped I was.

My cadaver boy duties required me to be on campus part of the summer. After learning that one more literature course would qualify me for a bachelor of arts degree, I took it that summer. I also took histology, the microscopic study of tissues.

As cadaver boy, I accepted and embalmed unclaimed bodies sent to the medical school from prisons, county poor farms, and mental institutions. Usually, these were the bodies of itinerants or of old, penniless, or mentally defective persons. An occasional body was willed to the medical school for research.

Joe Baughman of Kokomo, my predecessor as cadaver boy, taught me to embalm in one easy lesson. He also advised me to extract gold teeth. This may sound like robbing the dead, but bodies were given to the medical school so that students could learn by dissecting them. Body parts then were cremated, a process that destroys gold in the mouth cavity. Cadaver boys routinely checked mouths for gold plate, partials, or bridges. At the end of my year, I sold extracted gold to a dealer for $35. It all went toward school expenses.

After embalming, I put the bodies in formaldehyde in the basement vat room. The third-floor lab had twenty-eight dissecting tables. Four students worked on each cadaver—one on the head and neck, one each on the extremities on each side, and one on the chest and abdomen. After the bodies were dissected, I took new ones up. Students rotated so that each worked on four bodies in the year. One stormy night, I put four cadavers on a cart and wheeled it into the elevator to go to the third floor. At that moment, the power failed. I was a prisoner for about a half an hour with the four bodies. It was an eerie feeling.

I lived at Ella Springer's home that year. In addition to what I did to earn my rent, I had the NYA job, the cadaver boy's nominal pay, and the *Gray's Anatomy* book covers. I also made and reproduced an outline of my histology course and sold it for $1 a copy.

My roommate, Frank Whitlock, had annoying habits. I learned about one—swishing coffee around in his mouth—when Mrs. Springer began fixing us breakfast. (She enjoyed our company and charged us barely enough to pay for the food.) Across a study table from Frank, I learned of his other annoying habit—clicking his teeth. I think he had false teeth, but didn't check! Despite his shortcomings, Frank became a good friend.

I have fond memories of many fellow medical students, some of whom were poorer than me. Typical was Charles Eugene Green of Paragon, Indiana, whose undergraduate degree from Oklahoma Baptist University qualified him as a minister. To finance his medical studies, he pastored a country church about twenty-five miles from Indianapolis. His salary wasn't enough to pay tuition and fees. Unbeknownst to him, his classmates took up small collections to help. Rev. Green married at least fifteen class members while they were in medical school. A few years before his death, he wrote a book about his journey from the cotton fields to the practice of medicine. He mentioned me in it several times and included a picture of us.

A male quartet composed of Wally Bash of Warsaw, Joe Davis of Marion, Robert Craig of Gary, and Welbon Britton achieved near professional quality and sang many places, including Rev. Green's church.

Others friends were Britton, J. O. Price, and Alan Houser. As friends, we didn't do much together. In the first years of medical school, you don't do anything except study.

Our class included several bright women. One was Mary Craig of Indianapolis. Later Mary Tucker, she was the mother of Marilyn (Tucker) Quayle, wife of J. Danforth (Dan) Quayle, a congressman, senator, and vice president. Mary Tucker died of breast cancer. While Dan was vice president, his wife embraced the need for regular mammograms and research on the causes, prevention, and treatment of breast cancer.

Excited and worried as I began medical school, I quickly regained my composure. Taking the histology course in the summer helped, because I didn't have to take quite a full load in my first year. The difficulty of my studies was not a threat. Medical schools differ from law schools, which flunk students out after they're admitted. Most of those who get into medical school complete. The fallout usually is for medical reasons.

My courses were tough. Anatomy was especially so. I also had physiology and its lab, in which we experimented with dogs and drugs. I had microscopic neurology, in which we studied brain and spinal cord tissue under the microscope and learned the location of every nerve and muscle—where they start from and end, and what they do. It was memory work without much thinking. A lot of it would serve no purpose in practice. If one was going to be a surgeon, he had to know anatomy well. If one was going to be an internist, he had to know physiology well. However, every physician needed to know some anatomy and physiology, and that's why we had to take it.

Dr. Jacob A. Badertscher ("Jakie" to us) was an intense, stern professor teaching the dullest classes, including histology and microscopic neurology. Professor William J. Moenkhaus was a dull, boring physiology teacher. Dr. Harry B. Thomas, an anatomy professor and practicing physician, was more practical.

In spring, law school students (the laws) and medical school students (the medics) always had an athletic competition, usually touch football or softball. The prize was a thunder mug, a slop jar like those people put under beds and used at night instead of going to an outdoor privy. The victors put their name on the thunder mug, just as IU and Purdue put "I" and "P" links on the Old Oaken Bucket.

In 1938 we played softball, and I pitched. I wasn't fast, and I didn't fan many batters, but I was accurate and put lots of spin on the ball. Batters popped up a lot. With good fielding, my team usually won. We did that day. At the game's end, my team carried me off the field on their shoulders. A photographer caught that somewhat embarrassing moment, and the photo appeared in the 1939 *Arbutus*.

I believe I made all A's that year, but there may have been a B or two. I enjoyed learning about the body and its parts and how they function, but I disliked the stress of frequent quizzes and the not-too-friendly faculty.

I saw Beth only at Thanksgiving and Christmas that year. The semester break was about two weeks, but my cadaver boy duties prevented me from staying away from campus that long. Once or twice a semester, I hitchhiked home. Beth came to Bloomington only once, when I was a junior, for the Delta Chi sweetheart dance.

Late in my senior year, Beth and I decided to go ahead with marriage. I came home on Friday night, February 24, 1939. Since I would not be 21 until Sunday, February 26, my mother had to accompany me to the Lake County clerk's office to give consent to my marriage. No blood tests were required and there was no waiting period.

An elderly German-speaking minister, August Biester, married us at the Crown Point Lutheran Church on a cold, snowy Saturday evening. Only a few people were present. Beth's bridesmaid was a friend, Florence Ruffman. Harry Steinmann, Beth's brother, was best man. A reception followed at the Steinmann apartment. Beth and I then drove her mother's old car to Gary, about ten miles north of Crown Point, for our "honeymoon."

The next day, classmate Colin Elliott, who had brought me to Lake County, took me back to Bloomington. I never told him I was going to be married and never said I had been. He found out only when some-one noticed my wedding ring.

We made no plans for Beth to join me. She had a good job in Crown Point. It would be another eighteen months before we worked things out and could be together.

I was excited when I received my bachelor's degree, but anxious about the cost of the next three years. As noted, Beth was helping me with the big expenses—tuition and books particularly—even before we were married.

In the summer of 1939, we had the Steinmann apartment to our-selves. A detention officer at the Lake County Children's Home, Mrs. Steinmann stayed there during the week. Beth worked for the Depart-ment of Agriculture's Farm Security Administration. I worked at the Sears & Roebuck garage in Gary, mounting new tires.

Crown Point then was the "Gretna Green"—marriage capital—of the country. The county clerk's office was open twenty-four hours a day. Couples got licenses immediately, then walked to the office of one of Crown Point's many justices of the peace, and in minutes they were man and wife. Sitting by the apartment window, we often watched people go in and out of the courthouse, day and night.

At Indianapolis in the fall, I had a job at the Wheeler City Rescue Mission, then as now located downtown on Delaware Street, a mile from the medical school. I lived in a bare third-floor room with a plain desk and an iron single bed. Fellow "orderly" Edgar Thompson and his wife lived in an apartment across the street. He and I walked to campus every day—rain, sleet, or snow—carrying books and black dinner pails holding our mission-prepared lunches, usually a sandwich, an apple or orange, and a thermos of milk.

The mission now serves families and displaced children, but then it served transients—winos, alcoholics, and mentally ill men. Our nightly routine began about 9 P.M., after mandatory evening chapel. From ten to fifty transients went to the basement, stripped, showered, and filed through the sick call and inspection line. We listened to their medical problems and, if necessary, referred them to a doctor. We checked each man for lice. If they had that problem, we gave them blue ointment, the best treatment then available. Each man was handed a blanket and went to the dormitory room to sleep. Although we dispensed only aspirin and blue ointment, the work made us feel like doctors.

Life at the mission was simple. So were the meals. The cook, an alcoholic who I think sneaked a drink or two at work, did such a good job that he stayed for months. Usually we ate evening meals in the kitchen, but we didn't remain apart from the transients. We talked to them all the time, because they were lonely and needed to talk with someone.

Now working full time in Crown Point, Beth only occasionally was able to come to Indianapolis. I rarely got home to visit.

Medical school courses were tough, requiring lots of studying. In the first semester, we took gross pathology, studying organs in total. The next semester, we studied tissue under microscopes. We also studied pharmacology, bacteriology, and biochemistry. The latter is the study of the chemical composition of such things as body fluids. For a course called introduction to medicine, we had to buy another big text, *Cecil's Book*, which is to internal medicine what *Gray's Anatomy* is to anatomy.

We also were introduced to clinical work—medical history taking and physical exams. We got to see and examine patients, observe the skills of professor/doctors, and follow the head resident on rounds. We enjoyed that, but we had a sense of inadequacy.

The IU Medical Center was a much different place then. Riley Hospital for Children was one of the world's foremost children's hospitals, but it was much smaller. What then were the Long and Coleman hospitals now are used for other purposes. Still in use are the Medical Science Building and Emerson and Fesler halls. The latter was built the year I came to Indianapolis. Newer structures, including the modern University Hospital and the expanded Riley, now dwarf these older buildings. City Hospital, later Marion County General and now Wishard, was not part of the university, but we observed there.

The outstanding instructor in my second year of medical school was Frank Forry, a great pathologist and a wonderful teacher. A short, bespectacled, fast-talking doctor, he surrounded himself with tough assistants, one of whom we nicknamed "Black Mike." Dr. Forry was tough, but he wanted us to succeed. He kept prodding Frank W. Tinsley, the son of an Indianapolis physician, who was late on everything. Frank had reasons—he was married, with six children—but medical school professors don't accept any excuses. Dr. Forry once called Frank one of the best procrastinators he had ever seen.

Dr. Forry was a very fair grader. One of his assistants—Frederick Taylor, a practicing physician—took 10 points off my exam score for an answer that was wrong in a minor way. I missed an insignificant part of a multi-part question. Feeling that the penalty was disproportionate to the mistake, I took my paper to Dr. Forry. I told him I was bent on making Alpha Omega Alpha, the scholastic honorary for medical students. To do that, I said, I needed an A in pathology. The 10 points deducted on this exam, I told Dr. Forry, were pretty important. He looked it over and gave me back 5 points. That put my score in the 90s, and I got an A.

Another world-famous professor was Dr. Rollo Neil Harger, a chemist and Ph.D. who taught biochemistry and toxicology. Dr. Harger earned wide acclaim for inventing the Drunkometer, which helped fight drunken driving.

Our micropathology final exam was unique. A week in advance, we got a set of thirty slides of a deceased patient's tissues. Each set was different, so we couldn't help each other. Using the slides, we had to do a case history and determine the cause of death. Dr. Donald J. White, a kind clinical professor who practiced medicine uptown, gave me this oral exam. My slides showed extensive kidney damage. From several possibilities, I determined that ingestion of bichloride of mercury, a very poisonous toxic material, was the cause of death. Apparently I guessed right, since he gave me an A.

In this year, we spent time at the bedside of patients, working in groups of four with clinical instructors to learn the art of taking a history and doing physical exams.

Of all my medical school professors, the most outstanding was Dr. J. O. Ritchey. One of the country's foremost internists and a master diagnostician, he brought a patient from one of the hospitals to his classroom every week, took a medical history, did a quick physical, and then discussed his diagnosis and how he had arrived at it. Dr. Ritchey spent sixty-three years at the School of Medicine as an intern, resi-

dent, instructor, professor, department chair, and admissions committee chair. His knowledge of the science and art of medicine and his
high ethical standards made him every student's and every doctor's role
model.

While governor, I was with Dr. Ritchey often. By then, he was in
his early eighties, but age had not dulled his abilities. He died in late
1981, after I was out of the governor's office and teaching in the Department of Family Medicine at the IU Medical Center.

We liked Dr. Charles Owen McCormick, an obstetrician. He "in-
vented" the use of ether and oil enemas to curtail pain during labor.
The hot liquid was painful, and patients complained bitterly, but the
practice was not harmful and made labor a lot easier. Dr. Edwin Nicho-
las Kime, who taught topographical anatomy, had a mean reputation
and deserved it. George Samuel Bond, who taught cardiology, had a
loud voice that carried. We nicknamed him "Boom Boom" Bond.

That first year at Indianapolis was interesting, exciting, stimulat-
ing, demanding, and stressful. Once we were past it, absent total col-
lapse as a student, there was not much danger of flunking out. Still, life
as a medical student was tough. There were no study periods. We were
at the medical center from 8 A.M. to 5 P.M. and in class most of the
time. If not in class, we were at the hospital. I also had my mission
duties and an NYA job putting old, dusty medical school patient
records in order and filing them so they could be relocated. I got a lot of
paper cuts stuffing records into large Manila envelopes.

At noon in a large yard outside Emerson Hall, we played softball. I
usually pitched. Classmates on the other team got disgusted when my
relatively slow, screwy, spinning pitch made them pop up. They didn't
get many hits if my team had good fielders.

I seldom saw Beth. We wrote frequently and occasionally talked by
telephone. We kept looking for a way to make our home together, but
it came down to money, and we didn't have any to spare although Beth
was working full time at Crown Point.

As part of my ROTC training, I spent most of the summer of 1940
at Camp Carlyle, Pennsylvania, the Army's medical training center.
The Army wouldn't let Beth come, but she and her mother met me
when training ended, and we visited Beth's aunt in Philadelphia.

Upon my return, classmate Horace Norton urged me to apply for
a job at the Kregelo and Bailey Funeral Home in the 2200 block of
North Meridian Street. A poor boy from Plainville, Indiana, Horace
supported himself in medical school by working there and delivering

newspapers on campus. I applied and got the job after being interviewed by owner James F. Bailey (Mr. Kregelo was deceased).

The funeral home had three upstairs rooms. I suggested to Mr. Bailey that Horace use one and Beth and I one. The third room could be our kitchen. Probably anticipating that Beth could help with our duties, Mr. Bailey okayed the idea. I then persuaded Beth to come to Indianapolis. Finally we were together, although our living conditions were spartan. Beth had to carry water for all purposes from the bathroom to her "kitchen," which she furnished with cupboards made of curtain-covered orange crates. She did all her cooking on a hot plate and in an electric roaster.

Horace and I polished the brass signs almost daily, cleared the walks of debris, snow, and ice, and answered the phones at night. Beth assisted with hair and cosmetics, handled flowers, and helped answer the telephone.

The three of us had a cold breakfast, usually cereal, and brown-bagged lunch. (Beth quickly got a job in the Indiana Adjutant General's Office.) Beth cooked evening meals. If a body was in the funeral home, Mr. Bailey wouldn't allow cooking, since odors might reach the viewing rooms. In the evenings, Beth sat quietly in a chair, reading or working on her needlepoint, while I studied at my desk. Our only diversion was going to Tyndall Armory for professional wrestling or playing bridge with my medical school classmates Bob Bill, Clyde Botkin, and Welbon Britton.

If there was a body in the funeral home every three weeks, Mr. Bailey was doing well. Beth recalled a total of ten funerals while we lived there. A kind and gentle elderly lady stayed at the funeral home during the day and kept Mr. Bailey's agitations under control. We had to be there evenings and weekends. About 70, Mr. Bailey hid his good heart with outward gruffness and crabbiness. Twice he gave me $5 bills, first telling me to take Beth to a good restaurant, and then telling me to buy a hat because I didn't have one. I bought a beautiful black Homburg and still have it

Because I have somewhat rare B positive blood, I was asked to give blood for a local car dealer's leukemia-stricken father. I twice gave 750 cubic centimeters of blood—about a pint and a half. Usually, donors give 500 cc. The appreciative dealer practically gave us a Model A Ford, which Beth and I called our "blood car." It was old, but ran well. I drove it to medical school daily, picking up three students. They paid me 5 cents a day, more than enough to cover fuel costs with gas at 15 cents a gallon. We used the car for a two-week summer vacation in Michigan in 1941 and kept it until I got out of medical school.

We took an unbelievable eighteen courses as juniors in medical school. There were lots of lectures and quizzes. We gave physical exams at the hospitals. Except by observation, we received little training on the art of medicine, including bedside manners. Similarly, other than being reminded that the Hippocratic Oath governed our actions as doctors, we were taught nothing about the ethics of medicine.

As a junior, my grades were good enough to make Alpha Omega Alpha (AOA), the medical honor society. (AOA officers presenting me with a second pin while I was governor were surprised that I had an earned one. They probably thought anyone dumb enough to be in politics was not smart enough to have made good grades in medical school.)

In the summer of 1941, I returned to Camp Carlyle for six more weeks of Army training. Beth was able to go. It was a good time for us.

We functioned as general practitioners in the final year of medical school, devoting a few weeks each to internal medicine, orthopedics, obstetrics, and so on. We saw patients and prescribed medicines, always with a full-fledged doctor at our side.

We knew that war was coming. On Sunday, December 7, 1941, the Japanese attack on Pearl Harbor brought certainty. We were summoned to Emerson Hall the next day, where Dean Willis D. Gatch talked briefly to us before we listened to the radio as President Roosevelt asked Congress to declare war on Japan. The hall became totally quiet as everyone lapsed into deep thought about what lay ahead. Ours was the first class to graduate in wartime. Graduation even was accelerated so we finished in May.

Grace Blankenship, Dean Gatch's secretary, told me that my grades on the state boards were the highest of those taking them. Lasting two or three days, these essay exams were graded by practicing M.D.'s. Thinking I could gain a few points, I organized and outlined my answers before neatly writing them out. Apparently, I was successful.

At the Indiana University commencement the next month, I was one of 107 persons awarded an M.D. degree, graduating fourth in my class. Obviously I had a feeling of pride, but I was apprehensive about the future. Friendships from seven years of pre-medical and medical school studies were ending, so this also was a time of sadness.

At graduation, I also was commissioned as an Army first lieutenant. I was placed on inactive status for my internship, but knew that I later would serve. My hope was that I could do that in a hospital or in something directly related to medicine.

In Bloomington for my graduation were Beth; her mother Bertha Steinmann, and her brother Harry; all of my family; Beth's best friend, Florence Ruffman, and her parents, Mr. and Mrs. Louis Ruffman. There was no big celebration. Beth and I simply went home and relaxed until I started my internship.

✳ 3 ✳

Internship in South Bend

I INTERNED AT Epworth Hospital, now South Bend Memorial, the name that will be used here. Carl Culbertson, a former IU School of Medicine professor who had joined the South Bend Medical Foundation staff, recruited five of us. We knew and trusted Dr. Culbertson and felt good about interning at Memorial. Our internship began June 1.

My fellow interns were Dr. Eugene Buckingham of Indianapolis, later a family doctor in Bloomington; J. Colin Elliott of Middlebury, later a family doctor in Buchanan, Michigan; Salvo Marks of Hammond, later an ophthalmologist there; and Fred Kuhn of Plymouth, later a family physician in South Bend. (Dr. Kuhn started calling me "Buzz." I never knew how he came up with the nickname, but it stuck with my fellow interns and other doctors. Because of my resemblance to the actor, nurses called me Spencer Tracy.)

An internship's purpose is to put book knowledge to practical use, to learn by doing and by observing practicing physicians. As interns, we assumed patient care duties under a doctor's oversight. Exposed to every kind of illness, death, and dying, we learned how to handle patients and families faced with those realities. We alternated between medical, surgical, obstetrical, pediatric, genitourinary, and orthopedic units. We did detailed histories and physical exams on patients. We made rounds with doctors as they visited patients, observing their actions and asking questions. We learned the techniques of catheterizations, spinal taps, transfusions, and intravenous feedings. We drew blood. We applied casts. We learned to read electrocardiograms and X rays and to interpret lab results. We learned from nurses as well as doctors, especially in the emergency room, while responding to life-threatening emergencies.

All of us had emergency room first call every fifth night. Every fifth night, we had second call—that is, we were called if the intern on first call got really busy and needed help. If on emergency room duty, we went to bed about 11 but might be up four or five times. On Saturday nights, we stayed in emergency to handle a stream of people hurt in accidents, shot, or stabbed. Their injuries often related to alcohol use. We learned to do suturing very well.

In addition to emergency room duty, we made night calls on patients in our assigned units. For example, if on obstetrical service, we attended patients in labor if the attending physician was a teaching doctor. One of Memorial's OB physicians wouldn't let us assist, but most let us do normal deliveries, use forceps, repair episiotomies (incisions made in the vagina to make more room for delivery), and circumcise male babies.

Our morning starting time depended on the physicians with whom we worked. Some started at 7 o'clock, others at 9 or 10. If we wanted breakfast, we usually needed to get to the dining room between 6:30 and 7 to be clear for work.

We attended autopsies, usually performed by Dr. Alfred S. Giordano, the pathologist who headed the South Bend Medical Foundation's laboratories. Teaching us to approach autopsies like surgeries and to respect the bodies of deceased persons, he claimed that autopsies could be done in a tux and need not be messy. Dr. Giordano was a scholar as well as a doctor. The "father" of good medicine in South Bend, he was an outspoken advocate of quality care who staged seminars so that practicing doctors could get or stay abreast of new developments in medicine.

As interns, we learned that different doctors treat the same illnesses differently. We read up on diseases, especially unusual ones. Often, medical book language did not describe what we saw, especially when our patients had more than one disease. That taught us that the symptoms of one disease might mask those of another. Once a week, we made a clinical presentation on one of our cases.

Every day was long. Fourteen- to sixteen-hour days were common. We were on call at all times and were never really off duty. Each day was different. On one day, not a typical one, I was vomited and urinated on, got feces on my uniform while removing a fecal impaction, and had blood sprayed on me. (We always kept spare intern coats and white pants.)

There were a few overly demanding staff doctors at Memorial, but interns were not treated harshly. Our group did more than most interns, because at least twenty younger staff doctors had gone into the armed forces before our arrival. We relieved the pressure on the remaining doctors, especially in the emergency room and at night. Although interns, we were full-fledged physicians who could legally do anything any doctor could.

We received board and laundry services and lived in Memorial's intern quarters, two of us in one bedroom, three in another. There was a small lounge between the bedrooms. Our families could have come to South Bend, but the hospital had no family quarters, and we couldn't afford an apartment on our $15-a-month salary.

Beth tried to transfer to the South Bend Selective Service Board, but was reassigned to the Gary board and lived at Crown Point. About once a month, I took the South Shore Railroad to Gary, where Beth met me. I returned to South Bend on Sunday night.

Interns had no regular meal times. We rarely ate together. Kitchen personnel, especially a waitress named Flora, found us something to eat, and they even babied us with extra desserts if we had to skip a meal.

A memorable physician with whom I worked was Dr. David Bickel, an obstetrician. He let us do deliveries, but sat beside us, inspecting and supervising what we were doing. His teaching helped me considerably when I later went into practice. He taught us how to handle difficult deliveries using forceps or complications requiring other obstetric techniques. Dr. Bickel also taught me how to recognize delivery room emergencies requiring Caesarean sections.

Others who impressed us were Dale Pyle, a pediatrician; Alfred Ellison and George Green, both surgeons; and Carrol Hyde, a genitourinary specialist. Dr. Hyde was grouchy with interns and nurses, but he practiced good urology.

I knew Dr. Charles Walters, a surgeon at St. Joseph Hospital in Mishawaka, from medical school. I later referred surgical cases to him because he was so competent, and because St. Joseph was closer to Bremen than Memorial. When I next saw Dr. Walters on Okinawa, he had lost every hair on his body, probably due to the stress of round-the-clock surgeries on injured American soldiers. All his hair grew back after he came home.

A few physicians we knew as interns were not as competent. However, they practiced the art of medicine well, their patients loved them, and their results were good.

After internship, doctors went into practice or into a three-year residency at a large hospital. Today, all medical school graduates, even those in general practice, do three-year residencies. It now requires eleven years to go through pre-med, medical school, and residency, three years longer than for my generation. We've also come a long way from $15-a-month salaries. Residents now are paid living wages.

My internship ended on June 3, 1943.

❄ *4* ❄

Serving Uncle Sam

BEFORE GOING ON active duty, I spent a few days with Beth. On July 3, 1943, I reported to Carlyle Barracks. By train six weeks later, I went to Camp Cook, California. Located near Santa Barbara on a peninsula sticking out into the Pacific, it was so foggy, damp, and cold that we called it "Pneumonia Point." We wore winter uniforms even in summer.

On August 16th, I reported to Lieutenant Colonel William Williams of the 342nd Medical Group. I first was assigned as a collecting company's CO, then became CO of a medical clearing company. Medical groups had three collecting companies and one clearing company. In combat, collecting companies bring wounded soldiers to a clearing company's front-line station. Triage is performed there before wounded soldiers are sent to field hospitals.

Beth soon followed me to California, no small task with rationing. She and another soldier's wife drove thirty-five miles an hour on retreads in our old '36 Nash. At Camp Cook, Dr. and Mrs. Arnold Bachman and Beth and I lived in a house at Lompoc, near Solvang. During desert training near Indio, Beth and Bonnie Bachman lived in a small Desert Springs house. Unless assigned as officer of the day, we got off duty at noon Saturdays and spent the weekends with our wives.

We did real medical work. As an intern, I had assisted in numerous appendectomies, but never did one. Miles from nowhere, using a spinal anesthetic and equipment we would use in combat, I performed an appendectomy on a soldier.

Our Camp Cook and desert training involved simulations under combat conditions. I had my men practice setting up our multiple tents and equipment at night without lights. It was difficult, but they became adept at it. In the exercises, my men collected simulated "battlefield" dead and injured and carried them to the collecting station. The "injured" were treated there and sent to a field hospital, the "dead" to a simulated morgue.

In March of 1944, I was promoted to captain. After my unit moved to Camp Maxey, Texas, I volunteered for overseas duty. We moved to Fort Sam Houston at San Antonio, where the 10th Army was activated, and began preparations for overseas duty. Assigned as a headquarters cadre, I was in a medical unit handling sick calls under Dr. Glenn T. Howard, later of Alice, Texas, a major about 10 years older than I was.

At Fort Houston, we received—and I helped give—shots required before going overseas. To make them easier and faster to give, we filled a 10 cc syringe with vaccine, gave a cubic centimeter to each man, changed needles, and kept going until the syringe was empty. A colonel who had never practiced wanted to help. Handed a full syringe, he gave all 10 cc of vaccine to one soldier. Luckily, the latter developed only a very sore arm. The same colonel asked for medicine for a general with poison ivy or a similar problem. I gave him calamine lotion. The colonel asked, "What's the dosage?" I was heard to observe that the colonel probably couldn't run a one-pump filling station.

From Fort Houston, we moved by train to Fort Lewis, near Seattle, Washington. On August 26, 1944, we embarked for Hawaii on a crowded troop ship. On the six-day voyage, we were little more than serial numbers (mine was O-449690). On September 1, we disembarked at Honolulu and went to Schofield Barracks.

Beth was pregnant. When I left Texas for Fort Lewis, she returned home, staying at Crown Point until moving to my Uncle Daurcy's to be near my favorite obstetrician, Dr. Bickel. After thirty-six hours of rather hard labor, Rick was born at South Bend Memorial on August 19, 1944. A Red Cross field director's telegram sent to me at Fort Lewis said, "both fine no complications." However, Rick quickly required surgeries for a small cleft palate and a hypertrophic pyloric stenosis, a narrowing of the opening between the stomach and duodenum. He recovered well from both surgeries.

In Honolulu, I helped Major Howard with sick calls. We did jungle and amphibious landing training and learned about submarines, poisonous snakes, kamikaze planes, and the fanatical discipline of Japanese soldiers. I gave Colonel Jimmy Roosevelt, President Roosevelt's oldest son, shots his home physician prescribed. I investigated a soldier's suicide and treated an officer's collapsed lung. Other medical work was dull and routine—colds, rashes and malingering cases. For recreation we had a softball team, and I pitched. The catcher was Dr. George Finney, a noted Johns Hopkins surgeon.

At Schofield Barracks, the 10th Army headquarters staff was assembled. Although a lowly captain, I was one of the cadre, assigned to Plans and Operations. The 10th Army's original target was Formosa, but a decision had been made to bypass it and instead hit Okinawa. My role probably earned me the privilege—if it can be called that—of going ashore with my medical unit in the first few hours of D-Day.

Okinawa is the largest island in the Ryukyu chain, stretching from the Japanese island of Kyushu to Formosa (now Taiwan). Of its 454 square miles of land area, two-thirds is forested and mountainous. Planners seem to have chosen Okinawa as the invasion target because military intelligence underestimated Japanese strength. There were strategic reasons for the decision. Flying from Iwo Jima and Saipan, U.S. planes were bombing the Japanese mainland regularly. However, the distance to Japan from Okinawa (slightly more than 400 miles) is a fraction of that from Iwo Jima (1,200 miles). Okinawa's closeness to Japan also made it a better staging area from which to invade the Japanese homeland.

It took an interminably long thirty-nine days for our convoy to reach Okinawa. We lived in two-foot-wide, side-by-side hammocks under which we stowed duffel bags. We lost our physical readiness. Our ships zigzagged to reduce exposure to kamikaze attacks. When they came, we were herded below—below the water line, that is—and the hatches were fastened down. Had there been a hit, we would have had no way to escape. We heard ack-ack and machine-gun fire and the groaning engines of diving Japanese planes during the attacks. I later learned that a ship in our group was hit, but not sunk.

Task Force 58, the invasion armada, was the mightiest fleet ever to sail the Pacific. Kamikaze attacks took a toll as our ships sat offshore. Carrier and land-based planes and fleet guns bombed and bombarded the island for two weeks before the invasion began on April 1, 1945, the day President Roosevelt died. The Japanese elected not to defend the beaches, so the landing was relatively easy. Troops on our ship, including our medical unit, waited eighteen to twenty-four hours to land. I remember my amazement at the massive number of soldiers, support vehicles, and supplies going ashore simultaneously that day.

All hell soon broke loose. Fortified in hundreds of caves with multiple levels and openings, the Japanese were determined to fight to the end. As quickly as we bulldozed cave openings shut, they popped out of other exits. Flame-throwers became one of our best weapons. The northern three-fifths of the island was taken in less than two weeks, but it took ten more weeks to crack the six-mile line of fortifications from Naha on the west coast through Shuri to Yonaburu on the east coast. Driven to Okinawa's southern tip, many Japanese soldiers jumped off the high cliffs into the sea. Others, including General Mitsura Ushijima, the Japanese commander, committed hara-kiri. While the battle was in progress, we received word on May 8th of Germany's surrender.

Operation Iceberg, the battle for Okinawa, was World War II's last major battle and one of its bloodiest. More than 12,500 Americans died, and almost 37,000 were injured. Japanese dead exceeded 110,000. From 75,000 to 140,000 Okinawan civilians died. Americans lost nearly 800 planes, the Japanese more than 7,700. Kamikaze attacks inflicted heavy damage on the invasion fleet.

My worst memories of the campaign are images of truckloads of dead Americans, their bodies stacked like cords of wood, being taken to the rear for burial. One morning I saw forty or fifty Japanese dead, killed in a night attack on an airfield. The death of General Simon B. Buckner, the 10th Army commander, remains etched in my memory.

I witnessed the Japanese surrender of the Ryukyus to General Joseph (Vinegar Bend) Stillwell. For reasons unknown to me, an Army band played "The Old Gray Mare" and "Beer Barrel Polka" before the ceremony. In an area surrounded by Marines and bristling with troops and weaponry, Japanese representatives then marched out to take their places at the table. After the ceremony, there was an aerial parade. With others, I snapped pictures, but I was too far away for the individuals to be identifiable.

Another medical officer and I soon were sent to investigate the medical needs of captive troops. We used an LST (landing ship, tank). One end of the craft is little more than a big door that becomes a ramp when lowered onshore. On the LST, we did an emergency appendectomy, but it was easier because I was not the only physician aboard.

On our way to one island, one of the worst typhoons in Ryukyu history struck. The wind manometer, a type of pressure gauge, broke at

120 knots, or about 150 miles per hour. Tossed to and fro, our LST sometimes sat on the crest of three big waves. When the end waves dropped off, the ship was left teetering, then dropped precipitously into the ensuing trough. Our LST even collided with a destroyer after the two ships' anchors became tangled. We finally washed ashore on one of the Amamis, the northernmost island group of the Ryukyus. That experience was more frightening than the war itself.

My memories from that mission are of the dank, dark caves the Japanese used as hospitals and their messes, with big kettles of rice, often covered with flies. On returning, I turned in a seventeen-page report on the immediate and long-term needs of the Japanese forces for food, medical and water supplies, medical personnel, hospitals, and hospital beds.

DDT was used to kill mosquitoes and help control malaria. I once flew on a DDT spraying mission. Our plane went up, down, and in between the hills with its doors open. The plane's motion and the chemical's oily smell nauseated us. I also remember seeing Japanese ammunition loaded on amphibious "ducks" to be dumped into the ocean.

When atomic bombs were dropped on Hiroshima on August 6, 1945, and Nagasaki on August 9, 1945, we were completely surprised. President Truman's courage in using the bombs saved far more American and Japanese lives than both A-bombs took. A grim reality—that more bombs might fall—speeded the Japanese surrender on August 14, 1945.

The officers I remember from service were Medical Corps personnel. Major Howard, an easygoing, somewhat neurotic, quiet talker, was the CO of the 10th Army Headquarters Medical Detachment. Colonel Frederic B. Westervelt was the 10th Army surgeon general. Col. George Finney, earlier mentioned as our softball team's catcher in Hawaii, was a Johns Hopkins surgeon in civilian life. Captain Arnold Bachman of Columbia City was mentioned earlier. Lieutenant Colonel William Williams, the M.D. who commanded my unit at Camp Cook, was a Regular Army, spit-and-polish kind of officer who expected to be saluted every time, in a building or outside. I owe him for recommending my promotion to captain.

The war over, I was impatient to go home, but I stayed on Okinawa, probably because I did not go on active duty until mid-1943. There was little to do. I spent lots of time in a tent library, where I first read and memorized the *King Lear* quote. I investigated a complaint against a company commander. Colonel Westervelt asked that I be promoted to major, a field officer classification that carried a big pay raise. With our baby's surgeries, Beth and I could have used the money, but promotions were frozen, and mine never came through. Offered a promotion to major if I would stay in service at discharge, I declined.

In early January of 1946, I flew home on a cargo plane with backless bench seats. By way of Guam, the Johnson Islands, and Hawaii, we flew to San Francisco. From there, we rode eastward for three days on a badly equipped train with no showers or dining car. All of us wanted to rush home, but the train seemed to stop at every village.

We arrived at Chicago on a wintry day. Having had no shower for days, I felt dirty and probably smelled. I saw Beth before she saw me. We had a happy reunion, and she didn't complain about my forced lack of hygiene. We returned to Crown Point, where I saw my eighteen-month-old son, Rick, for the first time. In a week at home, I remained a stranger to him.

I then reported to Camp Atterbury, south of Indianapolis. For three months, I ran sick call and admitted patients to the base hospital. My discharge date was July 10, 1946, but I had a sixty-day furlough and left Atterbury in early May. My papers carry these notations:

Medical Officer General Duty;
Served with a medical collecting company, a medical clearing company,
and special troops, 10th Army Headquarters, in the Asiatic-Pacific
Theater of Operations
as well as Wakeman General Hospital, Camp Atterbury, Ind.
Examined, diagnosed and prescribed medical treatment for sick and
wounded personnel.
Service outside continental U.S.A.: 26 Aug. 1944 to 2 Jan. 1946.
Battles and Campaigns—Ryukyus
Decorations and Citations:
(1) American Theater Service Medal, (2) Victory Medal,
(3) Asiatic-Pacific Services Medal and (4) Japanese Occupation Medal.

My 201 (service personnel) file shows that I was immunized for smallpox, typhoid, typhus, tetanus, cholera, plague, and influenza and tested for immunity to diphtheria.

Finally released from the Army, I was ready to do what I had worked toward for most of my life—practice medicine.

⇒ 5 ⇐

Family Doctor in Bremen

BACK IN CROWN POINT, my son, Rick, finally accepted me as a family member. I also got reacquainted with Beth and my mother-in-law, parents, brother, and sisters. My younger brother, Dick, who had participated in the D-Day landing at Normandy, came home about the same time. Our parents were greatly relieved that both their sons had survived the war.

With a family to feed, I needed to begin a practice. Beth and I looked for a place where I could be a country doctor and still be reasonably close to good hospitals and consultative services. We also wanted a good place to settle down and rear a family.

We visited many areas. We chose Bremen because of its proximity to South Bend's Memorial and St. Joseph hospitals and Mishawaka's St. Joseph Hospital, and because I knew specialists in South Bend. Beth and I also liked Bremen's attractive homes, well-maintained businesses, excellent schools and parks, and many churches.

Bremen's only doctor, Dr. Homer Burke, was returning to the medical mission field. (Dr. Earl Cripe, also back from service, started practice in Bremen the same day I did.) I bought the old house that Dr. Burke had used as his office, purchased his equipment, furniture, and medical supplies, and bought medical instruments from a Bourbon physician's widow. The office had a large waiting room, two examining rooms, a medicine room, and a restroom on the main floor and a delivery room upstairs. I hired an office nurse, Bernice Crittenden, a secretary-receptionist, Lydia Heuberger, and an on-call OB nurse.

I also bought a small home, earlier the office of Dr. Wallace Buchanan, who did not return to Bremen after the war. Once remodeled, it became our first home. As I began practice, my goal was to be the most caring family physician possible. If I was available and conscientious and didn't gouge patients, I assumed that I would be as busy as could be.

I saw my first patient, Fred Lehman, in the evening on Memorial Day, 1946. His was an easy poison ivy case. My $1.50 charge for the office call included a bottle of calamine lotion. I kept fees at $1.50 for a few months, then slowly increased them until office visits were $5 and house calls were $7 by 1972. My initial fee for prenatal care, including the mother's six-week post-delivery checkup, her baby's first-month checkup, their night in the office's upstairs delivery room, and a nurse's services, was $35. By 1972, it reached $75. One reason I could keep fees so low was that malpractice insurance was only $15 a year. However, that cost soon zoomed rapidly upward.

I was busier than I'd ever imagined. Four or five doctors normally handle the work that Dr. Cripe and I had in our solo practices. My practice covered a twenty-five- to thirty-mile radius from Bremen north to Lakeville, Mishawaka, and South Bend, east to Nappanee, west to Tyner, Walkerton, Koontz Lake, and LaPaz, and south to Bourbon, Argos, and Plymouth.

Medical school gave me book knowledge and theory. The internship helped me apply that knowledge. In my first months of practice, I became my own teacher. The practice of medicine jibed with my medical school teachings, but we had not been taught how to run an office, schedule appointments, do consultations, write job descriptions, hire personnel, handle payrolls, deal with tax issues, and handle "hurt feelings and little jealousies" among office personnel. We also got little advice in school on how to integrate ourselves into our communities or keep up with new medical techniques and medicines.

My practice dealt mostly with upper respiratory and gastrointestinal illnesses, earaches, sore throats, arthritis, and common communicable diseases—"three-day" and "old-fashioned" measles, mumps, and chickenpox. In medical school, internship, and the military, I seldom saw such illnesses. I removed skin tumors, did "T&As" (tonsil and adenoid surgeries) and "D&Cs" (dilation and curettage surgeries), delivered babies, and did episiotomies in the delivery room. I assisted with surgeries on patients I referred to surgeons. I repaired lacerations of every kind and took care of simple fractures.

I handled 80 to 90 percent of all cases, referring the rest to specialists. I routinely made referrals on cases involving appendectomies, gall bladder removal, tumors other than skin tumors, complicated fractures, and medical or pediatric diagnostic problems. If I sensed that patients or relatives were overly anxious, or when patients did not respond to accepted treatment measures, I made referrals.

Referrals can be defensive. If patients sense that a physician is competent and caring, there are minimal legal dangers in practicing in a small town. In other settings, even with friendly patients and capable physicians, the dangers are greater. If a parent, spouse, or child is ill, it's a threat when the family member in charge says, "I don't care what it costs. Get my wife (or child or parent)- well." Doctors then must do expensive tests that won't show anything but will prove that the physician did everything possible.

On average, I delivered about 10 babies a month, or about 120 a year. Over twenty-five years in practice, I estimate that I delivered 3,000 babies. Long before it was common, I allowed husbands in the delivery room, warning them to sit or leave if they became lightheaded or dizzy. Few had to sit. Husbands and wives were thankful for this opportunity to share a special family moment, the birth of a child.

My office's upstairs delivery room had a labor bed, a delivery table, and supply cabinets. Unless patients wanted to go elsewhere, I delivered babies there, as Dr. Burke had, until Bremen Hospital became a reality. After staying overnight, my patients were carried down the narrow stairway on a stretcher by Johnny Siefer and Ernie Goss, employees of Huff Funeral Home, and taken by ambulance to the home of either Mrs. Jennie M. Bartels or Mrs. Francis A. Maurice. Those ladies cared for them until ten days were up. It was a far cry from today's immediate ambulation.

My typical day started at 6:30 A.M. with a quick breakfast at the town cafe. (Beth was busy getting the kids off to school.) After hospital rounds and house calls, I started office calls at 9 A.M. An emergency room call, a delivery, or seriously ill walk-in patient could put us behind. If we ran late, our secretary called the next patient. Morning and afternoon times were left open for catch-up. Over the noon hour, I worked in a house call or two, had a quick lunch, and returned to the office to see patients with appointments until roughly 6 P.M. After one or two more house calls, I went home, ate, listened to the news, and went to bed. Often I had a night house call or two.

I categorized patients in four groups—those with appointments, work-ins, walk-ins, and sneak-ins. We tried to stay on schedule for those with appointments. Work-ins were told to come in but were promised no specific time. They usually had high temperatures or were otherwise acutely ill. We saw them between appointments or by scheduling them in open appointment times. Most walk-ins were quite sick, and we cared for them as best we could. A typical "sneak-in" was a mother with an appointment who brought three kids along and said, "While I'm here, would you look at them, too?" If we had time, we did. If we didn't and they were not acutely ill, we suggested that they come back.

Patient loads depended upon the time of year. In a flu epidemic, if we had two or three imminent deliveries at the same time, if there was a major accident, if there was snow and ice on the ground, or if it was excessively hot or cold, we had more patients. My average daily patient load was about four patients on hospital rounds (not counting OB cases), four or five house calls, including those at night, and about twenty-five office patients.

I considered house calls an integral part of my practice. This was particularly true for Amish patients. Bringing a mother or two or three sick children to my office in a buggy was especially difficult for them. I could do a better job in my office, but an examination at home was better than none at all, and it was infinitely better than dragging a sick infant or an ill elderly patient out in bad or wintry weather.

For crippled or hypertensive older patients, I scheduled house calls—monthly, every other month, or every third month. Once these future house calls were noted in my appointment book, patients knew they could expect me at that time on that day. Serving twenty to thirty nursing home patients took half a day every month. Usually, nursing home patients' greater susceptibility to illness added an emergency call or two a week.

I drove myself on most house and emergency calls. If I was extremely tired and admitted it after an urgent call in the middle of the night, Beth drove. Nora Sausman, who lived alone two blocks away, came on short notice to stay with our children. At times, house calls were difficult. On one to an Amish lady's home up a long, muddy lane, my car got stuck. My patient's husband quickly pulled me out—with his team of horses.

In northern Indiana, snowdrifts and blocked roads are common in winter. In my car's trunk, I carried boots, gloves, a heavy coat, salt, and a scoop shovel. In the worst part of winter, I had chains on my tires. One night I got stuck near Buford Rowe's home, three or four miles out in the country. He probably heard me revving the car's motor, because

I had just started shoveling when he came with his tractor. Occasion-ally, perhaps trying to save a fee for an office call, people caught me at the post office or church or on the street and asked a medical question. If my patience was shorter than normal, my answer was: "Undress right now, and I'll check you."

Elderly patients were my pets. It took longer to examine them and deal with their problems, but they appreciated the attention. Elderly persons who accepted aging as a time to expect slowing and aches and pains and not to expect miracles were my least difficult patients. Babies were no problem except for their over-anxious parents. Children from two to eight years of age were less apt to be cooperative.

I am a great fan of the Amish people, a group of honest, friendly, tidy, hardworking, generous, religious folks. They handle most things themselves. If a family member is ill and can't afford needed care, all chip in. When an Amish family's barn burns, they put up another one in days. In twenty-five years of practice, I had only one Amish patient on welfare, an elderly alcoholic man.

The Amish do not use electricity, but most have indoor plumbing. They do not own cars, but some hire a vehicle and a driver for a vaca-tion or visit. They have no telephones, but often use the closest neigh-bor's in emergencies.

My Amish patients were no different than other patients. When they called, however, I knew they were really sick, because their call meant that their home remedies had failed. Amish children were good patients—either well-disciplined or very shy—and they never misbe-haved in my office or their homes.

Before Bremen had a hospital providing obstetric care, Amish women had babies at home. If an Amish man called or an Amish kid showed up at my home or office and said, "Come on out, Mom's sick," I knew I should take along my obstetric bag. After we got the hospital, the Amish were a bit reluctant to use it for deliveries. Once they started doing so, word quickly spread about how nice it was to have a baby there. Amish women still wanted to go home twenty-four to forty-eight hours after giving birth. At the time, I was reluctant to let that happen. In retrospect, they were ahead of the times.

The Amish became and remain ardent Bremen Community Hos-pital supporters. Each year, the hospital auxiliary stages a fundraising barbecue. The Amish supply wonderful homemade pies, attend in sig-nificant numbers, wait tables, and help clean up.

Amish patients never paid me on the spot for a Sunday call, but they were always at the door the next morning to pay.

My patients included two more than 100 years old. I did an appendectomy on a 90-year-old lady. I cared for five generations in one family and delivered children to three generations of several families. I enjoyed taking care of ministers, some of whom came back for physicals after moving away, possibly because I never charged them.

I once delivered the seventeenth child for one family. They couldn't afford to pay, and I didn't ask for anything. Being good people and wanting to do something, they left a chicken in a gunnysack in our garage. Wouldn't you know it, I ran over the chicken.

When medical problems or minor surgery was involved, I sent patients to Bremen Hospital. For major surgery, patients went to St. Joseph Hospital in Mishawaka or Memorial Hospital in South Bend. I always asked patients and their families where they wanted to go. Most preferred our local hospital, where they were babied and where relatives could visit easily. Even after major surgeries at Mishawaka or South Bend, patients often transferred back to Bremen in two or three days. Before the local hospital opened, patients needing hospitalization went to South Bend, Mishawaka, or Plymouth. Keeping patients in Bremen saved time for patients, families, and doctors.

There are hundreds of interesting anecdotes from my quarter-century in the practice of medicine, and a few memorable ones.

One patient, Delbert Snyder, broke his back and severed his spinal cord in a fall off a wagon. I cared for him as an intern at South Bend Memorial, then cared for him for many more years after returning from the service

I remember a family across the tracks that included about five children, the youngest a girl I had just delivered. Three or four days after she and her mother got home from the hospital, I was called to come see the baby. Her towheaded five-year-old brother met me at the door and said, "Come on in, Doc. My baby sister won't nurse and poops all the time." (I've substituted "nurse" and "poops" for his actual words.)

I once was called to the house of a young farmer, Richard Baker, whose illness had baffled physicians, including a South Bend specialist. When he was lying down, his blood pressure was okay. When he sat up, he fainted and his blood pressure dropped. He suffered dizziness. I had seen only one case as an intern, but Addison's disease came to my mind immediately. Tests showed that my hunch was correct. Cortisone treatments improved his condition dramatically. Since Addison's is a chronic disease, he had to stay on the medication. I felt proud that I made a rare diagnosis after others failed.

I delivered a set of twins whose combined weight was fourteen pounds. Wondering if that was a record, I checked the State Board of Health. The twins' birth weight was the second-heaviest in state history.

Occasionally, people conclude what they want. I carefully explained to the family of a farmer who had suffered a coronary occlusion, commonly called a heart attack, what had happened and what it meant. After I was through, a daughter said, "Well, thank God; I thought he'd had a heart attack."

A delightful little old lady who hadn't seen a doctor much came to me. Her daughter had told her that she would have to undress for the examination. We gave her a hospital-type gown to wear. When I came into the exam room, I saw that she had put on her pajamas.

One of my Amish patients was an 8- or 9-year-old boy with the biggest adenoids and tonsils I've ever seen. When he took a breath, he literally snorted. I convinced his parents that he needed a T&A (tonsils and adenoids) surgery. Two weeks later, my young patient came to my office for another reason. "Doc," he said, "I'm sure glad you took out my tonsils. Now when we play hide-and-seek, they can't find me."

The case of JoAnn Senff, born with a hole in the septum of her heart, was unique. She faced certain death without surgery. At age 14 or 15, when she was close to that point, we contacted Dr. Harris B. (Harry) Shumacker Jr., a heart surgeon and the chair of the Department of Surgery at the IU School of Medicine. He said immediate surgery had to be done.

JoAnn had the rarest blood type—A negative. Before surgery, we needed thirteen pints of that type blood. I obtained an A-negative donor list from the Red Cross Blood Bank, called those on it, and asked them to help. Some lived as far as a hundred miles away from Indianapolis, but no one turned me down—an example of the abiding goodness of people.

The surgery was successful. JoAnn needed a pacemaker, but she married and had two children, whom I helped deliver by Caesarean. She died at about age 45, before her children were grown, but had a longer, fuller life than otherwise would have been possible.

Within two years after coming to Bremen, my practice had grown so much that I was working eighty-hour weeks and had a house call or delivery most nights. I built a new office building in 1948, but it was obvious that what I most needed was help. Marshall E. Stine, a graduate of Washington Medical School in Missouri, joined my practice the next year. After Dr. Stine went into the service, Dr. Cecil R. Burket of nearby Wakarusa joined me in practice. As a South Bend Memorial intern, he relieved me a weekend or two a month and was familiar with my practice. He and his wife, Berniece ("Bunnie") Burket, a nurse, stayed at our home and used my office to see patients when he relieved me. On Dr. Burket's first day, I had a 104-degree temperature and tonsillitis and he had to go it alone.

After Dr. Stine's return, we formed a three-man family practice group. Drs. Stine and Burket were very competent, compassionate physicians. The three of us were remarkably compatible. (Dr. Stine passed away on April 14, 1999, at Naples, Fla. For the hospital newsletter, I prepared a eulogy that said in part: "From close personal experience, I can say that Marshall was a master at his job. He had the old standing virtues. He was well informed, conscientious, gentle and gracious. He was polite, attentive and a good listener—qualities that made him a good counselor to his patients. He was organized, considerate and reliable. He deserves to be called a true professional—one dedicated to his God, his family, his community, his friends and his patients.")

As our practice evolved, I added another nurse, a business manager, and a person to transcribe information from a recording device into which we dictated each patient's complaints, what our exam showed, and what we prescribed. This helped us keep our records current. Our business manager, William Helmlinger, served all three physicians. When I later left the group, he continued with Drs. Burket and Stine until retirement.

The group practice gave each of us time off. I took Wednesday afternoons, Dr. Burket Thursdays, and Dr. Stine Fridays. Every third weekend I was on call. Every third weekend I worked until Saturday noon and was on second call—the backup physician—for emergencies or major problems. Every third weekend, I was off from Friday night to Monday morning. The doctor on full duty covered office "walk-ins" at 11 A.M. Sundays. When they learned that a doctor was available then, a few patients who should have been to the office earlier or could have waited took advantage. Not many did, and the doctor on call could see all the patients needing treatment on a weekend in two hours.

When Dr. Jack Schreiner came to Bremen to practice solo, the community had five doctors and good medical coverage. All five were about the same age and retired about the same time. Several physicians saw that as an opportunity, and the community now has seven fine doctors in their thirties and forties.

My legislative service later required me to spend large blocks of time away from Bremen. These absences were unfair to my colleagues.

In 1964, I sold my office to Drs. Burket and Stine, put an office in the basement of my home at 304 North Center Street, and resumed solo practice. During legislative sessions, my former colleagues covered for me.

In solo practice, I made my own appointments and was able to keep on time. When patients called, I asked about their ailment. If they had a sore throat, I scheduled them for ten minutes. If the patient was a talkative older lady needing a physical and Pap test, I allowed an hour. Dressing and undressing—and talking—took a lot of extra time.

The 1965 Palm Sunday tornadoes, which took 139 lives in Indiana and caused massive property destruction, created medical problems that far exceeded any I had ever experienced except during the war. About 2,000 people were injured statewide.

Mrs. Calvin Grise of Wyatt was brought to our hospital on a door. A two-by-six-inch splintered board had sliced into her abdomen. Miraculously, it had not gone into the abdominal cavity, but had kind of split the skin over the abdomen. She also had a broken leg. It took us hours to get the wound cleaned and sutured and to set the fracture.

Bremen Community Hospital doctors and staff handled their share of tornado-related medical problems. Comparatively speaking, our hospital was busier than the larger South Bend hospitals, which saw about 100 patients. We saw about 30.

Events had an unsettling quality at times. I've always found it difficult to accept the deaths of young people, particularly those in auto accidents. While coroner, I was called to the west edge of Bremen, where an accident had taken the lives of two boys. Both were about 16 and barely able to drive. Just before the accident, they had tried to coax their good friend, our son Tim, into going with them. Tim knew he couldn't stay long after school without reporting home, so he didn't go. Beth and I were forever grateful that he didn't.

Dealing with a patient's death is difficult. I tried to be sympathetic and understanding and made it a point to explain to family members what had happened. I went to the funeral home to pay my respects and to create another opportunity for the family to talk with me about their loved one. It's a tight rope to walk. Being too emotional reduces one's ability to think and act professionally. Being totally unsympathetic looks (and is) cold and hard-hearted. Later, after losing loved ones of my own at too early an age to cancer, I came to think that—despite my best efforts—I might not have shown enough warmth and empathy. There is no greater trauma than losing those who occupy special niches in our lives.

I practiced in Bremen from 1946 to 1971. Running for and serving as governor later kept me from practicing. I've never regretted the fact that I did not specialize or practice in an urban area. Being a small-town family doctor involves a special, satisfying, and uplifting relationship. In Bremen, I was more than a physician. I was a friend, neighbor, fellow Kiwanian, band booster, and sports enthusiast like other townspeople. I no longer practice in Bremen, but I still enjoy a special relationship with its wonderful people.

Medicine has changed a great deal in the fifty-plus years since I started practice. I don't know when I realized that doctors must be both competent and compassionate. It's not enough to have competence without compassion, or vice versa. At some point, I also realized that some of the worst medical students were the best doctors because of the art of their practice, and some of the best students were poor doctors because patients saw their minimal charisma as cold and unfeeling.

Specialization and government intervention depersonalized medicine. Other factors, including shallow media coverage, make people expect the impossible—medical miracles on demand all the time. When things go wrong, people now sue, even if the doctor made an honest mistake or the problem was outside his control. Such developments negatively impact the practice of medicine.

The federal health care programs, Medicare and Medicaid, have been boons to patients and to some degree economic boons for doctors. However, the paperwork and occasionally goofy regulations associated with the two programs make doctors feel that someone is looking over their shoulder. This has altered the doctor-patient relationship and increased the cost of medicine.

Doctors had more charitable hearts when I practiced. Certainly, money counted, but not like it does now. At that time, doctors seemed more willing to donate time to free clinics for the poor. (Today's doctors might like to return to free clinic days, I suspect, if that would end the hassles in serving poor people.)

Despite the negatives, we see new and different miracles on an almost daily basis. I personally know many compassionate doctors. Fifty-plus years after I first began practice in Bremen, I still believe that the practice of medicine is the noblest of all professions.

Antibiotics are the biggest change in medicine in my lifetime. Sulfanilamide was a miracle drug when I graduated from medical school. I first heard about penicillin when Winston Churchill became ill in Africa or the Mediterranean, was treated with penicillin and made a miraculous recovery. Penicillin also gave the armed services a one-shot cure for gonorrhea. The tetracyclines followed. One after another, new antibiotics came along. Today's doctors have an array of infection-fighting drugs. There also are new medicines for hypertension, vaccines, and diagnostic tools like CAT scans and MRI's; advances in transplant surgery, renal dialysis, and laboratory procedures; new treatments for cancer, open heart surgery, birth control pills, and so on.

The first cases of AIDS undoubtedly developed in the sixties, but we did not know about them until later. We now seem to be at the start of the journey toward a cure.

In short, the changes we have seen in medicine in these last fifty years are a revolution, the end of which is not in sight.

Immense changes in medicine also have taken place in Bremen in my fifty-plus years there. A large crowd turned out when Bremen Community Hospital celebrated its fiftieth anniversary on June 16, 1997. The open house came seventeen days after my nephrectomy—removal of a cancerous kidney. Though still a bit under the weather, I had to be present, because I was there at the beginning. Drs. Stine and Burket and I were the speakers.

In 1943, Mr. and Mrs. William Myers started a nursing and convalescent center in a Bremen home. After Mrs. Myers's sudden death, the Church of the Brethren took over but couldn't handle the financial burden. The people of German Township and surrounding areas raised money, bought the home, incorporated the Community Hospital of German Township as a not-for-profit community hospital, and got it licensed by the state. The legislature authorized a small tax to help fund its operation.

Bremen needed a hospital. The community and surrounding area are twenty to thirty-five miles from Plymouth, Rochester, South Bend, Mishawaka, Elkhart, Warsaw, LaPorte, and Goshen, where there are hospitals. Accidents often occur on the heavily traveled roads that go through or near Bremen. Amish families in slow-moving buggies are vulnerable and can't make good time going to a hospital. Farm and factory accidents are numerous.

The State Board of Health once threatened to close the hospital because it was small. The community turned out en masse for a hearing, and the board's representative learned in no uncertain terms that Bremen needed and wanted its hospital. Even the Amish turned out. The hospital subsequently was re-licensed.

The hospital then had about fifteen beds. It was remodeled and expanded to twenty-three beds in 1958. In 1977, citizens dipped into their pockets to create a modern hospital with twenty-eight beds. The hospital was the first with OB convalescent rooms next to a nursery equipped with delivery drawers so that mothers can hold and feed their babies when they wish. In the early eighties, the community raised $800,000 to add the latest diagnostic and treatment equipment. In 1990, the hospital added an emergency department, more than doubled outpatient capacity, and added radiology, physical therapy, and cardiac rehabilitation.

South Bend and Mishawaka specialists of all types now spend a day a week in Bremen seeing patients. There are seven physicians, a long way from May 31, 1946, when Dr. Cripe and I began practicing as the new—and only—doctors in town.

Supply and demand remains the answer to attracting doctors to small towns. If U.S.-trained doctors prefer larger communities with more sophisticated hospitals and greater opportunity for specialization, then doctors trained outside the country have splendid opportunities as general practitioners in areas with unmet needs. Small towns advertise, build doctors' offices, and offer amenities because they understand the fierce competition for doctors. They want their own physicians. They should have them.

Government should not dictate where doctors practice, particularly after contributing to doctor shortages by controlling medical school subsidies and the number of medical students. From a public health standpoint, it's a risky business when policy makers ignore the plain truth that the pipeline takes twelve to fifteen years to deliver new doctors. However, there's nothing wrong with the federal government forgiving the educational debt of doctors who practice in inner cities and underserved rural areas.

Closed-circuit TV and other types of remote consultation with specialists may mean more rural areas without doctors in the future. Bremen would have faced that danger if its physicians and townspeople had lacked foresight. Luckily, as a rapidly growing bedroom community, Bremen's increasing need for medical services will support the hospital and hold good physicians. Other towns may not be as fortunate.

On a personal level, our family found Bremen to be the "good town" promised by the signs at the town limits. Its good schools, parks, and churches reflect the values of its thrifty, honest people, many of whom are of German descent.

In a small-town practice, finding time for family is a difficult challenge for which there is no medical school preparation. Beth did most of the child-rearing. Without ever complaining, she was our children's mother, part-time father, chauffeur, disciplinarian, and counselor. Most of the responsibility for school activities fell to her.

As much as possible for a busy country doctor, I tried to help. I cooked breakfast on Sunday mornings so that Beth could get the kids off to Sunday school. I did the yard work. In winter, I shoveled our walks. Our house was on a corner lot, so there was twice as much sidewalk to clear. I also cleared sidewalks for an elderly couple living next door.

We tried to do things as a family. An example was our annual trip to a tree farm to cut a Christmas tree. Even when it was snowing and cold, the kids enjoyed it. We had room to display a large tree, and our children thought "bigger was better." Once they spied the one they wanted and we began cutting it, they learned that bigger wasn't necessarily easier. However, everyone took a turn with the saw.

I tried to see that our children participated in sports. Basketball was king then, and there was no football. Our boys were able basketball players, but too short. Rick made the first team as a senior but usually sat on the bench. Judy was a high school yell leader for four years. Although our sons didn't play, we attended basketball games far and near. My older boys and I played church league softball. I played softball until age 48, when I tore a calf muscle. I was on crutches with a painfully swollen leg that was black and blue from my toes to my thighs. I coached Little League. I was, and am, a spectator at high school and college basketball and football games.

I spent less time with my children than I wanted, but I have wonderful memories from their earlier days. They might prefer that I remain silent about their occasional mischief, but some of the things they did are fun to talk about now.

Judy had a playhouse that she and a neighbor girl enjoyed, but we discovered that the girls were hiding there to smoke cigarettes. Settling on a non-physical remedy, I bought a pack of cigarettes, took Judy into our living room, and told her we were going to smoke the entire pack together, one after another. Pretty soon she didn't feel so good, and neither did I. To my knowledge, she never smoked again.

I once came close to clobbering my second son, Tim. Hearing a back stairway creak about two o'clock one morning, I grabbed a heavy coat hanger, sneaked to the top of the steps, and flicked on the light. There was Tim, who had climbed out a window to the carport roof and slid down a support post to the ground. To get back, he had to come by the normal route. As a "reward" for his nocturnal tour, I grounded him for several days.

As a teenager, Rick had difficulty staying focused. He had ability and intelligence but lacked the desire to excel in his studies. In high school, he did only what he had to do to earn acceptable grades. This carried over to college. Once he married and went back for a master's degree, he proved his ability by making straight A's.

After Rob's kindergarten teacher told us that he couldn't see the blackboard, we had his eyes checked. He got glasses the day we went on a Chicago trip. I recall his astonishment at what he could see as we rode the South Shore and saw one of the first 3-D movies, *The Wind-jammer.* I felt guilty for not recognizing my own child's vision problem.

Beth and I were very proud of our children. I still am. Anyone who knows them agrees that they are the kind of people we hoped they would become. Before Beth's death, they gave us six wonderful grand-children. The number since has doubled.

Our oldest son, Rick, earned his bachelor's degree at Indiana University, Bloomington, and his master's degree at St. Francis College, Fort Wayne. In 1966 he married the former Sandra Kay Todd, born at Taylorsville, Indiana, on June 30, 1944, and a daughter of Maurice and Evelyn Todd. Sandy teaches at River Falls (Wisconsin) High School. Rick coaches basketball and teaches at River Falls College. Their children are Matthew Timothy Bowen, born July 27, 1971, and Michael Todd Bowen, born June 27, 1974.

Born at Bremen on January 6, 1947, our daughter Judy attended Purdue University before her marriage in 1966 to David L. McGrew, born at Nappanee on April 16, 1946, and a son of David and Mildred McGrew. An industrial engineer, he managed R. R. Donnelly Publishing Company operations in several locations. He now is CEO of Xyan, an on-demand printing and imaging firm. The McGrews live in Philadelphia. Their children are Richard Todd McGrew, born December 5, 1966; Nicole Lee McGrew, born August 7, 1969; and their adopted daughter, Monique Noel McGrew, born in Korea on August 15, 1977.

Born at Bremen on September 12, 1948, our second son, Tim, earned his B.S. degree from Indiana University. He owns and operates a printing firm at Statesville, North Carolina. With his first wife, Jackie Norris of Elkhart, he had two children, Amy Elizabeth Bowen, born May 27, 1976, and Angela Kay Bowen, born May 15, 1980. In 1984, at Davidson, North Carolina, Tim married Ann Brandes, born at Davidson on April 3, 1954, and a daughter of Roddy and Marguerite

Brandes. Their children are Timothy Brandes Bowen, born February 20, 1992, and Nathaniel Brandes Bowen, born October 3, 1995. They reside at Cornelius, North Carolina.

Our youngest son, Rob, born at Bremen on July 31, 1952, earned his bachelor's degree at IU and his J.D. degree from Valparaiso University. He practiced briefly in Columbus before being elected as a Marshall County Court judge. After unsuccessfully running for secretary of state, he returned to private practice for a few years and then was elected to the Marshall County bench, where he still serves. In 1980 he married Patricia Ann Pflanzer, born at Beech Grove on December 27, 1957, and a daughter of Raymond and Alice Pflanzer. Their children are Andrew Robert Bowen, born April 12, 1984; Christopher Otis Bowen, born September 6, 1985; and Elizabeth Alice Bowen, born February 11, 1992. The Rob Bowens reside next to me at Donnybrook.

Although an avid sports fan, I never had time for the usual sports. In my first year in Bremen, I tried golf, but I was called off the course so often that I switched to yard and garden work. Strictly for my own pleasure, I played the organ and piano. My children may have been humoring me when they said they enjoyed lying in bed and listening to me. They often were there before I got home from night house calls or emergencies.

I collected anecdotes, pithy bits of wisdom and humor. I still have several containers full, sorted by subject matter. They come in handy for speeches.

Our family has been active in the Bremen community and Marshall County. Beth served on the Blueberry Festival Committee. We both held medical association offices. Beth was treasurer, vice president, and president of the Indiana State Medical Society Auxiliary. I also served on the education board at our church, which operates a school.

I joined the Kiwanis Club soon after arriving in Bremen. While active, I had thirty-five years of perfect attendance. The premature death of the father of three young boys made me realize that as many as twenty boys were in like circumstances. While I was club president, this prompted me to start a program in which we assigned a Kiwanian to each boy. On a regular basis, the Kiwanian took his protégé to a game or on a picnic or did something fun. Members also ensured that their protégés had good shoes, warm clothing, and an occasional treat. To my disappointment, this program died out after a few years.

Beth was everyone's mother. A good example was one of Rick's classmates, a young man from a fine, hard-working family. He wanted to go to college, but his parents were dead set against it. After he refused to get a job in the foundry where his father worked, he was "invited" to leave home. Between his senior year of high school and his first year of college, and between his first two years of college, he lived with us. Beth did his laundry, loaned him money, and provided moral support. He earned bachelor's, master's, and doctor's degrees and now is superintendent of the Bremen schools.

Beth was a devout Lutheran. My family attended the United Brethren Church in Fulton. There was no UB church at Francesville, so we attended a Methodist church there and in Crown Point. At Bloomington, before I knew Beth, I attended a Lutheran church and enjoyed it. That made it easier for her to "convince" me to adopt her Lutheran faith. The only thing that bothered me about Lutherans was their use of a common communion cup. I saw that as a health issue, especially if flu was going around. I finally gave our minister, Rev. Ernest Eggers, a signed blank check to buy a communion set in Chicago. It was a hit with most of the congregation. Rev. Eggers gave older diehards a choice—they could have the communion cup or tiny individual cups.

Our closest friends in Bremen were LeRoy and Thelma Hirstein. Thelma taught two of our children in elementary school. Roy drove a gas and oil delivery truck and a school bus. The most honest, dependable, and conscientious person I've ever known, he was my Kiwanis mentor, a superb Kiwanian himself, and a devout Lutheran. The Hirsteins had no children, but they were like second parents to ours—especially Rob, our youngest. Roy, Thelma, Beth, and I sat together at basketball games and traveled to away games together. As a softball umpire, Roy was an outstanding role model for all fans and participants. At least once a summer, we went to Chicago for a White Sox baseball game and to the Lake Michigan beach at Michigan City. When I couldn't go, the Hirsteins were my surrogates.

Other close friends, all members of our church, were Mr. and Mrs. Buford Rowe, Mr. and Mrs. Eldon Roeder, Mr. and Mrs. Howard Seifer, and Mr. and Mrs. Richard Miller. The first three were farm families. A Studebaker executive, Dick Miller later ran a Bremen insurance agency.

For many years, twenty members of our church had a pinochle club that met monthly. The Millers, Hirsteins, Rowes, Roeders, and Seifers were active participants.

Nora Sausman, the older lady who often babysat for our children and was like another grandmother to them, was so much a family member that we included her in Christmas dinners and other get-togethers. (Her contribution was the best croissants I ever ate.)

In my years of practice, real vacations were rare. The only way a physician can relax is to get out of town. That's never easy. Arrangements must be made for another doctor to take calls, and OB patients due to deliver must be told which doctor is substituting. Our most memorable vacations were to Indiana, Michigan, Wisconsin, and the Canadian lakes.

This period—when I was practicing and Beth and I were rearing our family—was fulfilling and rewarding both personally and professionally. I've always said that work isn't work if you enjoy what you're doing. I was busy doing what I enjoyed. My only regret is that my practice, politics, and government kept me from spending more time with my children. I now realize that Beth carried a far greater share of the load of rearing our family than she should have. I supplied the wherewithal, but she had the most important task.

This also was a challenging period. I became accustomed to long hours, lost sleep, and missed meals. I learned to remain calm and unflustered and to be patient with and tolerant of others. I learned when to be tactful and when to be stern and decisive.

In short, as a doctor, father, and neighbor, I learned a great deal that would serve me well in public life.

⚶ 6 ⚶

First Public Service: Coroner

DAD WAS A Democrat, Mom a Republican, so I could have gone either way. Dad ran unsuccessfully for county surveyor in normally Republican Fulton County. After retiring from teaching, he twice was elected as Aubbenaubbee Township trustee.

Feeling that President Roosevelt's policies were making people too dependent on government, I became a Republican about 1940. Dad kidded me, saying I was immature and politically unwise. Kidding him back, I said I had seen the light. When I ran for governor, Dad gave me his full and enthusiastic support. I always voted. I also served as a precinct committee person, and Beth as vice committee person, for four years.

In 1952, my precinct committee person, Theodore Schweisberger, and Marshall County Republican chair Stewart Robertson asked me to run for county coroner. Our county medical society thought that a physician should fill the position. I didn't seek the job, but I agreed to take my turn without a thought about where it might lead.

I had no primary opponent. My fall opponent was P. R. Irey, a short, stocky doctor with a good practice in Plymouth. I knew the coroner would be a physician no matter who won, so I didn't campaign much. I credited my easy 9,381 to 6,049 victory to the fact that Marshall County usually elected Republicans. Until someone pointed it out, I was unaware that my 3,332-vote victory margin was better than that for any candidate except President Dwight D. Eisenhower, who received 20 more votes in the county than I did.

Neither did I know that this victory was to be the start of a long run of electoral successes. From 1952 to 1976, I won twenty of twenty-one primary and general elections—ten of ten contested and uncontested primaries and ten of eleven contested and uncontested general elections. If conventions are included, I had an overall record of twenty-one out of twenty-three.

A coroner investigates causes of deaths, those that are accidental and some that are not. I learned from a State Board of Health statistician's call that the deaths of elderly persons who die after breaking a hip are accidental. However, a coroner's focus is to look at all accidental deaths and identify those in which foul play may be involved.

One of my first cases involved a Plymouth boy who had accidentally shot his little sister. Another involved a cave-in that took the life of a man working in a deep trench with no side supports. My examination showed that he had suffered horribly as he struggled for air after dirt clogged his mouth and air passages. Another involved a two-year-old boy who drowned in Lake Maxinkuckee at Culver while visiting his grandmother. The deaths of five or six persons in a Culver home fire were yet another.

The case I remember most ruined an entire Christmas Day. Early that morning, on the road separating Marshall County from St. Joseph County, a man's body was found on the Marshall County side. That made it my case. At Nussbaum Funeral home in Walkerton, my examination showed what looked like thumb and finger marks on the man's throat. The marks proved to be just that when special photographs were taken. I needed an autopsy, but it took some doing to get a pathologist from the South Bend Medical Foundation to do one on Christmas Day. The autopsy showed that the man had been choked to death. There was no other physical evidence. Investigators later learned that the murder resulted from a gay lovers' quarrel, and they made an arrest. The murderer was convicted and sent to prison, where he died a few years later.

Cases like this show why death investigators need to be trained. At one point, I asked the Indiana State Medical Association (ISMA) to encourage doctors to run for coroner. Indiana did not—and still does not—require coroners to be physicians. I told ISMA and others that many suspicious deaths were too quickly being labeled as accidental.

I proposed that Indiana employ pathologists as full-time medical examiners, give them additional legal and investigative training, and assign each of them to a region of the state. My proposal went nowhere. Political people, especially county and state party chairmen, disliked the proposal because it would take the office out of politics. The General Assembly did try to respond, mandating that doctors serving as coroners be paid one and a half times the salary of non-medical coroners, but that didn't solve anything.

When I served, the coroner's salary was $600 annually. I had thirty to thirty-five cases a year. Because bodies cannot be moved until the coroner investigates, I had to leave what I was doing and immediately go to the death scene. Obviously, the $600 coroner's salary didn't repay what I lost by leaving patients.

There was nothing enjoyable about being in the presence of death, but my first experience in public life was worthwhile. Being coroner didn't teach me much, but it stirred my further interest in state and local government.

⇛ 7 ⇚

Winning (and Losing) Elections

WHILE I WAS coroner, I groused about many things. County GOP chair Robertson, precinct committee person Schweisberger, and others told me that if I was so concerned, I should get more involved. Their appeal to my sense of responsibility led to my candidacy for the Marshall County seat in the Indiana House of Representatives.

The seat had become vacant when Bremen attorney R. Alexis Clarke decided not to run. Clarke had earlier replaced Plymouth businessman Eugene Stanley, who resigned after being elected to the seat in 1954. At first, Clarke's decision meant there would be no incumbent in the race, but Stanley later decided to run for his old seat.

With a busy practice and four children to feed, clothe, and educate, I could not have served if the General Assembly had met as long then as it does now. The legislature then was in session for just sixty-one calendar days every two years. It rarely convened on Saturdays and never met on Sundays. By forsaking long vacations and getting time off from my medical partners, I could serve. I proposed to Drs. Stine and Burket that I practice on Saturdays and take Sunday calls to relieve them. They were supportive.

A House member's salary then was $1,200 a year plus 5 cents a mile for trips to and from Indianapolis. Serving would be a money-losing proposition, since I would have to live in hotels and eat in restaurants

in Indianapolis and would lose income from my medical practice. However, I saw that as a small price to pay for the opportunity.

I did not know that forces allied with Lieutenant Governor Harold
W. Handley and opposed to Governor George Craig had urged Stanley
to get in the race. I was not allied with either group. I didn't even know
there were such factions. There were no dominant issues. I talked to
people about education, health, roads and highways and the state's
need to live within its income and control taxes. I prepared a handout
card that pledged me to:

1) Study both sides of every question.

2) Solicit and listen to the information and desires of the people of
Marshall (later Fulton and Starke) County.

3) Ask myself the following questions:

Is it morally right?

Is it good for Marshall (Fulton and Starke) County and the State of
Indiana?

Will it furnish the greatest good to the greatest number?

Who will it hurt? How much? What can be done to remedy it?

Does it conform to rules of good sound judgment and economic
principles?

4) After this preparation, study and guidance, vote according to my
own reasoning and the dictates of my own conscience.

When they later saw a copy of my creed on my desk in the House chamber, Frank White, who wrote "The Hoosier Day" for many Indiana
newspapers, and Wayne Guthrie of the Indianapolis *News* wrote com-
plimentary columns.

On primary day, the polls closed at 6 P.M. Precinct workers usually
ate, then counted the paper ballots "by hand," a tedious process that
took hours. After all the ballots were counted and the totals checked,
inspectors brought the ballots and tally sheets to the county clerk's
office. A copy of each precinct's tally sheets went to the local headquarters of both parties, where running counts were kept. Enthusiastic
election-night crowds usually stayed until the wee hours of the morning to learn the final results.

With one precinct out, I trailed Stanley by 40 to 50 votes. The
strong turnout in that Bremen precinct, the largest in German Town-

ship, probably made it late in reporting. When it came in about 1:30 a.m., it made me a winner by an apparent 21 votes. After the official canvass, my margin ballooned to a 30-vote difference, 1,692 to 1,662. Since I was not then well known outside Bremen, my victory was a surprise.

My fall opponent was Bremen merchant Lester Leman, a fellow Kiwanian, patient and friend. I campaigned door to door, usually in late evenings and on Saturdays, attended local Republican meetings, and spoke to the Farm Bureau, mothers' clubs, the League of Women Voters, school and church groups, service clubs, and other groups. I advertised in the Plymouth daily and the Bremen, Argos, Bourbon, and Culver weeklies and on radio, and I distributed yard signs and bumper stickers. Not counting time and lost practice income, my total expenses were under $150, all out of my pocket.

I won 9,020 to 6,615. Although happy with the large margin, I was sorry that Lester had to lose. He kiddingly told people that he had lost because those who liked me had overwhelmingly voted for me, and those who didn't like me had voted to get me out of town.

The only unusual aspect of the primaries from 1956 to 1970 was Stanley's all-out attacks on me, using full-page *Pilot-News* ads. His reasons remain a mystery. The "louder" he got, the quieter I became, even reducing the size of my ads. Stanley's tactics so turned people off that I went from a 30-vote margin in 1956 to 701 in 1958, 1,264 in 1960, 1,950 in 1962, 2,864 in 1964, 2,634 in 1966, 4,232 in 1968, and 3,037 in 1970.

The strongest of many strong general election opponents was my 1958 opponent, Forrest N. (Banty) McLaughlin, a well-known and well-liked Plymouth insurance man. We waged a clean, competitive campaign. The political climate was unfavorable for a Republican, but I expected to win. When the votes were counted, however, I had lost by 4 votes, 7,296 to 7,292—the only time I ever lost in a primary or general election.

People suggested a recount. I disliked losing, but I liked the idea of a recount less. If I asked for one, I felt that voters would see me as a crybaby or a poor loser. I knew that the House's own recount, which would come after any done at my request, would increase the number of voters who blamed me for wasting time and money on a recount.

Other than a strong Democratic tide and McLaughlin's popularity, we came up with several reasons for my loss. The candidacy of Donald Bowen of Indianapolis for an Indiana Court of Appeals judgeship was the principal one. In those days, state, county, and township ballots were separate pieces of paper, handed to voters as they went into the voting booth. The House race was on the county ballot, the appeals court judgeship on the state ballot. We felt that many people probably thought they were voting for me when they voted for Donald Bowen. Although not well known in Marshall County, Donald Bowen did very well there. This confusion may have cost me 200 to 300 votes.

Beth and I worked hard to register Amish people, especially my patients. We got a few registered. The last four voters in my home precinct were Amish. When they counted the ballots, election workers found that the top four involved votes only for township trustee, the officeholder who could most influence the operation of Amish schools. Had the four Amish voters voted in the House race, I feel they would have voted for me.

I lost several votes when a 92-year-old lady died the night before the election. She had voted absentee, but her ballot rightfully was not counted. Understandably, her death and the need to make final arrangements kept her seven children and many grandchildren, all of whom lived in the county, from the polls.

After the election, I asked Fred Berger, a Bremen area farmer, if he had voted. He said he and his wife hadn't because they didn't think I needed their votes. Little did they know!

I later used my four-vote loss to make the point that every vote counts, and to urge everyone to vote, no matter what their politics.

Between 1958 and 1960, I attended political meetings and made a few talks. When asked if I was going to be a candidate, I didn't deny that I planned to do so.

I won the next six general elections handily. In 1960 and 1964, Banty McLaughlin again was my opponent. In 1962, my opponent was George Schricker of Plymouth, son of former governor Henry Schricker. Others were John Kizer, son of state senator Marshall Kizer (1966), and Ralph Ringer, a well-known Plymouth-area farmer (1968). The 1960 and 1962 elections were the most difficult. I was unopposed in 1970.

My House district changed twice. From 1956 to 1962, it included only Marshall County. In 1964, it included Marshall and Fulton counties. From 1966 to 1970, it included Marshall and Starke counties. The 1964 and 1966 boundary changes resulted from the U.S. Supreme Court's "one man, one vote" decision requiring equal population in legislative districts. The changes gave me a larger area to represent, more people to contact, and double the number of political events to attend.

8

Doctor in the House

WHEN I CAME to Indianapolis, I had no personal agenda. None of the bills I introduced was earthshaking, but each sounded fair and needed when it was explained to me.

In addition to the budget, right-to-work and daylight savings time bills aroused strong feelings. The right-to-work bill simply said that a worker didn't have to belong to a union to be employed in the building trades. Debate on the bill created animosity between labor unions and businesses and industries and their organizations, including state and local chambers of commerce. My seatmate, Marion merchant James O. (Jack) Murrell, carried the bill. Opponents carried signs in the State-house that said, "Murrell, drop dead," or something equally hateful. I supported the bill.

Daylight savings time was an urban-rural issue. The most telling argument was that in some months, kids would wait in the dark for school buses. Opponents thought the bill was foolish—one only had to start an hour earlier to get an extra hour of daylight.

Governor Harold Handley proposed near-elimination of the state property tax levy. Local governments collected most property taxes, but this small change was welcome. Back then, I don't remember bitter wrangling over budget bills like we see today. After the House Ways & Means Committee hammered out a budget bill, most legislators from both parties voted for it on the floor. The only exception I remember was Rex Minnick, a legislator from Brazil. He became known as "Red Finger Rex" because he almost always pushed the button on his desk that turned on the red light signifying a "no" vote.

In my first session, I learned that a legislator must "bird dog" a bill to get it passed. A bill can fail at any step—in committee, on second or third readings in either house, or in a conference committee. At that time, House speakers had almost dictatorial control over bills introduced in the House and Senate bills coming to the House. The speaker could—and often did—assign bills to a committee where he knew the chair would not give them a hearing. He could—and often did—refuse to hand bills down for a passage vote.

George Meyers, who knew the legislative process well from his long service as House attorney and parliamentarian, helped me learn the ropes. At one point in my second term, I mentioned to him that I would like to be speaker someday. He quietly encouraged me.

When I came to the House, George was about 60 and had health problems. I often checked his blood pressure, and I once arranged for him to be seen at the IU Medical Center. Other colleagues also came to me with aches and pains. I listened and wrote an occasional prescription or referred them to another physician. One time, I made a call to the hotel room of Warsaw legislator George Fisher to check his wife. She was seriously ill, and I got her taken to an emergency room. Hospitalized for several weeks, she regained her health and outlived her husband. He was grateful to me.

In my first term, George Diener of Indianapolis was speaker. To become speaker, a member must be in the majority caucus, establish good relationships within that caucus, be a person of his word, and be known as fair and knowledgeable. Having seniority helps.

House minority leader Birch Bayh of Terre Haute obviously wanted to further his upstream political ambitions. He later was to be a three-term U.S. senator. I didn't know Senate president pro tem John Van Ness, a Republican from Valparaiso. Senate minority leader Matt Welsh, a Democrat from Vincennes, was a quietly effective gentleman whose qualities soon would make him governor of Indiana.

In the 1957 session, I served on several committees. Public Health Committee chair Earl Aders of Elkhart leaned heavily on my knowledge as a physician when it came to public health bills. Other legislators also consulted me about public health legislation.

In 1957, the GOP controlled the House, 75-24, and the Senate, 33-17. Governor Handley and Lieutenant Governor Crawford Parker were Republicans. This complete control required us to be productive and harmonious and we were. With little infighting, we passed a reasonable budget and the right-to-work bill.

Governor Handley's friendliness made it easy to work with him. He awed me. He was a good governor, and history has treated him badly. Governor Handley urged the building of Indiana's portions of a north-south Chicago-to-Louisville road and an east-west Cincinnati-to-St. Louis road. He saw the need for an Ohio River bridge at New Albany, oversaw building of the $30 million State Office Building, got $2 million earmarked for land for a Lake Michigan port, and established a school of veterinary medicine at Purdue University. His advocacy of increased gas taxes earned him the label "High Tax Harold," and his ill-fated Senate run in the middle of his term as governor marked the end of his political career.

The 1957 session infected me with what I came to call my "incurable disease." I learned that I liked public service and enjoyed its implicit challenge—making the right things happen for the people of Indiana.

After sitting out the 1959 session, I returned to the House in 1961. There were no pressing local problems, so I had no local bills. That allowed me to get reacquainted with the members I already knew and get to know the many new faces there.

I chaired the Public Health Committee. We reported thirty-one House and Senate bills to the floor. Those with the slightest chance of improving public health survived.

The speaker assigned me to four other committees. He probably named me to Labor because I had voted for the right-to-work law and was unlikely to vote to repeal it. I served on Judiciary B Committee, the "graveyard" committee. The speaker, who assigns all bills, always named a "Judy B" chair who would sit on bad bills—give them no hearing or, if heard, see that they never came to a vote. Either way, the bills were dead unless the full House "blasted" them out of committee, a rarely used procedure. "Judy B" later was abolished. I also served on the Education Committee, whose members were pressured constantly on teacher salary recommendations by the Indiana State Teachers Association, the most powerful legislative lobbying group.

In 1960, Democrat Matt Welsh won a slim victory over Lieutenant Governor Parker for governor. Republican Dick Ristine of Crawfordsville was elected lieutenant governor. The stern and harsh but effective S. Hugh Dillin of Petersburg was president pro tem in the Senate, where Democrats held a 26-24 majority. Wendell Martin, a gentlemanly Indianapolis lawyer, was minority leader. In the House, Republicans held a 65-34 advantage after a legislator's death reduced the number of members to 99. Dick Guthrie of Indianapolis was the speaker. Bayh was minority leader.

The mixed political complexion created potential for dissension, but the 1961 session was more harmonious than expected.

During the 1961 session, I had it in mind to run for speaker if re-elected in 1962. I felt Marion County was too dominant, particularly in the House, where it had the speaker and a generous share of committee chairs. There was a real urban-rural tension in the body. Most non-urban legislators approved of a country doctor taking on the big-city speaker, but it made the big-city folks nervous. In mid-1962, I mailed a brochure to GOP House candidates and made "house calls" on them. Once winners were known, I contacted them by mail, by phone, and in person. I had a cookout at my Bremen home and meetings for legislators living in the Lafayette, Fort Wayne, Indianapolis, and other areas.

Paul Myers, my 1957 and 1961 seatmate, warned me that I faced an uphill battle. Seeing that I intended to go ahead, he urged me to "grab the bull by the tail and take what comes." He then presented my name to the caucus. The vote was Guthrie 35, Bowen 20. I quickly assured Representative Guthrie of my full cooperation. He could have punished me, but reappointed me as Public Health Committee chair and named me to the Education, Public Policy, Legislative Procedures and Military Affairs & Memorials committees.

The House leadership that year was mediocre. Charles Edwards of Spencer was majority leader. Owen Crecelius of Crawfordsville, a mustachioed retired colonel who spoke and acted like a first sergeant, was caucus chair. Minority leader Bob Rock of Anderson was looking for his next political opportunity. In contrast, the Senate leadership was good. On the Republican side, Russ Bontrager of Elkhart was president pro tem, and Roy Conrad of Monticello was caucus chair. Democrat Marshall Kizer of Plymouth was minority leader. All were fine legislators and good men.

In the 1963 session, debate on whether a tax increase was needed was a minor battle. The major one was about what taxes to increase. A Republican senator's death reduced the GOP's majority to 25-24, making it impossible to pass any bill without the vote of at least one Democrat. The Constitution requires 51 House and 26 Senate votes to pass a bill—a "constitutional majority." Stakes were so high in 1963 that this was a tough hurdle.

Governor Welsh submitted a $1.2 billion balanced budget but

asked us to consider $450 million more in "special needs." (In a seat with a vote, one must separate "wants" from "needs.") The sixty-one-day regular session ended in an impasse, and the governor immediately called a special session. Late in it, hush-hush negotiations produced a compromise that would impose the state's first sales tax at a 2 percent rate. A 2 percent adjusted gross individual income tax, a 2 percent corporate net income tax, and a 50 percent increase in the business gross receipts tax also were part of the compromise.

After soul-searching, I voted for the package. If a tax increase was unavoidable, I felt the public saw a sales tax as less obnoxious. Still, the finish was a hair-raiser. On the special session's 40th day (the 101st overall day), Senator Walter A. Baran of East Chicago was ill and could not be present. As a result, only 48 senators were on the floor when the conference committee report on the sales tax bill came up.

The Senate tied 24-24. Whereas a 26-vote constitutional majority is required for Senate adoption of a bill, a conference committee report can be adopted by a majority of those present and voting. This left the decision to Lieutenant Governor Ristine. "To get this session over with, and to get the state moving forward again," he told the body, "the chair votes aye." Ristine's courage may have cost him the governorship in 1964, although a national Democratic landslide probably was a greater factor. To this day, I regret that the bright and able Dick Ristine never was governor. He would have been a great one.

We stopped the clocks for a full 41st day and part of a 42nd day to let the mechanical parts of the process catch up. Those 103 stress-filled days were expensive—I had to live in the Claypool Hotel and forgo medical practice income for an extra 42 days.

There were small consolations. I played a significant part in increasing mental health funding against the wishes of Ways & Means Committee chair John Coppes. Irving Leibowitz, editor of the Indianapolis *Times*, was known for his harsh judgments about the General Assembly, but he named me as one of the five best legislators of 1963 based on factors of conscientiousness, effectiveness, and responsibility. After a draining, bitterly contentious session, these were small things to take home.

Although I won re-election to my House seat in 1964, the election was a catastrophe for Republicans. Utilizing what I still consider to be dirty campaign tactics, President Lyndon B. Johnson won a massive victory over Barry Goldwater. (In my heart, I still know Goldwater was right.) Lafayette attorney Roger D. Branigin was elected governor. Democrats won control of both houses of the General Assembly.

As the only Republican House leader to survive the landslide, I was an automatic favorite to lead the GOP caucus. In politics, however, you don't wait for a draft or take anything for granted. Before the election, I again called on potential winners. Afterwards, I re-contacted all twenty-one actual winners. On organization day, for whatever it was worth, House Republicans elected me as their minority leader.

For me, the 1965 session was a totally new experience. I was in the House minority for the first time, and the opposition also controlled the Senate and the governor's office. Young House Democrats were hungry for action and power. Their aggressiveness was epitomized by Marion County's "young Turks," who launched what the media labeled a power grab, intended to drastically alter the way the capital city ran.

New House speaker Dick Bodine came from Mishawaka, Bremen's neighboring city. The South Bend *Tribune* often praised the fact that Dick and I worked together for the state's good even though we were from opposing parties. As minority leader, my aim was to be constructive. I drew criticism for not jumping up to rant about all Democratic proposals. It was a fact, however, that the opposition's 78-22 majority allowed them to do anything they wanted if they stuck together. Their huge majority also doomed every Republican proposal, even those with merit.

Our band of twenty-two Republicans stayed together. That and the fact that the Democrats went overboard set the stage for a GOP comeback in 1966 and 1968. House Republicans focused attention on the bad elements of bills that the Democrats rammed through. A specific example was a reapportionment bill, which the majority tried to draw to ensure a perpetual Democrat majority. This political greed was to backfire on the Democrats.

Senate Democrats and Governor Branigin exercised better judgment than radical House members and softened some House actions. However, for House Republicans, if only because of our small numbers, 1965 was not a good year.

☙ 9 ❧

Leader of the House

IN 1966, I had a strong opponent in John Kizer, son of state senator Marshall Kizer of Plymouth, but I expected to be re-elected. Thinking that the GOP might regain House control, I traveled the state seeking support for a leadership role. (I tried to live by an unwritten law in politics—that you notify party officials in advance of your visit and its purpose. This created a friendly reception even when those officials didn't like my ideas or me.)

When I announced for speaker, I was the second candidate, feisty John Coppes of Nappanee having announced four days earlier. He made no secret of the fact that he again wanted to be Ways & Means Committee chair. He made it equally clear that the one who promised him that chair could expect him to withdraw as a candidate for speaker and support his benefactor. Coppes did not like me because I had led a group that in 1963 overcame his objections to increased mental health funding. That prompted Coppes to call me a "yellow-bellied bastard" in the Republican caucus. He knew I wouldn't name him to the position he coveted and didn't ask me to do so.

Typical of my efforts to win support was a trip to see Dick Boehning, a Lafayette lawyer just elected to the House. He and his wife, Phyllis, were friendly and gracious. Dick and I discovered that we both were Francesville High School graduates, and that we had many mutual friends. I came away with no commitment, but more optimism.

Hearing good reports in my travels, I told a reporter that the GOP would control the House, 52-48. I underestimated our numbers. On election day, a 78-22 Democrat majority became a 66-34 Republican majority. Between the election and organization day, I again personally contacted returning and new Republican House members.

My real opponent was not Coppes, but Charles (Billy) Howard of Hamilton County, one of the "donut" counties around Indianapolis. Howard did not announce for speaker until the Marion County and other urban delegations promised support, a pledge he thought was tantamount to election. To Howard's credit, he refused to promise Coppes the Ways & Means chair. Coppes then said he intended to vote for me.

There was electricity in the air as we moved into the caucus. I was counting on the vote of Roger Jessup of Fairmount, who wasn't even in the room as the meeting time neared. To my relief, Jessup arrived a minute before we started.

On the first ballot, Coppes and Boehning voted for me. When ballots were counted, it was obvious that I needed their votes, and Jessup's, for Howard and I tied, 33-33. The caucus quickly went to a second ballot and I won, 34-32.

I don't know what happened. One person may have shifted to me, or several members may have changed their votes with the net change favoring me. My opinion is that only one vote changed that day—the vote of a Marion County legislator. Perhaps it was my fellow Lutheran Charlie Bosma of Beech Grove, or my good friend Ray Crowe of Indianapolis, famed as the coach of Crispus Attucks teams that won two state high school basketball championships. My opponents may have overestimated their strength, but I didn't misjudge mine, and I expected a close vote. My only uncertainty was Boehning's vote. Coppes's was a bonus. So was the extra vote on the second ballot. (After the vote, at least six members sidled up to me and whispered, "I was the one who changed my vote to you!")

I now see my election as speaker as the single most important event of my political life—a defining moment. Had I not been elected and not served six years as speaker, I would not have been in position to win election as governor. Boehning, Coppes, Jessup, either Crowe or Bosma, and the others who voted for me fashioned my political future that day. I became the fourth doctor to serve as speaker. (My predecessors were John W. Davis of Sullivan County in 1831, 1842, and 1851,

George W. Carr of Noble County in 1848, and Jonathan W. Gordon
of Marion County in 1858–59.)

An ambitious young Indianapolis attorney and a Howard ally, Bill
Ruckelshaus, was elected as majority leader. In 1968, after just one term
in the House, Ruckelshaus lost a bid for the U.S. Senate. President
Richard M. Nixon then appointed him as assistant U.S. attorney general. Later the Environmental Protection Agency's first administrator,
he also served as acting FBI director before returning to Justice in time
for the "Saturday Night Massacre." In that Watergate chapter, President Nixon ordered Attorney General Elliott Richardson to fire Special Prosecutor Archibald Cox. Richardson refused and was fired. General Alexander Haig, Nixon's chief of staff, then directed Ruckelshaus,
as next in the Justice chain of command, to fire Cox. Ruckelshaus refused and also was fired. As his later accomplishments show, Bill was a
talented, very capable individual.

Once the dust settled, I asked each member to note five committee
preferences. Too many members wanted to serve on the more important committees, but I honored everyone's first or second choice and
named everyone to about four committees.

The 1967 session was productive. The battle over the choice of
sites for a proposed new medical school was the most interesting issue.
To deal with doctor shortages in rural areas and small towns, an inter-
im legislative committee had recommended creating a second medical
school to increase physician supply. Terre Haute, Fort Wayne, Gary,
Evansville, Muncie, and South Bend were all competing to be chosen.
Each local community and chamber had a bill. Each intensively lob-
bied legislators from outside their areas. These non-aligned legislators
became referees, trying to remain fair and impartial in this difficult debate. So that no area would have an advantage, I decided that the
House would hear all six bills on a single day. Noise in the chamber and
the traffic in and out of it were so great that I ordered the doors closed
during the debate. The vote on each bill was the same—no city could
muster the fifty-one votes necessary for passage.

The issue went nowhere until a proposal was made to integrate science programs at six universities with IU's program. In concert with
the medical center, the six universities would accept twenty to thirty
students for the first year of medical school. (The second year later was
added for some sites.) Students would spend the second, third, and
fourth years at the IU Medical Center. Glenn Irwin and Steve Beering,
who successively served as dean of the IU School of Medicine, played
major roles in developing the plan. Other medical school figures, the

Indiana State Medical Association, and legislators contributed ideas. I take a little credit for helping to get the bill in final form and shepherding it through the House. After passing the Senate, it was signed by the governor.

An important but non-controversial medical bill created regional family practice residency programs in several large Indiana hospitals to educate family doctors and improve the quality of family practice. Our expectation was that doctors supervising the family practice residency programs would have to keep current just to answer inquisitive young doctors' questions. As a result, residents would get the benefit of the latest medical knowledge and practice. We also felt that locating the first (and later the second) years of medical school in six major Indiana cities would stimulate supervising family practice physicians to volunteer to teach classes and oversee some aspects of resident training.

I had no trouble seeing Governor Branigin when needed. He helped me deal with many problems, including one big one. A beautician from my county told me that the large beauty salon "chains" were trying to reduce competition from small shops in homes and farm homes. Unable to get the General Assembly to pass legislation, they had convinced the Board of Beauty Culturists to propose rules requiring separate entrances and bathroom facilities for salons, imposing stiff continuing education requirements, and so on. After satisfying myself that the board had no statutory authority for such an action, I took the matter to Governor Branigin. He muttered a mild oath (not "egad" or "shucks"), said he would put a stop to such nonsense, and did. Every visit I made to Governor Branigin's office was entertaining, for he had a tremendous wit.

A proposed constitutional amendment to permit the General Assembly to decide how frequently, when, and for how long it meets was adopted in 1967. It passed again in 1969, and Hoosiers ratified it at the polls in 1970. By law, the 1971 General Assembly then set session limits and frequency. In odd-numbered years, sessions begin on the first Tuesday after the first Monday in January and must end by April 29 (originally April 30). In even-numbered years, sessions start on the same schedule and must end by March 14 (earlier March 15). Bill introduction starts on organization day. Recesses are allowed. The law's original specifics on the number of session days later were removed as unnecessary.

In 1968, the GOP increased its majorities to 73-27 in the House and 35-15 in the Senate and elected Secretary of State Edgar D. Whitcomb as governor. My loss to Whitcomb for the nomination lurked in the background as the 1969 session began. A coterie of big county party chairs, led by Indianapolis kingmaker L. Keith Bulen, ramrodded a slate headed by Whitcomb through the convention. The actions of convention chair Frank Millis, a Whitcomb supporter who tightly controlled the convention and prevented my supporters from demonstrating in my behalf, still irked me.

A handsome, ultra-conservative Seymour attorney with a record of World War II heroism, Whitcomb was elected after the war to the Senate, served as an assistant U.S. attorney, and in 1966 was elected as secretary of state. That office was the launching pad for his successful 1968 campaign for governor.

His every act as governor was closely monitored, and even arranged, by Don Tabbert, a former U.S. attorney. Still, I felt that he and I could work together. In his campaign, Whitcomb pledged to hold the line against any increase in state-level taxes, but the 1969 session still seemed like a good time to restructure the tax system to remove at least part of the cost of public schools and local government from the property tax.

I had been grousing for years about the unfairness of Indiana's property tax system, which was put in place when property still was the primary indicator of wealth. With levies increasing 10 to 12 percent annually, I believed that we ought to fund public education and local government with revenue from broader-based state-level taxes.

On February 10, 1969, I spoke at the Columbia Club to the Northern Indiana Economic Development Council. This was a routine opportunity to rub shoulders with South Bend–area friends. My remarks were similar to those I had made for years. They were not, nor did I intend them to be, a "blockbuster" speech. I did not throw the gauntlet of property tax reform at the feet of Governor Whitcomb. I made no adamant demand for property tax relief. I said that property taxes were out of hand, that we should consider some form of property tax relief, and that returning balance to the tax system required fundamental change. My only error may have been a closing question: If not now, when?

Those present included Jack Colwell, a respected political writer for the South Bend *Tribune*. The Associated Press disseminated his report on my remarks statewide. My comments became the most controversial subject of what some called the "bloody 69th." I heard from several sources that my remarks had angered Governor Whitcomb. His people immediately cast me as a liberal tax raiser. That was a baseless accusation—even fiscal conservatives agreed that reform was needed. Restructuring taxes with no increase in total tax burden is hardly a liberal position. If anything, such a change could make it easier for people to own homes, a desirable—and conservative—objective.

Until the General Assembly met, I didn't fully realize the depth of my disagreement with Governor Whitcomb on property tax relief. In retrospect, I believe he knew little about the property tax system, had made no attempt to learn more, and did not recognize the need for reform. I never heard him say anything about the benefits of property tax reduction as he complained about raising other taxes to offset property taxes. I never heard him say that public education and local government were being financed out of the wrong pocket, or that it was wrong for farmers and businesses to pay property taxes even if unprofitable. I never heard him say that farmers and homeowners—especially older homeowners—were paying a disproportionate share of the cost for public education. I never heard him say that 10 to 12 percent annual increases in property taxes were slowing expansion by businesses and industries, which needed certainty that property taxes would stop going up or even go down. All I ever heard was a kneejerk "No, no, no."

If nothing was to be accomplished on property tax reform in Governor Whitcomb's term, I feared the situation would require drastic action after he left office. I also recognized that property tax relief was an issue on which I could base a 1972 campaign for governor.

In 1969, a property tax relief program passed the House. Two Senate Republicans—John Shawley of Michigan City and Joe Harrison of Attica—voted against suspension of the rules and prevented its consideration in the Senate. Shawley's vote was no surprise, but Harrison's was. I held no animosity toward either of them—they had to vote their consciences and their constituents' wishes.

Similarly, I held no animosity toward Governor Whitcomb. He was the beneficiary, not the perpetrator, of the 1968 convention's slating outrages. I tried to cooperate with him, except on property tax relief, on which we could not agree. He did his best to live up to his "no tax increase" campaign pledge, I felt. I also believed that his closest advisors—Bulen, Tabbert, and others—dictated his actions, reactions, and moves too much.

After property tax relief died in the Senate, the House refused to go along with the booze and cigarette tax increases that Whitcomb wanted. By then, House members wanted to give the governor exactly what he had promised in his campaign and said he still wanted—no new taxes. The General Assembly did impose a 7 percent upper limit on property tax increases to reduce the rate of increase.

A proposed amendment to the Constitution to permit governors to serve successive four-year terms was adopted for the first time. Since 1851, no governor had done so. (Governor Henry Schricker served two terms and eight years, but sat out four years between terms.) This first step was followed by adoption by the 1971 General Assembly and voter approval in 1972. The amendment was to give me an opportunity to be the first modern governor to seek and win a second consecutive four-year term.

For 120 years, every new governor had been a "lame duck" when elected. Governors now can pursue their agendas into a second term—if they earn it. Two of the governors who followed me—Republican Robert D. Orr and Democrat Evan Bayh—served eight years. The third, Governor Frank O'Bannon, a Democrat, now is completing his first term.

The annual sessions amendment passed for the second time, and it was sent to the voters in 1970. This amendment caused lots of criticism. Wags only half-facetiously suggested that the legislature ought to meet two days every sixty-one years. Diehards found annual sessions hard to accept. However, the General Assembly decided that the "board" of an entity with a multi-billion-dollar budget ought to meet at least once a year. Critics now claim that the only difference between short and long sessions is their length, but the real culprits are those who abuse the original concept that short sessions should deal with emergencies. The General Assembly needs to return to a strong committee system in which chairs decide when a real emergency exists, act accordingly, and take the heat for their decisions.

Also adopted were constitutional amendments making supreme and appellate court judges appointive and giving the auditor, treasurer, and secretary of state four-year terms. Uni-Gov was created for Marion County, and time has proven it to be beneficial. The only valid complaint may be that by exempting police and fire departments and not including schools, it did not go far enough. Even with the exclusions, however, Uni-Gov was a very big bite. If police and fire had been included, the bill surely would have failed. With schools included, it absolutely would have failed.

I placed the Uni-Gov bill on the House calendar based on the time my office received it, and I intended to hand it down in order. Local officials got antsy when I didn't hand the bill down as quickly as they wanted. Urging people to call me, Mayor Richard G. Lugar gave out my office and hotel telephone numbers. Beth and I were so deluged with calls that we moved from the Claypool Hotel to the Atkinson. Had caller sentiment determined the bill's fate, it would have died. By a 12-1 margin, Vi Walker's tally showed that the "aginners" were call-ing. The Indianapolis *Star* carried an editorial cartoon labeled "Foot and Mouth Disease" showing Mayor Lugar with his foot in his mouth. Although unhappy about Mayor Lugar's gaffe, I still handed the bill down, and it passed.

In this session, we changed the motor vehicle tax from property to excise. As many as 20 to 25 percent of all vehicle owners were evading personal property taxes by licensing their vehicles in other states. The new excise tax was to be based on the original value and age of vehicles and collected when plates were purchased.

In spite of tensions between the governor and the General Assem-bly, the session was productive and the final results were good.

The 1970 elections reduced GOP majorities to 53-47 in the House and 29-21 in the Senate. The slim House margin demanded more party coherence in the 1971 session. (As one of the 53 Republicans, I could vote, but speakers usually vote only when needed to reach a constitu-tional majority. A few times, I voted on bills of great interest to me.)

Even by 1971, there was no consensus on property tax relief. If a tax had to be raised, Hoosiers seemed to favor the sales tax. Although Indiana's 2.5 percent rate was one of the nation's lowest, taxpayers were not enthusiastic about proposals to increase personal income taxes. Marion and Allen County officials wanted a local option income tax so they could do more in Indianapolis and Fort Wayne. House members were not opposed, but felt that all counties should have an option if any did.

In such times of uncertainty, strong people step forward. If there ever was a better person than John Hart of Indianapolis to design and carry property tax relief legislation, I don't know who it would be. Hart was a giant in physical size and a giant when it came to state budgets, finance, and property tax relief. A homebuilder, he under-stood how high property taxes adversely affect home ownership and the economy.

John developed and steered a set of bills through his committee and the House that raised sales and income taxes and used the income as an offset against property taxes. To ensure that the program worked, he included property tax controls. The bills provided for a graduated income tax, an idea not well received by Republicans in general or Senate Republicans in particular. Unlike the so-called "progressive" federal income tax, which taxes high-income taxpayers at higher rates, Indiana's income tax is flat-rated. I preferred no graduation but recog-nized that graduated rates would be more palatable to House and Senate Democrats. The media quickly labeled John Hart's package "Supertax."

The legislation had pluses and minuses. We could not guarantee that property taxes would decline, and Hoosiers, particularly newspaper editors, doubted that property taxes would go down or stay down. They figured that sales and income tax increases would be just that. Business and industry didn't care for the proposed corporate net income tax hike. Senate President Pro Tem Phil Gutman generally sided with Governor Whitcomb. House Republicans Ned Lamkin of Indianapolis and Thames Mauzy of Warsaw shuttled back and forth between the chamber and Governor Whitcomb's office, giving him advance notice of planned actions and the House's mood on them.

When the package went to Governor Whitcomb, he vetoed it, claiming that only a third of the new revenues would go to property tax relief, and that property tax relief distributions would leave insufficient dollars to fund the state budget. I always felt that Governor Whitcomb was an honest man, and I never doubted that he believed what was in his veto message, but he was dead wrong. The House unsuccessfully tried to override the veto.

Otherwise, the 1971 session was productive. Legislators swallowed hard to accept some federal mandates, but accept them they did, and they generally were responsible on other issues.

In an action related to the earlier medical school rivalry, the General Assembly created the Commission for Higher Education to gather the facts that legislators and state officials need to sort out inter-institutional rivalry, finance, and equity issues. CHE was to be a coordinating board, not a board of regents, but university trustees and presidents opposed the bill. Understandably, they disliked the idea of someone looking over their shoulders and having input—before the fact—on new sites, programs, and buildings.

A sidelight of the 1971 session was formation of the "1288 Club," named for the bill that Governor Whitcomb vetoed. Members came from organizations or firms supporting property tax relief. They were Fred McCarthy, Indiana Manufacturers Association; Charles Van Nuys, Indiana Retail Association; Bob O'Bannon, Indiana Telephone Association, son of the former senator of that name and brother of Governor Frank O'Bannon; John V. Barnett, Indiana State Chamber of Commerce; George Applegate, East Chicago Chamber of Commerce and later the Gary Chamber of Commerce; Pat Clancy, Indiana Gas Association; Daniel Fisher, Eli Lilly & Co.; David Davis, Indiana

Petroleum Council; George Doup, Indiana Farm Bureau; Bill Colbert, Indiana Rural Electric Membership Cooperative; and Richard Stein, Eli Lilly & Co., and later with Public Service Indiana.

The 1288 Club served as my advisors and actively worked for property tax relief until it became a reality. After I left the governor's office, members still met socially, even holding a "reunion" in Washington while I was H&HS secretary.

The short session in 1972 met expectations by being short, as it was supposed to be.

In late 1971, I announced for governor and made it known that I would not file for a House seat. If I didn't win nomination for governor, then so be it. I had served fourteen years in the House. I was only the third person in Indiana history to serve three terms as speaker— following James Knapp (1929–31, 1939–41, and 1941–43) and Hobart Creighton (1943–45, 1945–47, and 1947–49)—and the second speaker to serve three consecutive terms. I had presided over more sessions and session days than any predecessor.

Ed Ziegner, political editor of the Indianapolis News, used to say that lawmaking is not the exclusive province of legislators. The governor is part of the process. Dependent on his will and vision, he sets and influences the General Assembly's agenda to some extent. Ziegner reduced the lawmaking formula to simple terms—51 votes in the House, 26 votes in the Senate, and the governor's signature. That's not far off the mark.

There are still other players. By far the most important are the millions of Hoosiers who look to the General Assembly for fairness and equity and occasionally for help. As conduits of information to Hoosiers, opinion leaders, and watchdogs over citizen interests, the media play a critical role. State and local officials are very influential.

Lobbyists almost always are mentioned negatively but are an important part of the process. Some lobbyists are paid, but many are unpaid volunteers. Some are amateurs, others professionals. Some play hardball. Others use a sophisticated, softer approach. There is an occasional bad lobbyist, but most lobbyists I've known are principled men and women who vigorously represent their clients' interests and never get close to the wrong side of the line dividing right from wrong. It's easy for me to admit relying on lobbyists to help me achieve my objectives while speaker and governor.

Too many Hoosiers have a distorted, incomplete picture of the General Assembly's members. They believe that legislators spend all their time eating free lunches and attending parties, that they live to grab power, that their only interest is higher pay, that they are secretly beholden to special interests, especially big campaign contributors, that they take open and hidden advantage of their office, and that every decision is made on a political basis, not on the basis of what's best for Hoosiers.

This impression is false. On the whole, legislators are conscientious, smart, honest, and well-intentioned people who work hard to get elected and equally hard to do what's in the best interests of Hoosiers. For example, although opposed to legalized gambling, I never questioned the integrity of those supporting it. I knew that before legislators went on a bill or voted for it, they had resolved questions of conscience. Legislators are people. When elected, they remain imperfect like the rest of us. As long as they try to do their best as legislators, and the right thing for their constitutents, we can ask no more.

From their colleagues, legislators expect friendliness, honesty, integrity, and the kind of helpful attitude that arises out of genuine respect. They expect their colleagues to be even-tempered and gentle. A highly developed code of honor and legislative etiquette operates among legislators who are ethical, honest, and committed to public service. (Not all those elected to the General Assembly have those attributes, of course.)

Since legislators become experts on various public issues, good legislators expect their colleagues to share their expertise. Good legislators write off colleagues as poor public servants only if they talk on every bill, fail to keep their word, engage in personal attacks instead of making sound arguments, or engage in dishonest acts.

Many legislators frequently eat lunches—and breakfasts and dinners—on someone else, and there is no shortage of parties for legislators. However, most legislators, probably the majority of them, prefer quiet time away from even subtle lobbying. (Some lobbying is not so subtle.) I did some of my best thinking alone or with my wife over a quiet meal.

It's a fact of political life that campaign contributors get extra attention. Legislators need contributions to mount campaigns. Any good legislator tells contributors that all they can expect is an open mind. A good legislator listens to all sides, applies common sense to the facts and arguments, and votes his conscience.

An incorrect impression of endemic and continuing corruption of the legislature also exists. The cases of two major Republican legislative leaders in the late 1970s are proof that corruption occurs. However, in all my associations with the General Assembly, I felt a corrupt act occurred only a handful of times. (Even then, proving it was another matter.)

Finally, there is an impression that the legislative process is like a boxing match, and that someone always wins at someone else's expense. That is another misleading impression. Robust, honest debate lies at the heart of the legislative process. There is great ethnic, cultural, and geographic diversity in the General Assembly. Members of the northwestern Indiana delegation differ in their views, interests, and objectives from members of the Indianapolis, Evansville, Fort Wayne, and South Bend delegations. The ideas of big-city legislators are different from those of legislators from small towns and rural areas.

When these men and women come to Indianapolis, they begin a session-long debate on issues of importance to Hoosiers. From that, a consensus develops around what the state's needs are, what can be done within the state's resources to meet those needs, and what's best for Indiana. Ultimately, legislators reach the point of legal consensus—Ed Ziegner's 51 House votes, 26 Senate votes, and the governor's signature.

The diversity of legislators is a safeguard against dominance by a single geographic, political, or economic sector. Over time, that diversity produces good results, not always what everyone agrees with but what everyone can live with—at least until the next session.

A bit of blame for these misunderstandings may rest with the news media, but I have no complaints about the Statehouse press corps. They did their job well, and I got along with them fine. My policy was always to be available, honest, and frank with them.

Old-timers in the press corps were dependable and accurate. Younger, newer faces were less apt to be so. I held many print media veterans in high regard, including Ed Ziegner, Jack Averitt, Gerry LaFollette, and Bill (Moose) Roberts of the Indianapolis *News*, Jack Colwell of the South Bend *Tribune*, Hortense Meyers of United Press International, Ike Miller of the Associated Press, Paul Doherty of the Indianapolis *Star*, Gordon Englehart of the Louisville *Courier-Journal*, Bob Flynn and Bob Sievers of the two Evansville newspapers, and Bob Ashley of the Gary *Post-Tribune*. I greatly admired radio newsman Bob Rutherford. Many others probably deserve mention.

I remember being aggravated once. That situation involved a newsman who was so good that he knew as much as budget directors about state budgets and finance. The reporter, Jack Averitt, was and is a good friend. Jack covered a legislative conference at Minneapolis that I attended as speaker. All the participants attended a conference dinner. Later, Jack wrote something like: "While many people are going hungry, legislators are here dining on steaks and champagne." That seemed more sarcastic than warranted, and it sort of ticked me off. What did he expect the host to do—feed us mush?

Looking back, I believe that legislators made many contributions to improving the lives of Hoosiers. It's difficult to sort out what was most important, because so many creative and innovative programs were considered and enacted. If pressed, I would list the following:

• Using amendments to modernize the state's 1851 Constitution, make the General Assembly and state government more effective, and improve local government. In this category are annual legislative sessions, four-year terms for the auditor, treasurer, and secretary of state, bipartisan selection of Indiana supreme and appellate court judges, allowing governors to succeed themselves, Uni-Gov, and reapportionment. The 1851 Constitution needed only fine-tuning to remove anachronistic language.

• Improving the state's higher education system. Included are the creation of Ivy Tech State College and the regional campuses of Indiana and Purdue universities, the Higher Education Commission, the State Scholarship Commission (now the State Student Assistance Commission), the medical education plan and the family practice residency program through the IU School of Medicine and other cooperating institutions, the school of architecture at Ball State, and the school of veterinary medicine at Purdue University.

• Providing a foundation for Indiana's future economy. In this category are the Ohio River bridges, the beginnings of a port system, partial construction of the interstates and other road improvements, and a start on professionalizing the Department of Commerce to make it the state's instrument for promotion of economic growth.

• Meeting the underlying needs of Indiana's people. The particulars of this ongoing accomplishment are deeply embedded in the biennial budgets.

• Holding down the overall tax burden. Indiana remains a low-tax state.

Indiana is fortunate that so many good men and women served as legislators. It may be foolhardy to single out individuals, but a few deserve mention as memorable people and legislators. (Those memorable for "showboating," for speaking on issues without being prepared, or for being flaky and undisciplined will go unnamed, as much as they deserve negative "recognition.") A few of those that I rank among the best of the best are:

• Paul Myers—not because he authored many bills, or spoke often or eloquently, but because he taught others so much. You admire some individuals because they are good, gentle, and kind people. Paul was such a person. There was no wiser or better counselor. One time I went with Paul to his home in Parke County, from which he drove daily to Indianapolis when the House was in session. That night, I helped him with his chores. I remember how tenderly he cared for a horse that was more than 30 years old and looked every bit of it. Paul told me the horse had been a faithful old friend, and he'd keep him as long as the old fellow seemed comfortable. That was the kind of person Paul Myers was.

• Glenn R. Slenker, a Monticello lawyer and the dean of the legislators with whom I served. He kept horehound candy in a glass container on his desk, took off his shoes and scratched his feet a lot, and still passed the candy around. When he got up to speak, everyone listened because they knew that he knew his stuff.

• James Allen, an attorney from Salem, a Delta Chi fraternity brother, and a former speaker of the House. He was a quiet, polite, and extremely able legislator.

• John Hart of Indianapolis, the most ardent and articulate advocate of property tax relief. Despite his size, he was a gentle, soft-spoken man, so sincere that on occasion I saw a tear or two trickle down his cheek as he presented arguments on the floor.

• Dick Boehning of Lafayette, who still looks ten years younger than his real age. As House majority leader while I was speaker, he stood tall, although he physically is my kind of man—very short. An effective legislator and a fine human being, he was someone whose judgment I trusted and on whom I leaned heavily for advice and counsel.

For their knowledge, loyalty, and ability, I admired Republicans Kermit Burrous of Mexico in Miami County, who followed me as speaker; John Donaldson of Lebanon, an able legislator who organized last session day activities; Eldon Lundquist of Elkhart and Joe Cloud of Richmond, excellent legislators who were together so much that colleagues called them the "gold dust twins"; Philip Warner of Goshen; and Harriett (Bailey) Conn of Indianapolis. Democratic members memorable for their gentlemanly deportment and effectiveness were Fred Bauer of Terre Haute, Austin (Buzz) Barker of Attica, Joe Bruggenschmidt of Jasper, John Frick of South Bend, John Mitchell of Flat Rock, Dick Bodine of Mishawaka, and Jimmy Hunter of East Chicago.

I am less familiar with the Senate, but can't resist mentioning old-timers like Russell Bontrager of Elkhart and Ruel Steele of Bedford and those of later vintage: Jimmy Plaskett of New Washington, Joe Harrison of Attica, Jim Young of Franklin, Morris Mills and Larry Borst of Indianapolis, and Bob Mahowald of South Bend.

The General Assembly could not function without the professionals in the Legislative Services Agency and the permanent and session staffs of both houses. Council analyst Ray Rizzo helped me with speechwriting and served as troubleshooter, counselor, and wise judge of how things were going while I was speaker. My personal secretary, Vi Walker, did a whiz-bang job of scheduling me and running the office. It's impossible to name everyone on the House staff, but I owe much to Sharon Thuma, the principal clerk. To that list, I add George Meyers, a quiet dynamo who served as parliamentarian and whose knowledge of the legislative process was indispensable; David Bahlman and Bob Skinner, who as attorneys for my office read bills and advised me of draftsmanship problems or issues of constitutionality; and my administrative assistant, Ralph Rader, a former House member who was the "keeper of the bills" and my legislative calendar.

Some final thoughts on the General Assembly and the legislative process:

The General Assembly is a co-equal branch of state government. As a legislative leader, I felt the legislature lacked stature and pushed for full partnership with the other branches. As governor, I concluded that the General Assembly was powerful enough.

My experience in both branches strengthens my belief that it is too easy to override a governor's vetoes. It takes only 51 House votes and 26 Senate votes, the same number needed to pass a bill. I once proposed amending the Constitution to require 60 to 67 in the House and 30 to 34 in the Senate, but the idea went nowhere. It remains a good idea.

There should be a constitutional amendment requiring the issuers of mandates to pay for them. If the state requires local governments to do something, it should pay. (If the feds mandate the states to act, they should pay.) I'd also like to see an amendment to the Constitution defining the exact purposes for which property taxes can be used.

I remain optimistic that the legislative process will meet the state's future needs. At times, the General Assembly will fail Indiana's citizens on specific matters. At times, it will be slow to provide solutions. Over time, however, the General Assembly's history is that it will take the right steps and correct failures, sometimes by crafting better laws, and other times by being forced to act by voter pressure or the ballot box.

But it will happen, because the system works.

✣ 10 ✣

First Campaigns for Governor

FAR BACK IN the corner of my mind, I had first thoughts about running for governor when I was House minority leader; but I never divulged them, even to Beth. I started thinking seriously about running in 1967, in my first term as speaker, after the news media, legislators, and local people suggested that I give it a try.

Newsman Harry Kevorkian of WNDU-TV, South Bend, and the Plymouth *Pilot-News* first floated the idea. Local support came from Ida Chipman, Bill Gee and Bill Young of Plymouth, and Bob Osborn of Culver, friends of long standing. Legislators included Dick Boehning, Howard Barnhorst of Kokomo, Quentin Blachly of Valparaiso, Kermit Burrous, Arthur Coblentz of Liberty Mills, John Donaldson, Ralph Dunbar of Osgood, Ralph Heine of Columbia City, Wayne Hughes of Hudson, Harold Mertz of Logansport, Ellsworth Peterson of Ligonier, Mike Rogers of New Castle, Jack Smitherman of Mooresville, Jack McIntyre of Bloomfield, and John Thomas of Brazil. My Speaker's office staff—Vi Walker, Ray Rizzo, Ralph Rader, Bob Skinner, and Dave Bahlman—and Sharon Thuma, principal clerk of the House, supported the idea.

The only physician who was an early supporter was Wilson Dalton of Shelbyville, but encouragement and support came from most county medical societies. Once I became a candidate, much of the early money came from physicians. (Early contributions are the "mother's milk" for a healthy, successful campaign.)

An intense interest in good government was the reason for my decision. I guess I had ego enough to feel I could be a good governor. Coupled with my legislative experience, my physician's training was a good qualification. Public health underlies much of what state government does. It's especially pertinent to the state's roles in public, mental, and animal health, but also comes into play in welfare, corrections, water quality, and the training and certification of medical professionals and paraprofessionals.

In late 1967, I assembled a small, inexperienced group. Mrs. Chipman became my campaign chair. Bill Gee, the Marshall County GOP chair, was a natural to join the group. Others were Bob Hutchins, a wheelchair-bound polio victim and editor of the Plymouth *Pilot-News*, Alexis Clarke, and Osborn. Long-time friend Clarence Long of Indianapolis made suggestions, but we lacked the money and staff to implement most of them.

We ran the campaign from Ida's living room in Plymouth and my home at 304 North Center Street in Bremen. Not one person in that campaign received even a single dollar for their work. I don't recall what we spent, but it was under $35,000. We couldn't afford paid staff or outside help. (I hired a professional to do an important speech. His $200 charge for something no better than I could have written put a crimp in our budget.)

If voting went past a first ballot, I might have a chance to win. If I failed, I knew I had four years to take a second shot. My 1968 run wasn't just to lay a foundation for 1972, however. Once I decide to do something, my nature is to pursue it single-mindedly—another example of Bowen "determination," alias "stubbornness."

I knew how to count votes, something I needed to do especially well in the governor's race so that I could arm myself with a realistic assessment of delegate strength. My approach in 1968 was not to count friendliness as support. People went in a "no" or "undecided" category unless they said, "I'm absolutely for you," or asked, "What can I do to help?"

I had a single theme—that Indiana should remove the burden of public education and local government from property taxes. I saw this as shifting some of the burden to state-level taxes that more fairly treated income and profits, not increasing total taxes. Property taxes had jumped at a rate far greater than inflation—10 to 12 percent annually—and were becoming ruinous. (The "rule of seven" provides an idea of the danger for taxpayers. With compounding, spending at 7 percent annually doubles outlays in seven years. In some locales, rates were rising more than twice 7 percent.)

My campaign strategy focused on state convention delegates, whose identities would not be known until the next May's primary. Delegate lists from earlier conventions showed many repeaters. I put them at the top of my list and traveled the state to see them. In the six months prior to the convention, I logged 25,000 miles, visited all 92 counties, contacted about 1,800 people, and talked to scores of party leaders and influential Republicans—mayors, bankers, other businessmen, lawyers, and organization heads. At every opportunity, I attended Lincoln Day dinners and took speaking engagements.

Beth went with me, and she often took the wheel so I could catnap. I am not a smoker; however, to keep awake on long trips, especially at night, I occasionally lighted up a cigar. From that indiscretion, I acquired small burn holes in my topcoat and trousers.

Knocking on the first delegate's door was the hardest. The more face-to-face contact I had, the easier it became. For many delegates, a face-to-face talk with a candidate prior to the convention was a first. I respected the position of delegates who wanted to remain uncommitted pending caucuses, but I asked them and delegates already pledged on the first ballot to vote for me on a second ballot. Many promised to do so.

My delegate search was aggressive. I would go anywhere at any time to talk to delegates. After dark in Posey County in southern Indiana, I once went through fields to a pond to talk to a delegate fishing there. In Switzerland County, I forded a creek to see a delegate. I caught the Miami County GOP chair before breakfast—in bib overalls and barefoot. I found a Fulton County man on the roof of his garage at King's Lake. To get close enough to talk, I had to go between two dogs—a hound on one side, a police dog on the other. I decided the hound was the lesser threat, but it was a bad decision. When I got close, he bit me on the behind. Luckily, his teeth didn't get through my topcoat, and I was not injured. His owner and I then talked.

I probably won some of these delegates' votes. Rural delegates and members of organizations like the Farm Bureau were apt to support me because of my property tax reform position. Physicians were supportive, but few became delegates. Labor delegates did not support me because of my vote for the right-to-work law. Indiana State Teachers Association–affiliated delegates did not support me, but many teachers did. Least apt to support me were the large county Republican chairs who had brokered a secret alliance to ensure that each of them got a candidate on the 1968 state ticket. If they stuck together and their delegates voted as instructed, they knew that their alliance could carry the day.

I learned that some party leaders don't even pretend to be fair. Bill Gee drove us to a southern Indiana rally at speeds that had Beth and me on edge but were necessary to get there on time. At these events, candidates usually are introduced and allowed to speak briefly. Wearing his county chair hat, Bill told the emcee I would like to speak. However, we were in the domain of Eighth District chair Seth Denbo, one of Indiana's most colorful political figures, and a person known to use any tactic to gain an advantage. He was supporting my principal opponent, so Bill's request was ignored, and so was I.

In a late 1967 coup, Vigo County and Seventh District GOP chair Buena Chaney became the state party chair, replacing Charlie Hendricks. Chaney was part of a large county coalition assembled by L. Keith Bulen of Marion County. Friendly with all factions, I was too politically innocent to realize what the "pols" knew—that the change practically ensured Secretary of State Edgar D. Whitcomb's nomination for governor.

Bulen recruited delegate candidates whose names began with the letters "A," "B," or "C." Their names appeared first on the ballot, so they usually won. Bulen's candidates then often resigned. Under party rules, county chairs fill the vacancies. Many county and district chairmen used the power to appoint replacement delegates to further their ends. Bulen employed it in a way that perverted the process.

(Bulen still heads my short list of people, in or out of politics, for whom I harbor ill feeling. I found it satisfying to be elected speaker in 1967 despite his behind-the-scenes efforts to defeat me. After he ruthlessly scuttled my 1968 effort to win the governor's nomination, it was even more satisfying to beat back his desperate efforts to sabotage my second effort in 1972. After the 1972 convention, and as recently as 1994, he claimed that he delivered the votes that gave me the nomination. This was an outright falsehood. The Marion County delegates voting for me in 1972 did so as a direct result of my personal visitations—specifically to Wayne Township, where my friend Charlie Bogdon was chair.)

The state chair change lengthened the odds against me. In retrospect, it's probably a good thing I was naïve and stubborn. Had I known the deck was being stacked so much, there might not have been a 1968 "practice run." Without that baptism by fire, I could not have built the political following and strength to win in 1972.

Ed Whitcomb never made an overture to me to become his running mate, although the Indianapolis *Star* suggested that he had in "Behind Closed Doors," its Sunday political gossip column. The item, published on January 21, 1968, hurt my campaign by suggesting that I couldn't sustain my bid for the top spot, that Whitcomb was so far ahead that he was thinking about a running mate, and that I might be willing to accept the number two spot. The column was little more than a collection of distortions, half-truths, and falsehoods.

Bob Mooney's "Politics in Perspective" column in the *Star* on the same day dealt with Whitcomb's and Robert L. Rock's announcements for governor on January 23rd. This was a formality—everyone knew that they were running, and that I was announcing on January 24th. Mooney didn't mention me or two announced candidates, Democrat Dick Bodine of South Bend, former House speaker, and Republican Earl Butz of Lafayette, former dean of the Purdue University School of Agriculture. That hurt, too.

I was making headway with delegates. Reception in my one-on-one "house calls" was so good that by late March, I saw a faint hope of an upset if no one won a first-ballot victory. (Blows to my campaign yet to come made it obvious later that I had no chance.)

On May 25, 1968, three and a half weeks before the June 18 convention, big county chairs held a slating session at the Michigan lodge of O. C. (Mike) Carmichael of South Bend. Although professing neutrality, Chaney was present, as was party treasurer Dick Folz of Evansville. (Called while on vacation, Bulen supposedly objected to slating but was overruled.) Attendees agreed to keep secret the names of those present and those slated and the fact that a meeting was held. When a fundraiser was held for the slate, an invitee tipped off Ed Ziegner, who wrote a story for the Indianapolis *News*.

Slated were Whitcomb for governor, Folz for lieutenant governor, Bill Salin of Fort Wayne for secretary of state, Lake County and First District GOP chair Theodore L. (Ted) Sendak for attorney general, and John Snyder of Washington for re-election as treasurer. (Later added were Trudy Slaby Etherton of South Bend for auditor and Dick Wells of Valparaiso for re-election as state school superintendent.) For "unblessed" candidates like me, Ed Ziegner's story was important intelligence, but hardly good news.

Shortly before the convention, the Associated Press asked the GOP county chairs who would be the nominee for governor. Twenty-five of the 49 responding chairs picked Whitcomb, 20 Butz, 4 me. The next day's headlines proclaimed Whitcomb as winner apparent. I don't blame AP for taking the poll and distributing the results, but the story had a dampening effect on my campaign. Since 25 county chairs had said I was their second choice, the poll confirmed the favorable effect of my contacts and strengthened my hope that a first-ballot deadlock might make me a compromise choice on a second ballot.

On arrival in Indianapolis, I tried to remain optimistic. Each candidate had hospitality rooms the night before the convention. Mine drew lots of delegates, but didn't match my principal opponent's traffic. It was clear that the delegates believed Whitcomb would win the next day, but many of them encouraged me to hang in there for a second ballot.

Hope dies hard. I went to the convention floor thinking there still might be a miracle. In that huge hall, the big county bunch again flexed their muscles in ugly fashion. Old-line Republican Frank T. Millis, the convention chair, let a Whitcomb demonstration go on for what seemed like forever. After my nomination, he gaveled down those whooping it up in my behalf in less than two minutes. Convention planners also placed my supporters on bleachers far off to the side and high up, limiting the ability of delegates to see and appreciate their efforts. Obviously, fairness was AWOL from the floor that day.

The convention had 2,224 voting delegates. The winner needed one-half plus one, or 1,113 votes. I hoped Whitcomb would fall 100 votes or so short, and that Butz and I could split the rest, forcing a second ballot. Instead, Whitcomb got 1,260 votes and won easily on the first ballot. I came in second with 527 votes, a good showing. Butz got 429. I got a few more votes than the pros thought I would from places like Marion and Lake counties.

Before the convention, I had written out two sets of remarks—one to use if I won, the other if I lost. After the vote, I went to the podium, thanked those who had supported me, and told the delegates that I assumed that they were not against me, but were more for Whitcomb that day. My conciliatory remarks drew vigorous applause from the delegates.

All those on the slate were nominated with Whitcomb and elected in November.

The loss did not embitter me. Looking back, I now think that it may have been a good thing, although I readily admit that I didn't think so then. Had I won and been elected, I could have served only one term. In 1972, the year I was elected governor, Indiana's constitution was changed so that governors could serve two consecutive four-year terms.

My loss made me more determined to mount a stronger 1972 effort.

Over the next four years, my 1968 contacts helped me do that. I may have been an outsider to party leaders in 1968, but that was not true of delegates, rank-and-file Republicans, and some county and district chairmen. Some of the latter, even those who supported Whitcomb, left town feeling that they "owed me one" and promising themselves to repay me at some future time. Some people also came away from the convention feeling that the days of "king-makers" were over, and that I represented a new generation of Republicans.

(Indiana moved away from back-room politics when the General Assembly passed a direct primary bill in my first term as governor. Republicans urged me not to sign it, but I did. Both parties still might be choosing major candidates at conventions if they had been less subject to manipulation by power brokers. "King-makers" forget that political parties exist to nominate and elect candidates who will govern honestly and effectively. Making the process a game of power politics was a major error in judgment.)

Even after losing the 1968 nomination, I still was speaker. That was my platform for another effort to win the governor's chair, and a vantage point from which to watch the new administration. I often wondered whether it was Whitcomb's administration or Don Tabbert's and Keith Bulen's. Tabbert, especially, seemed to have inordinate influence on decision making. However, except for his deaf ear on tax restructuring, the new governor did his best, and I have no serious criticisms of his performance.

The minute the vote was announced at the 1968 convention, I decided to run for governor in 1972. A few days later, I called my long-time friend Clarence Long and said, "Let's get started." Clarence contended that I had started my first campaign too late, with too little staff, money, and experience. Although a bit naïve about power politics, he was right about the seat-of-the-pants nature of that first campaign.

We formed a strategy group—the "kitchen cabinet." Members were Long, Boehning, Skinner, Will Hayes of Crawfordsville, Charles Gaus of Anderson, and Brad Grubbs and Henry DeBoest of Indianapolis. The son of movie "czar" Will Hayes, Hayes was the mayor of Crawfordsville. An Indiana Bell Telephone executive, Grubbs was one of my closest friends. Gaus had become concerned about funding schools from the property tax during his long service as attorney for the South Madison Community School Board. DeBoest was vice president for corporate affairs for Eli Lilly & Company. Long was my long-time friend, and Boehning was my former House colleague. Skinner worked for me in the House.

The group's members were to keep abreast of campaign plans but stay detached from day-to-day activities so they could judge how the public received my messages, offer criticism of what was or was not going on, and suggest alternatives. The kitchen cabinet defined the end goal as winning nomination on the first ballot in 1972 and advised high visibility as an initial strategy. When the legislature was not in session, I was almost invisible. I had to practice to make a living, so getting visibility around the state meant politicking at night and loss of sleep. My driver and cheerleader, Beth, kept me going.

I let party leaders know I was running, with or without their blessing. I felt confident about my prospects. I held many IOUs, and there was lots of delegate sympathy left over from 1968. Being speaker gave me credibility and visibility and ensured that I got more speaking invitations. The property tax relief tiff between Governor Whitcomb and me was a plus, although I disliked being in opposition to his "no general tax increase" position.

As 1971 neared its end, everything looked favorable. More Hoosiers now agreed that there was a property tax problem and that something needed to be done about it. My name recognition inside the party was better. Party people and the media saw me as the front-runner. With an overall strategy and a plan, and with well-developed ideas for campaign materials, we were well ahead of other candidates. The number of volunteers and campaign contributions increased rapidly, the latter to the point that we could hire staff. (For the campaign, I had three self-imposed rules: I wouldn't run it; I wouldn't spend my own money —although I did shell out some; and I would always be candid with the media.)

I wanted to retain my 1968 base-delegates who had voted for me and those who would have if a second ballot had been needed. Many "repeater" delegates were in my corner. Before the primary, I told them I was running and focused my post-primary contacts on those who had not been delegates in 1968. To build my base, I encouraged supporters to run.

On November 29, 1971, I announced my candidacy from the front porch of our home at 304 North Center Street in Bremen. A large and enthusiastic crowd that included news media and party leaders was present despite the cold, windy, snowy weather. My family, including my parents, stood with me as I announced my hope of becoming Indiana's forty-fourth governor. Students displayed large posters of support. It was a fun day and a good beginning.

In the spring of 1972, J. B. King, an attorney with the Indianapolis firm of Baker & Daniels, became my campaign manager. One of Indiana's most knowledgeable tax lawyers, J. B. was a member of the Republican Action Team assembled by Keith Bulen to oust H. Dale Brown as Marion County GOP chair and set the stage for Richard G. Lugar's successful 1967 campaign for mayor of Indianapolis. He had helped John Hart and House Republicans write property tax relief bills while I was speaker, and he had impressed me with his knowledge, common sense, and efficiency. His connections to the Marion County GOP organization were a plus, because out-staters dominated my organization.

My "jack of all trades," Ray Rizzo, a formidable idea man, was a principal architect of the campaign, participated in every phase of it, and recruited Bill Watt, an aide to Lieutenant Governor Folz and a former Associated Press newsman.

In 1968, Bill Colbert produced a campaign button with black horn-rimmed glasses on a white background and the words "I'm for Him." In 1972 and 1976, he produced more creative buttons. One looked like an actual button and said just "Bowen Button." Another featured an arrow and the words "Bowen Arrow." I disliked his "Bremen Demon" button and asked that it not be used. When we ran out of other buttons, we used it anyway. To my surprise, criticism was non-existent, demand strong, and the supply soon exhausted. Colbert's most remembered 1972 button may have been the one that read "He Hears You." People thought it captured the fact that I listen carefully, and to all sides, before acting.

For the 1972 campaign, my treasurer was Bob Osborn of Culver. Bill Young of Plymouth was finance chair. Both were businessmen, long-time supporters, and friends of long standing. I knew I could trust them to keep fundraising and financial record-keeping straight and in keeping with Indiana law.

Gerald (Jerry) Olson, executive director of governmental relations for Cummins Engine Company, was a key individual. He earlier had been involved in the campaigns of George Romney and Nelson Rockefeller for president, John Lindsay for re-election as New York City mayor, and Dick Lugar for re-election as Indianapolis mayor. When I found myself shuttling back and forth across Indiana without getting much done, it was obvious that I was wasting time on travel. Jerry integrated my schedule so that multiple events were held the same day in the same area. That preserved my time for better uses.

One-hundred-dollar-a-couple fundraisers were an everyday thing. Clearing $1,000 was a standard goal, not always reached. Such events are hard work. My right thumb and little finger were often painfully swollen because people would grab that hand and squeeze very hard. To minimize or prevent pain and swelling, I learned to grab first and squeeze hard myself. (For politicians, this is a common problem. In 1972, after being nominated for governor, I went to Washington for a campaign photo with President Richard M. Nixon. As I was ushered into the Oval Office, the president swore at the fellow who had just left. He had squeezed Mr. Nixon's hand so hard that he was in pain.)

Jim Garretson, a Carmel High School teacher, chaired an issues research group composed of Dr. John Seffrin, then a professor at Purdue, but now the executive vice president of the American Heart Association; Bob Marshall, now an Indianapolis businessman; Carmel teacher Hans Gundersen; attorney Randy Foxworthy, now with the Simons; Tom Kinghorn of Muncie, now Ball State's vice president/finance and treasurer; ISTA lobbyist Dick Dellinger of Noblesville, later a House member; Frank Abercrombie, then an American Fletcher National Bank officer, and now with Fannie Mae; Tom King of the Indianapolis Chamber, now an Indianapolis utility executive; the late Ron Hinchman, law clerk to Judge Paul Buchanan; and Fred Swift of the Noblesville *Daily Ledger*.

Prior to the convention, Noblesville *Daily Ledger* editor Jim Neal was elected GOP state chair. As party secretary, he presided at the 1966 House caucus when I was elected speaker. I knew that Jim would be neutral and fair, and I expected him to be a superb chair. He was exactly that. I shed no tears for Neal's predecessor, John Snyder, whose pitched battle with Governor Whitcomb had embarrassed Republicans, irrespective of their factional alliances. Eventually, concern about their feud and what it might do to the party's chances in 1972 led to a consensus that saw Snyder's resignation and Neal's election.

My opponents at the 1972 convention were Senate president pro tem Phil Gutman of Fort Wayne, Public Service Commission chair W. W. (Dub) Hill of Indianapolis, and Owen Circuit Court judge William T. Sharp. (Former House majority leader Bob Webb of Arcadia announced for governor but later dropped down to lieutenant governor.)

A former College Life Insurance Company executive, Hill had served in the House and Senate before becoming a state government troubleshooter for Governor Whitcomb. Sharp was a former administrative assistant to Governor Whitcomb and Marion County Municipal Court presiding judge and was the unsuccessful 1959 Republican candidate for mayor of Indianapolis against Charles Boswell. Gutman was a lawyer.

Whitcomb and Bulen supposedly supported Hill. Seen as an "egg-head," Hill did not play well with convention delegates. (He would have been a good governor, I think.) Sharp declared late, at the urging of Bulen, who probably hoped to create a stalemate into which he could insert Sharp as a compromise candidate. Whitcomb was saying freely that he could not support me, but he never really did much for Sharp. With Bulen's support, Gutman could have been my strongest foe. Without it, he had few supporters outside the Fort Wayne area. Lieutenant Governor Dick Folz did not run and quietly supported my candidacy. (He and Whitcomb may have had a falling out that soured him on politics. Hindsight also suggests a health problem, since Folz died only thirteen months after leaving office.)

Bulen's failure to focus on one candidate and stick with him, and Ed Whitcomb's strange reticence, probably affected the eventual outcome in some way.

In the lieutenant governor's race, my heart was with my close friend Representative John Hart of Indianapolis, but I left the decision to the delegates. The most compelling reason was that my opponents had used steamroller tactics to squelch my hard work and high hopes of winning nomination for governor at the 1968 convention. I did not want it said that I did in 1972 what I had condemned as unfair in 1968. There also was a political reality—that endorsing anyone other than the Eighth District's "favorite son," Senator Bob Orr, would cost me the support of Evansville-area delegates. By staying neutral, I held that support.

J. B. and I felt that I was a winner before convention eve maneuvering began on June 22. My decision to let the delegates choose the nominee for lieutenant governor probably cemented my victory. To win, we needed the votes of 1,042 of the 2,082 delegates. J. B. and I counted close to 900 solid votes and 300 to 500 probable supporters. If our assessment was accurate, we needed only 225 of the probables.

On the night before the convention, an elbow-to-elbow crowd packed my convention center hospitality suite. Ida Chipman, Bill Colbert, and others did a superb job planning the function. Bremen High School's swing choir performed with enthusiasm. We served hot dogs, soft drinks, and popcorn and passed out buttons, paraphernalia, and "Bowen for Governor" hats. My mom and dad wore their fedoras proudly and were thrilled by the sheer energy in that big ballroom that night. The crowd's enthusiasm conveyed an important message—that no one looked strong enough to take the nomination from me.

We used several creative wrinkles, most of them the product of Ida

Chipman's fertile mind, on the convention floor the next day (June 23rd). Hundreds of persons whom I had delivered while practicing wore "Bowen Baby" T-shirts. This time my supporters got to show their enthusiasm, and a thunderous demonstration erupted when I was nominated.

The convention was an anticlimax. On the first ballot, I received 1,243 votes, far beyond the 1,042 needed. Sharp had 364, Gutman 354, and Hill 108. Bob Orr needed three ballots to win nomination for lieutenant governor. Also nominated were Ted Sendak for re-election as attorney general, Marilou Wertzler for re-election as courts reporter, and Harold Negley for state school superintendent.

The fall campaign began the minute the convention ended. J. B. and I never doubted that we would win, but we knew we faced major challenges in staffing up, fundraising, media relations and campaign advertising, and volunteer organization. Everything fell into place, and we moved ahead without a major hitch.

Former governor Matthew E. Welsh of Vincennes and Indianapolis was my opponent. He was highly regarded and much better known. An early poll showed that only 16 percent of Hoosiers even knew my name. There is a simple reason: Only a governor has what Teddy Roosevelt called the "bully pulpit" all the time.

At Bill Colbert's suggestion, we engaged Garrison Jasper Rose & Company of Indianapolis to do our advertising. The agency prepared a half-hour "mini-documentary" focusing on my early life, family, practice, and House service. The presentation was long, wasn't a hard sell, and wasn't issues-oriented. It aired before Labor Day, the point when the "pols" believe that people start thinking politics. However, it quickly improved my name recognition.

In 1972, the national ticket became a major plus for Hoosier Republicans. President Nixon was at the height of his popularity, although the Watergate burglary already had occurred. Democrats chose George McGovern, a left-wing South Dakotan. It was a poor choice and looked even more so when McGovern had to pick a running mate twice. His political philosophy and bumbling didn't set well, and sentiment quickly swung to the Republicans. That helped candidates at every level.

I made hundreds of campaign stops. Jim Garretson suggested the Generators, a group of fine young musicians who entertained wherever I appeared and were a huge hit. To get around, we used a car, a mobile home, a van, and planes. On many days, we traveled 600 to 700 miles. My driver was a pre-law student, Paul Mannweiler. I like to take credit for his later service as a House member, speaker, and minority leader. In 1972, Paul had less lofty duties. His first job after we reached a destination was to find a restroom, his second to find a Dairy Queen so we could get a chocolate shake. The latter was as important as the former was necessary.

Conserving time was essential, so flying was necessary. One trip between two small southern Indiana airports was downright dangerous. At the airport from which we were departing, the fog was so heavy it was hard to see your nose. We were using a small plane. Our destination airport had no runway lights or tower. My young, confident pilot said not to worry. "We'll make it," he said. It's easy to get up, and we did. En route, he made the kind of calculations pilots make in these circumstances—something he called "vectoring." He soon said, "This is where it ought to be." Sure enough, there "it" (the runway) was. However, there is something totally unnerving about seeing the ground for the first time when you're only a few feet above it. Facing such a trip today, I would drive.

As we were landing at Fort Wayne's Baer Field in a storm one night, a crosswind pushed the airplane wildly one way and then the other. On our first shot at landing, the plane's wheels bumped the ground, but the wind was tilting the wing dangerously close to the ground. How the pilot did it, I'll never know, but he took us back in the air again. He then made a second, uneventful and—thankfully—successful landing.

Beth accompanied me on most trips. She was popular on the campaign trail and had a way of making friends quickly. In the campaign's last few weeks, when there were too many requests for me to handle, Beth became my surrogate. My boys and my daughter, Judy McGrew, and her husband, Dave, also made appearances.

Governor Welsh worked as hard as I did. We often bumped into each other, usually at joint appearances or "debates." Matt never stooped to negatives, but he understandably criticized my positions and property tax relief proposals. We were asked most about our positions on legalizing marijuana and abortions. These questions still are being asked thirty-eight years later. Matt was handicapped by the sales tax enacted while he was governor, but his biggest handicap was McGovern's unpopularity.

My worst negative came from Governor Whitcomb, who called my property tax relief plan nonsense and said that we would find out the hard way that it wouldn't work.

On Election Day, I remained in Bremen, relaxed because I knew I had given the campaign my best. At 6 p.m., Beth and I went to the Legion home at Plymouth to watch returns. The early trend was strongly Republican. Beth and I soon left by private plane for an Indianapolis victory celebration. On the way, we tried to find the right words to say to those who had made my victory possible. We finally realized that a simple "thank you" from the heart says it best. As tired as Beth and I were, our night of celebration was so special that we almost wished that it never would end.

For J. B., Beth, and me, the victory was no surprise. Initial GOP polls had shown Matt Welsh ahead by a substantial margin, but my probable percentage of the vote rose with each succeeding poll. By fall, I had passed Governor Welsh. He recovered a bit, but never regained the lead. Final polls indicated an easy win. The record margin—more than 303,414 votes out of 1.2 million cast in the gubernatorial race— did surprise us. Bob Orr, Ted Sendak, Harold Negley, and Marilou Wertzler won. Dick Lugar defeated incumbent R. Vance Hartke for the U.S. Senate. President Nixon racked up the largest vote total (1.405 million), margin (697,000), and winning percentage (66.5 percent) and won all 92 counties.

Of all those involved in the 1972 campaign, Beth made the greatest contribution. Politically literate and astute, she was my daily inspiration, encourager, and advisor. Without her, I could never have made it through the campaign.

J. B. King would come next. The campaign's real brains, he made all the tough calls. A side benefit of the 1972 campaign is that it brought together J. B. and Ann Wantz. A volunteer, Ann worked in my campaign on scheduling—getting me where I needed to be on time. In that role she met J. B., and they became friends. After she joined my staff in the governor's office, she and J. B. were married. They now have two fine sons.

Jim Neal was another key figure. Under his leadership, the party supported my campaign in every possible way. Bill Young of Plymouth, finance chair and fundraiser, and Bob Osborn of Culver, campaign treasurer, were superb. After that, it's a tie between the incomparable Ida Chipman, Bill Gee, Ray Rizzo, Bill Watt, Bill Lloyd, Paul Mannweiler, the Generators, many county and district chairs, Jim Garretson and his issue researchers, my "kitchen cabinet," particularly Clarence Long and Brad Grubbs, the 1288 Club members, and many others. (I owe a lot to McGovern, too.)

Jim Neal planned to serve as GOP state chair only through the election. I asked him to stay on, and he agreed. Two days after my victory, I named Rizzo, Bill Lloyd, Bob DeBard, and Watt as executive aides. A Bloomington attorney, Lloyd already was on Whitcomb's staff for transition purposes. DeBard had been a campaign aide. I also announced that Vi Walker, my long-time personal secretary, would be my executive secretary when I moved into the governor's office.

I had to select department heads after evaluating those who had served Governor Whitcomb, find new talent, develop a legislative program, get bills drafted, and prepare legislative messages. There was no "honeymoon" with the Statehouse press corps. They were immediately inquisitive—as they should have been—about my new administration.

To help with personnel, Jim Neal chaired an advisory committee that I divided into "Big P" and "Little P" sub-groups ("P" standing for patronage). "Big P," chaired by Jerry Olson, screened for major positions, and "Little P," chaired by Bill Gee, screened for lower-level positions. Other members were Betty Rendel of Miami County, the state vice chair, and county chairs Lavon Yoho of Greene County, John Sweezy of Marion County, Virgil Scheidt of Bartholomew County, Quentin Blachly of Porter County, and Tom Milligan of Wayne County. Rizzo, Watt, DeBard, and Lloyd served ex officio.

To make big decisions, we needed to get away from distractions. The Republican State Committee allowed us to go at party expense with our spouses to Long Boat Key near Sarasota, Florida. Bob Orr, J. B. King, and I were present throughout; Jim Neal was there most of the time. Senators Gutman and Walter Helmke and Representatives Burrous, Hart, and Jack Guy joined us briefly. Participants worked to identify people to head state agencies.

The full committee and I then processed appointments. I wasn't about to make a clean sweep of Whitcomb officeholders, but those who did not support me at the convention had to go. I did not keep Millard F. (Bud) Renner, commissioner of administration, or Joseph Root, Bureau of Motor Vehicles commissioner. I agonized about James Mathis, who had been an excellent revenue commissioner. The decision came down to persons of equal quality—Mathis and Ivy Tech vice president Don Clark. I went with Clark, whom I knew and trusted, and he performed with integrity, dedication, and loyalty. With hard work, we made about forty appointments and reappointments by inauguration day.

I did not want a chief of staff arrangement in my office. My top aides and I met with Roy Jumper, a specialist in organization management with Indiana University's School of Public and Environmental Affairs (SPEA), and Ed Williams, an IU administrative vice president.

I settled on a cabinet-style arrangement giving each aide equal authority and equal access to me. After assessing talents and interests, I then assigned departments to each aide. They were told not to dictate, but to serve as liaison between agency heads and me, and to help agency heads get to me if problems arose. Each aide then was told to do a cram course on his or her agency, including how to react to emergencies.

By inauguration day (January 8, 1973), we were ready to begin.

Inauguration day itself was filled with excitement for Beth, our family, and me. After a morning prayer breakfast, between 4,000 and 5,000 people jammed the second floor of the Statehouse near the Rotunda and lined the third- and fourth-floor railings to watch the inauguration. On the platform or up front were major officeholders, General Assembly leaders, members of Congress, four former governors (Ralph F. Gates, George N. Craig, Matthew E. Welsh, and Roger D. Branigin), the outgoing governor, Edgar D. Whitcomb, and his wife, Pat, and Barbara Handley, the widow of Governor Handley.

Beth sat beside me. My parents, brother and sisters, children, and grandchildren were in front of us. The ceremony was anything but boring, but a photographer caught a yawn by our two-year-old granddaughter, Nicole McGrew. Her photo appeared in many papers.

We shared the spotlight with new lieutenant governor Bob Orr and his wife, Josie, and Attorney General Ted Sendak and his wife, Tennessee. (Harold Negley, elected state school superintendent, and Marilou Wertzler, re-elected court reporter, started their terms at a different time.)

When Jim Neal called me to the podium, I introduced my family, saving Beth for last. I then told that huge crowd that she was the individual whose help had been part of every achievement I had ever had in my life, including my election as governor.

Joe Kotso, my Lake County coordinator and later the Lake County and First District GOP chair, swore me in as Indiana's forty-fourth governor. Lake County normally delivers huge (25,000 to 50,000 vote) margins to Democratic gubernatorial candidates. In 1972, I lost Lake County by only 5,600 votes, the closest any recent GOP gubernatorial candidate had come to winning there. Despite its Democratic leanings, Lake County often casts more Republican votes than any area of the state except Marion County.

I chose Kotso to administer the oath of office to show my appreciation for his work and to relay a message to Lake County's people that I would not forget them. As governor, I later made dozens of Lake County appearances, listened to the concerns of its people, and tried to help with their problems. I feel I treated Lake County and other counties in the state's far reaches—northwest Indiana, the Evansville "pocket area," and the area around New Albany and Jeffersonville—well and fairly. However, I acknowledge that they feel neglected, and understandably so. Their TV news diet comes from stations across the border, whose anchors seldom inform Hoosiers even minimally about what's going on in Indianapolis or in Indiana state government.

Inauguration day was one of those times you want to preserve in every detail. I remember sitting on the platform, looking at that large, happy, cheering crowd. I remember Beth holding the Bible, and looking so proud, as Kotso swore me in. I remember the reception line after the ceremony—because I shook so many hands that mine again was sore and swollen for days. I remember the quiet dinner and family celebration Beth and I had with our children and my parents at the University Club. And I remember the wonderful inaugural ball, attended by about 4,000 persons.

More than anything else, I remember sitting down for the first time in that big black chair behind the governor's huge oak desk. I remember looking around that big room at the portraits of former governors lining the wall, the huge state seal woven into the carpet, and the view through the long windows facing Capitol Avenue.

In the late afternoon, I signed my first letters. My name was typed at the bottom over the word "governor." It was then that it came home to me—I now actually was the governor. At that moment, I knew the effort to get there had been worth it.

❧ II ❧

First Steps and Property Tax Relief

As I TOOK office, my objective was to be an honest, fair, and compassionate governor who was a good listener. Those first days were exciting, but I knew I had asked the people of Indiana to believe that I was capable, and that it now was time to do the job.

Hindsight tells me that a governor must be a decisive problem-solver, have good character, and be willing to lead politically, governmentally, and symbolically. A public official's most important traits are honesty and integrity. These are the foundation of credibility, a public leader's most precious commodity. A governor cannot lead by trying to please everyone, straddling the fence, or trying to come down on both sides of it. He must lead by making decisions based on common sense and tempered by compassion.

A governor's symbolic leadership role requires him to support and lend his name to worthy causes, to challenge people to do good deeds, to honor and recognize people of achievement, and to help constituents believe that they have the power to make their state a better place. Governors are cheerleaders and father figures.

Politics is an honorable profession, and most politicians operate with good intentions. As party leader, a governor cannot play politics—he must help keep it clean.

I was fortunate that my predecessor had left me with no major problems. Whatever differences Governor Whitcomb and I had, he took care of business reasonably well.

The General Assembly's session began in mid-November of 1972, and a "governor's budget" developed by the State Budget Committee was on the table before I took office. This was Governor Whitcomb's budget, not mine. My immediate challenges were to:

- implement my property tax relief goals;
- finalize my positions on the biennial budget and prepare speeches to lay out my program and discuss my budget proposals;
- complete the job of organizing my administration; and
- set the tone for my new administration.

While I was seeking nomination for governor, my call for property tax relief was a general one. After I was nominated, my aides suggested using "visible, lasting, and substantial" to describe my property tax reform goals. These became familiar words to Hoosiers, but neither my advisors nor I defined what they meant or what we intended to do. I had pledged myself to work hard for property tax relief in the campaign, but took care not to promise it outright. As governor, I now had to pursue it. If I failed to get some sort of property tax relief in the first legislative session, the media's judgment would be rightfully harsh. It wouldn't be difficult to write the headline: "Bowen fails to deliver property tax relief."

Going into the session, I had advantages. I personally knew almost every member in both caucuses of both houses. We respected each other. Our occasional disagreements were good-natured ones. The 1972 landslide gave Republicans strong majorities in both houses. (I had this luxury in half my years as governor—in 1973, 1974, 1979, and 1980. From 1975 through 1978, the opposition controlled one house.) I've always worked well with legislators of the other party, but it's easier when a governor's party controls both houses. If the opposition controls one or both houses, it can block a governor's program, and nothing holding the slightest promise of political advantage will get through.

As we confronted the property tax relief (PTR) challenge, the first question was who should be on point. The only logical choice was John Hart of Indianapolis, the House Ways & Means Committee chair. His role as chair and his knowledge and talents made him the best person to present and defend a PTR package. A builder, John shared my belief that rapidly rising property taxes reduced the ability of Hoosiers to own and improve their homes and Indiana businesses and industries to expand and create jobs.

Bill preparation started before I took office, to allow our proposals to be filed early. John Hart got the best available help, inside or outside state government. J. B. King was a principal advisor, but Rizzo, Lloyd, Thomas, Donaldson, Ed Thuma, Burrous, Boehning, and others contributed. Strong controls were a major element in the bills. This was not a new idea, since John had included controls in the bill that Governor Whitcomb vetoed in 1971.

Rates or levies can be controlled. Rate limits let taxes increase as assessments go up. Levy limits freeze the dollars that can be raised. Put simply, rate limits are a half-step toward controlling property taxes, levy limits a full step. For schools, the primary culprit in rising property taxes, we proposed going to levy limits. This was major medicine.

Implementing major changes in the state's tax structure required decisions on many sub-issues. For example, almost everyone wanted to exempt food from the sales tax but differed on what "food" was. Was it soft drinks, candy, snacks, and restaurant meals, or just groceries? In broad terms, the program I proposed called for:

- increasing sales and corporate net income taxes from 2 percent to 4 percent;
- permitting a 1 percent local option individual income tax, with counties required to "opt out";
- imposing tight controls on the ability of local schools and civil units of government to increase property taxes; and
- establishing two boards, one for local schools and the other for all other local units of government, to enforce the controls.

Revenues from state-level tax increases would flow into a fund dedicated to reducing property taxes by at least 25 percent. In localities adopting the local option tax, property tax reductions could reach 35 to 40 percent when the program was phased in fully.

Democrats soundly criticized the proposal. Vitriolic criticism came from newspapers and some Republicans. Whitcomb said the program wouldn't work. Indianapolis *News* editor M. Stanton Evans sounded strident alarms in his paper. Opposition by the *News* and the Indianapolis *Star* put capital city Republicans in a politically dangerous position. (Most stuck with me, but I was disappointed that John M. Mutz, then a senator, voted "no" on final passage.) Lafayette industrialist Herman Andre, who headed the Taxpayers Lobby of Indiana, was downright obnoxious in his opposition.

House members passed the four PTR bills with votes to spare. The biggest reason was John Hart. Trusted and respected, he was so persuasive that House members believed him when he said the program was needed, fair, and justified.

In the Senate, there was less trust. Some Republican members opposed tax increases for any purpose or were on the fence on property tax relief. The Senate's more leisurely pace also allowed PTR opponents time to bombard senators with negative messages.

President Pro Tem Gutman didn't work against the package, but he didn't do much to get it passed. Some suggested that this was his payback for losing the governor's nomination in 1972. This sounds plausible, but lacks validity. Senator Gutman was wrong in saying that I didn't help. I called in wavering Republicans to discuss why I thought the program was a good one, and why they should support it. True, I didn't twist arms or threaten anyone. I believe legislators have a duty to vote their consciences and their constituents' wishes.

When the Senate completed its debate on the PTR package, it initially had only 22 votes for passage. Republicans Charles Bosma and Leslie Duvall of Indianapolis and Leo Sullivan of Peru switched their votes to "yea," creating a 25-25 tie. As president of the Senate, the lieutenant governor breaks ties. Bob Orr quickly provided the 26th vote. The final count on the other three bills was identical, with Bob Orr casting the deciding votes.

The Senate made amendments, so the House had to concur (agree) or dissent (disagree) with them. A dissent meant going to conference committee, a step involving major risks. I favored conference committee consideration because Senate amendments were substantive. The media played up the Senate's cut in property tax relief from 25 to 20 percent, but my biggest complaint was a significant loosening of the controls.

The House dissented to send the bills to conference committee. These bipartisan four-member committees have one legislator from each caucus in each house. All four must sign a report, and both houses must adopt that report for the bills to go to the governor. A stalemate developed there. I then suggested that we float a final proposal for an up-or-down vote. Hart, King, and I agreed on the contents. J. B. put the proposal's language into conference committee report form. Its major provisions would:

- increase the sales tax from 2 to 4 percent;
- increase the corporate net income tax from 2 to 3 percent;

- gradually phase out the old corporate gross income tax on business;
- provide for a local option income tax at rates from $1/4$ to 1 percent, with counties able to opt in (rather than being required to opt out)
- exempt groceries but not restaurant or carry-out food, candy or carbonated drinks from the sales tax;
- freeze property taxes at the 1972 level; and
- guarantee a 20 percent credit on property tax bills.

As the House Republican conferee, Hart carried the proposals to the conference committee and battled for their acceptance. Conferees agreed to report them to the House and Senate floors. The House quickly gave its approval, although all Democrats and at least twelve and sometimes one to three more Republicans voted "nay."

Senate approval was another matter. I did what I could to sway Senate Republicans, and I talked to a few Democrats. Senator Wayne Townsend, a Democrat from Hartford City and a large-scale farmer and property taxpayer, was sympathetic, but he planned to seek his party's nomination for governor and didn't want to create a stumbling block for himself. Other senators later told me that he tried to get Democrats and wavering Republicans to vote for the package. (Senator Townsend ran for governor in 1984, but lost to Bob Orr.)

When the conference committee report on the sales tax bill was handed down in the Senate, Senators Bosma, Duvall, Mutz, and Sullivan—all of whom had voted for the bill's earlier version—voted "nay." Senator Joseph Harrison of Attica, who had voted "nay" when the bill first was considered, voted "yea." The result was a stunning 22-26 rejection of the report. At that point, most people felt that property tax relief was in rigor mortis. John Hart quickly pointed out that "until midnight [of the last day of the session], the patient is critically ill but with the possibility of recovery."

The day before the Senate was to consider a new conference committee report on a Friday the 13th (of April), I had a brief visit with an old friend, Senator James M. Plaskett, a Democrat from New Washington. We talked about the PTR package, but he gave no indication whether he would vote for or against the bills. The same day, another old friend, Senator Robert E. Mahowald, a South Bend Democrat, talked with me about funding for the Northern Indiana Children's Hospital and the South Bend bypass. I had campaigned in favor of both objectives, so I told Senator Mahowald I would do everything that I could to advance them. I do not recall discussing the PTR package with him, but my staff undoubtedly did.

When the conference committee report on the sales tax bill was handed down, 7 of the 30 GOP members—Duvall, Sullivan, Mutz, Shawley, Joan Gubbins, Bob Shaeffer, and Earl Wilson—and 18 Democrats voted against adopting it. Senators Mahowald and Plaskett "crossed over" and voted "aye," creating a 25-25 tie. Once again, Lieutenant Governor Orr was on the bubble. He quickly cast an "aye" vote and the report was adopted, 26-25.

In rapid succession, the Senate adopted the three other conference committee reports by 26-23 votes. Senators Mahowald and Plaskett again voted "aye" on each report. Their votes pushed total "ayes" to 26, so Bob Orr did not have to break more ties.

Suggestions were made that I had struck a deal with Senators Plaskett and Mahowald in exchange for their votes. I did not do so and neither man asked me to do so. Interviewed after the historic votes, both said they voted as they did because they thought it was the right thing for Indiana. I had no reason then, and I have none now, to doubt their word.

The importance of Bob Mahowald's and Jim Plaskett's "ayes" cannot be minimized. It took great courage for them to break party lines. The fact that both were defeated at the next election is evidence enough that they risked their political futures. I remain grateful for their courage, their willingness to put the people's interest above their own and above politics, and their willingness to take the political heat for their votes.

Bob Orr's votes also were courageous. Early in the session, Bob and I discussed the possibility that the opposition might try to box him in so that he had to cast deciding votes. If so, Bob said, he could be counted on to vote right. When ties developed in the first go-around, his political future was on the line, but Bob Orr kept his word and voted "aye" three times. Even more than Senators Mahowald and Plaskett, he was putting his political future at stake again when he cast his fourth tie-breaking vote.

Had the reports not been adopted, the news media would have suggested—correctly—that even the Republicans among the General Assembly members did not support my property tax relief initiative. They also would have deduced that other elements of my program were doomed. The long-term effect of a few key votes, as these were, still amazes me.

There were multiple ironies in the situation. Senate Republicans made it necessary for two Democrats to vote "aye" on the sales tax conference committee report. Only after Senators Mahowald and Plaskett voted yes, as we wanted them to, did Bob Orr have an opportunity to supply the last vote, as we wanted him to, and as Democrats hoped to force him to do. Finally, because the program became popular, Bob Orr's tie-breaking votes were a positive that helped him win election as governor in 1980.

Forcing Bob Orr to vote for tax increases, Democrats believed, would put him in a bind like Dick Ristine had faced. So much, I think this says, for traditional political wisdom!

So everyone knew that the PTR program was reducing property taxes, we required bills to show total property taxes before the PTR credit, the amount of the credit, and the net amount. There was apprehension about whether we could actually deliver relief, but I had devoted time to the issue for so long that I felt confident.

Predictably, Andre's Taxpayers Lobby filed a nuisance suit, and the Indianapolis *Star* jumped in to support him editorially. We were too busy to give the action much attention. Andre and his group eventually lost the suit.

I appointed J. B. (Heavy) Kohlmeyer of Lafayette and Don Pratt of Rockville to head the control boards. Kohlmeyer was one of the state's top property tax experts; Pratt was a very able former House member. Both had the ability to separate needs from "wants" and the courage to say no to "wants." After Kohlmeyer resigned for health reasons, I named James T. (Tom) Robison of Frankfort as his successor. David Davis of Indianapolis, Bill Long of Lafayette, and Howard Goodhew of South Bend later held one of these positions.

Starting in 1974, Hoosiers saw property taxes go down by 20 percent or more. The program made our tax system more equitable, reduced reliance on property taxes for schools and local government, made it more appealing to own a home, and lessened business fears that expansions would increase taxes without regard to profitability.

Proposition 13, a California property tax reform initiative, came along after Indiana reformed its property tax system. The national media treated it as if it were the first property tax reduction effort. There was no fanfare when we did a better job much earlier.

As time went on, reassessment made changes in the controls necessary. However, the General Assembly also began creating exceptions. By the time my eight years in office ended, there were eighteen different ones. In my last address to the legislature, on January 8, 1981, I warned that continuation of that trend could mean future property tax disaster, but the General Assembly kept nibbling away at the controls in the 1980s and 1990s.

It hurt a lot that Hart wasn't around to remind legislators that they needed to keep property taxes under control. (He resigned from the House in mid-1973.) Legislators never fully understood how their actions affected property tax controls. Over time, opponents nickel-and-dimed the controls to death. Changes were presented as a way to "help" with a "problem," and legislators felt good about voting "aye." No one mentioned that the legislation would loosen the controls and increase property taxes.

I believe the PTR program lasted longer than could be expected, and the facts show that it did. A 1996 report by the non-partisan Indiana Fiscal Policy Institute indicates that property tax collections increased 73.2 percent—better than 10 percent a year—from 1988 to 1995. In constant dollars, with inflation removed, the seven-year increase was about 7 percent annually. By contrast, statewide property tax collections did not reach the 1973 freeze-year levels in constant dollars until 1995, twenty-two years later. Even in unadjusted dollars, statewide property taxes did not reach freeze-year levels until 1988.

However, property tax "creep" from the cumulative effects of legislative nibbling at the controls once again has become a rapid rise. More than a quarter of a century after achieving property tax relief, we have come full circle. The issue is back with us.

❖ 12 ❖

Budgets, Surpluses, and Other Challenges

My second challenge as I took office was to develop my own budget proposals and other legislative initiatives.

The dominant legislative issue in odd-numbered years was—and still is—the budget. By placing dollar values on public functions and purposes, the budget defines and limits what state government does. Budget making is a complex process, full of sound and fury, but much more disciplined than most people believe.

Governors have major roles in budgeting. On a year-round basis, the governor's fiscal agent is the bipartisan State Budget Agency, a small group of professionals who develop budget strategies, watch revenues and expenditures, make recommendations to the governor and legislature, and monitor every agency's day-to-day activities. The budget director may be the most critical person to any governor. I was fortunate to have two of the best—Edison (Ed) Thuma and John Huie.

As mentioned, a "governor's budget" was in place as I took office. The debate over the PTR package intensified the normal budget debate. The reason was that the PTR program's elements drastically changed the way the overall budget was constructed.

Revenue forecasting is a step in budgeting. Forecasting requires making assumptions about where the state and national economies are headed. That is akin to rolling the dice. However, Indiana has an enviable revenue-forecasting record. Outside experts, mostly economists, evaluate trends and project them into the future. A non-partisan technical group takes the economists' scenario and develops reasonable estimates of future tax revenues. Bill Styring, then on the Budget Agency staff, later a State Chamber vice president and now a senior Hudson Institute fellow, was a key figure in this process.

Other states routinely puff up forecasts to make room for more spending. When projected revenues fail to materialize, they must drastically cut spending, drastically increase taxes, or both. Indiana's budget problems in the eighties were less serious than other states' and were due to a downturn in Indiana's manufacturing-based economy, not to fictitious revenue estimates.

In Indiana, both sides of the political aisle agree that revenue should be estimated carefully. They accept the economists' scenario and the technicians' number-crunching as the best available figures on which to base a two-year budget. With these matters off the table, the governor, his budget director, and the General Assembly's fiscal experts need only agree on spending levels and the appropriate surplus to get to a budget. That's not easy, but it's easier to start from an agreement about how much money is on the table.

The budget debate always focuses on spending and surplus levels. Like any governor, I had ideas about what was important and what was not, and feelings about what a prudent surplus was. For emergencies and economic downturns, I wanted a larger surplus than most legislators did. This security blanket let me sleep a little better.

Maintaining a reasonable surplus became an accepted practice. After I left office, the creation of the rainy day fund institutionalized it. While I was governor, we also created a tuition reserve fund to handle cash flows associated with large payouts to school districts. This fund now also is institutionalized in the budgeting process.

Republican legislators generally sided with me in maintaining an adequate surplus. Democrats were more likely to push to spend extra money. One of the problems with spending money just because it's "in the bank" is that the increases become part of the base for the next biennium. The General Assembly normally fixes budget increases for the future biennium at a percentage of the spending in the current biennium. To paraphrase a famous quote, add a million here and a million there, and pretty soon you're talking about real money! The other problem is that spending down the surplus minimizes the available cushion when there is an economic downturn and projected revenues fail to materialize.

Over time, I came to believe that we ought to return funds above the amounts needed for state government operations and a safe surplus to taxpayers. In 1979, I was roundly criticized for proposing what some called a "peanut-sized" refund of $15 a person. However, millions of taxpayers received the refund, and the total refunded was a very large sum. Government often takes too much from taxpayers, but it rarely gives anything back. The fact that our novel effort was unappreciated has little to do with whether it was right for taxpayers. I thought it was right then, and I still think so today.

As governor, I never was afraid to spend for real needs. Before doing that, however, I wanted to be certain that we had been careful to separate "wants" from needs.

I take pride that in 1979, my next-to-last year in office, Indiana ranked fiftieth in the nation in taxes collected from individuals. Mind you, we had that ranking six years after we increased state-level taxes to reduce dependence on property taxes. I consider our position as a low-tax state to be another of my major accomplishments as governor. (We still have a low total tax burden, but not as low as it once was.)

My third challenge as I became governor was to complete staff and department head appointments. With "Big P" and "Little P" committee input, I quickly filled other key positions. Many incumbents were retained, especially in number two and three spots. Most agency and department heads were my choices. As capable as I considered them to be, I knew that performance would be what counted. I quickly learned that I would repeat the process of identifying and qualifying people over and over again. State government has many employees, turnover is high, and there always are vacancies to fill.

I drew criticism for naming former legislators like Pratt, Boehning, Jim Gardner, Cloud, Jim Young, and Maurice McDaniel to key positions. However, it was easy to defend their appointments. I knew their capabilities, knew them as doers, and knew that they would keep their word and be loyal.

For example, Governor Whitcomb's employment security director was John Coppes. Some wondered why I even considered him, but I reappointed Coppes after we reached an understanding of what I expected. He performed well, with one embarrassing exception. The media reported that he took long lunch hours to play poker in an agency office. Fearing that he would be fired, he was very apologetic. I was urged to fire him and perhaps should have, but my soft heart kept me from it. Instead, I made him forfeit a week's wages and forgo a merit increase. He straightened out and served nine and one-half years before retiring in mid-1978 after suffering a debilitating stroke. To the best of my recollection, the other legislators all served loyally and effectively.

Vi Walker, my executive secretary, chose some of my support staff and organized them to respond to phone calls, visitors, and correspondence. As my buffer, she also decided who needed to talk directly to me and who could be referred to aides or department heads. Since she screened information coming to the office, she also was a key person in identifying and resolving problems. If she saw situations needing attention, she alerted the responsible aide. She also screened correspondence, channeling it to aides for action and preparation of responses.

My final challenge as a new governor was to set the right tone for my administration. The day after my inauguration, I called the department heads together and told them that I expected high standards of performance, responsiveness to the General Assembly without lobbying, and caution in dealing with lobbyists. I suggested that they decline free trips offered by vendors, persons, or companies with which their agencies did business or which they regulated, and that they decline all but consumable gifts of nominal value, like candy. At a second meeting, I said that I also expected them to be open and cooperative with the news media.

These sessions were an inoculation against bad or stupid behavior. Since I remember only three instances in which behavior required me to take action, my messages must have gotten through. Coppes's poker playing was one instance. Another required me to release a second-echelon individual. In the third, I admonished one of my aides, Jim Smith, who one night did too much partying and was involved in a minor auto accident. Two agency heads resigned, one at my request. Otherwise, the behavior and decorum of the "Bowen administration family" was quite good.

❧ 13 ❧

Managing for Results

As GOVERNOR, MY management style was an open and candid one. In return, I expected openness, truthfulness, competency, and loyalty. I seldom made significant decisions without consulting the aide responsible for the area involved, and often the entire staff.

The cabinet-style staff organization worked well. From the start, I met regularly with my executive staff. Attending the meetings were my executive aides, Mrs. Walker, the budget director (Ed Thuma and then John Huie), the commissioners of administration and revenue (Ray Sanders and Don Clark), and Lieutenant Governor Orr. I wanted Bob Orr there so he would be aware of everything and could, if something happened to me, carry on without disruption. Don Newman, director of the Indiana Washington liaison office, was among those who sat in occasionally. Others attended by invitation.

We met three times weekly, promptly at 9 A.M., around my big conference table. (One wag remarked that it was big enough to "seat fifteen, but only sleep six.") What was said at the table was to stay in the room, but no effort was made to police that understanding. Typically, there was no formal agenda. I usually had a short list of things to discuss. Then each person was given a chance to brief the others on events, problems, and opportunities in his or her area, or to ask others for advice and judgments. This process allowed us to test our thinking against the group and let everyone make suggestions. I encouraged candor and got spirited back-and-forth exchanges that occasionally became heated. My staff knew that I would weigh both sides before deciding—then or later—how to proceed.

I tried to see the big picture and keep details from obscuring it. However, I was—and still am—a perfectionist. That has probably made me more detail-oriented than I should be. I personally read, reviewed, and signed almost every response to every letter. I rarely sent letters back for better answers, but I frequently returned them for factual, typographical, or grammatical errors. My staff marveled at my ability to spot typos. They learned that I disliked split infinitives and sentences ending with prepositions. Once they had redone a few letters, they quit making those kinds of errors.

State government is a huge, incredibly complex organization, with thousands of employees and a multi-billion-dollar operating budget. It's hard to describe its breadth. Much of what gets done is vital and necessary, but is done routinely and goes unnoticed until something goes wrong. Most of state government's work produces no headlines. For example, citizens never read about the patients who are successfully treated in mental hospitals. They hear only about the problems in such institutions.

Within this framework, a governor is more like a CEO than a manager. He establishes broad goals and objectives within which his managers—department and agency heads—find the best ways to accomplish what he wants done.

As I look back over my years as governor, I see a half-dozen major accomplishments, and many other areas in which we made significant progress. I've mentioned two of which I'm proud—property tax relief and maintaining Indiana's position as a low-tax state.

After property tax relief, my most popular accomplishment probably was upgrading Indiana's park and recreation system. Beginning in 1974, we started the biggest park-improvement program in the history of the Department of Natural Resources (DNR), the agency that operates Indiana's state parks, recreation areas, state memorials, state forests, nature preserves, the state museum, and other related properties and facilities.

Once one of the nation's finest, Indiana's park system slipped badly after World War II. As neighboring states made major investments in park and recreation facilities in the 1950s and 1960s, we lagged behind. I had no idea of the extent of our neglect as I took office, but Bill Watt gave me the sorry details. This was a situation in which money was the answer. DNR director Cloud and his associates developed a realistic list of needed improvements, and in 1974 the legislature appropriated $12.7 million over and above its 1973–75 appropriation to start what became a continuing park improvement program.

Our effort wasn't limited to upgrading parks. We wanted every Hoosier family to be within driving distance of a park. To achieve that, we opened Potato Creek, Wyandotte Woods, Harmonie, and Hardy Lake parks and began developing White River State Park, an innovative linear park in the heart of Indianapolis. A little-noticed addition was more than forty nature preserves. We added new memorials, the most notable being the Wright Brothers Memorial in Henry County and the Ernie Pyle Memorial at Dana.

We increased the number of rooms in the inns at Brown County, McCormick's Creek, and Turkey Run state parks, renovated the Spring Mill State Park inn, and installed new food-service facilities at the Dunes State Park. We built two new swimming pools at Brown County State Park, one at the Abe Martin Lodge and the other near the north entrance. We constructed new pools at the Clifty Falls, Turkey Run, Ouabache, Harmonie, and McCormick's Creek properties. We built a swim beach at Potato Creek State Park. We built or reconstructed new walking and bicycle trails, nature centers, picnic areas, shelterhouses, boat docks, family cabins, group camps, and campgrounds, including the first winterized group camp at Wyandotte Woods.

By the time I left office, major improvements had been made at every park, and a variety of recreational facilities were close to every Hoosier. For its strong support, the General Assembly deserves credit. For the rapidity with which it made improvements and their quality, DNR deserves credit. Our park investments were not truly large, but they still pay dividends. I take great pride in these improvements.

Brookville and Patoka Reservoirs were completed. These and older reservoirs control floods, provide water supply, and create opportunities for recreation. By the time I took office, the popularity of reservoir building was waning. The remaining proposed sites in Indiana might have made good facilities, but enough was enough. Building a reservoir takes lots of farmland. It destroys an area's natural beauty. Acquiring land for a reservoir often requires the use of eminent domain, the highly unpopular practice of taking private property for a public purpose after an owner refuses to sell.

As the man in the middle, I decided that construction had to be justified on all three grounds—flood control, water supply, and recreation—and that expected benefits had to justify costs. All the proposed reservoirs fell short, so I supported their de-authorization. That brought heat from proponents and praise from opponents. De-authorization of Lafayette Lake prompted the hottest and loudest debate. Congressmen John Myers and Floyd Fithian both wanted it, but the cost-benefit ratio was not good.

A proposal to create a Dunes National Lakeshore was a major skirmish. The principal issue was how much land the federal government would take. First District congressman Adam Benjamin of Gary helped construct a compromise that pleased neither the feds nor us, but it was one that both parties could accept.

The Corps of Engineers proposed to canalize the Wabash River and define navigable streams to include every rivulet in America. The latter would have given control of all waterways to the Corps. Indiana knew something about canal building—we went broke trying to do it in the state's earliest years. Both proposals were laughable, so the Corps went away empty-handed.

Another accomplishment was the creation of a statewide emergency medical services system. Before I took office, funeral homes provided emergency ambulance services in many locales, usually out of a sense of community service. (Some may have hoped that families who lost someone would turn to them for funeral services.) Hearses were used to transport injured people to hospitals. Those operating them had no special equipment or training. Funeral directors usually lost money providing these services.

Increasingly, funeral directors were facing a potentially huge legal liability for mistakes in handling medical emergencies. (It is a sad fact of life that those apt to sue didn't care if the funeral homes were trying to provide a public service.) As I came to office, funeral home directors were rapidly pulling out. The problem was most pronounced in smaller communities and rural areas. In larger communities, paid and volunteer firemen trained in EMS procedures provided the service and did it well.

To look at the problem, I convened a Governor's Conference on Emergency Medical Services in mid-1973. Its participants recommended legislation to:

- create a statewide system of emergency medical service response centers, relying on existing hospitals;
- create an EMS Commission to set standards for the centers, training standards for EMS personnel, and equipment standards for ambulances, specifically life-saving equipment and two-way radio; and
- adopt 911 as a statewide emergency response number.

I supported this proposal because it dealt with a real need. Feeling threatened, firemen in larger cities opposed the legislation. Taking their cue from the firemen, some urban area legislators opposed the bill. The most adamant was Senator Gubbins of Indianapolis, where firemen provided sophisticated emergency medical services.

The EMS bill passed. My first commission appointments included my good friend Buford Rowe of Bremen. Earlier, a piece of farm machinery had turned over on him, pinning him underneath. He remained there until I got to his farm to supervise his being moved and avoid further physical damage. A conscientious man with a good sense of humor, Buford served well and was a popular commission member.

I brought Phil Martin of Lafayette from another agency as the new Emergency Medical Services Commission's staff director. He and the commission did their job well. A quarter of a century later, qualified personnel provide quality emergency medical services in every part of Indiana. Ambulances are equipped with appropriate life-saving equipment and two-way radios. The universal emergency number is 911. It's impossible to estimate the value of lives saved and injuries minimized by well-trained personnel using properly equipped ambulances, but I consider the EMS system one of the finest legacies I left to the people of Indiana.

Another major accomplishment was the state's landmark medical malpractice law. As I assumed office, a rising tide of medical malpractice lawsuits was threatening medical care in smaller communities, where one or two physicians practice. A good example involved the only doctor in the town of Topeka. Although near retirement age and financially able to retire, he hadn't planned to do so. Defending himself against a frivolous malpractice suit left a bad taste in his mouth. He went from wanting to continue serving to an "I don't have to put up with this" attitude and retired, leaving a small community with no doctor. The same scenario was occurring elsewhere.

A few bad doctors deserve to be sued. However, bad doctors were not the nub of this problem. The problem was lawyers, working on a contingent fee basis, who went for every "deep pocket" in sight. The increasing numbers of malpractice suits included borderline and even spurious cases. The hope of the attorneys (and perhaps their clients) seemed to be that doctors and insurance companies would settle rather than fight an expensive court battle, or that sympathetic juries, faced with medical situations they did not understand, would decide the suits emotionally and award large judgments.

The surge in malpractice suits set off an upward spiral in insurance premiums, which soon became exorbitant. By the time we set out to address the problem, some insurance companies were refusing new clients, including doctors coming out of medical schools, and were canceling the policy of any doctor sued for malpractice. These factors had implications for health care in every community, not just the small ones.

Medical and non-medical groups, including community organizations and chambers of commerce, formed statewide groups to find solutions. (Trial lawyers opposed any change.) Not surprisingly for a small-town doctor, I decided to use my pulpit to stimulate corrective action. Although my administration proposed the medical malpractice reform bill, an urban legislator—the late senator Adam Benjamin, a Gary Democrat—worked hardest for its passage. (Regarded as one of the finest legislators ever to serve in the General Assembly, Benjamin later served in Congress until his sudden death at too young an age.)

The bill that passed limited maximum medical malpractice awards to $500,000 and the filing period to two years. Recognizing that it might take years for birth damage from alleged malpractice to appear, an exception was made for infants and young children, in whose behalf suits could be filed until age eight. A panel of physicians, chaired by an attorney, was to examine the validity of malpractice claims. Its findings were admissible in court. Fees paid annually by doctors and hospitals financed a patient's compensation fund. The state became the insurer of last resort for doctors unable to obtain malpractice insurance, usually those entering practice, at rates higher than the norms.

No one was happy with the final bill. That told me that it steered a middle-of-the road course and probably was good law. Amendments have since been made to increase the maximum awards and set a six-month limit on the time a malpractice panel has to act.

Today, medical malpractice premiums are much lower in Indiana than in most states. Statistics show that the law works fairly for patients, doctors, and attorneys, although trial lawyers still want award limits removed and still object to limits on attorneys' fees. The law is a national model. For twenty years after it was enacted, I had many personal contacts and inquiries about the law. The first question usually was: "How did you get it done?"

My list of accomplishments also includes what we did in transportation. Most visible were our efforts to eliminate "killer highways"—the stretches of roads where statistics showed that accidents, injuries, and fatalities were most likely to occur—and to complete every Indiana mile of the original interstate system in a shortened time frame.

The "killer highways" were U.S. 31, which needed four-laning and a bypass around South Bend, and Indiana 37 and U.S. 41, which needed four-laning. Best illustrating the need was a one-lane bridge with a stoplight on U.S. 31 near Rochester. We completed major elements of the killer highway projects and moved the rest along. We also completed other major road projects too numerous to mention.

The interstate completion project resulted from the ingenuity of my former House colleague Dick Boehning, who chaired the State Highway Commission. Late in 1973, responding to the energy crisis, President Nixon signed a law allowing gasoline fees and other vehicle-related user fees for mass transit for the first time. The law established a new allocation formula that penalized states that built interstates. Under the new formula, the fewer miles a state had completed, the more money it got and vice versa.

Indiana had forty-seven miles of remaining interstates to build at an estimated cost of $39 million. Included were the ten miles of Interstates 65 and 70 that form the "spaghetti bowl" in downtown Indianapolis and other high-cost segments. Boehning's analysis of the legislation's fine print showed that its allocation formula would so stretch out federal funding that it would take ten years to complete the last Indiana interstate miles.

Our first reaction to the allocation formula was outrage. On its face, it wasn't fair to Indiana. As time went on, reality set in. The states that benefited most from the new law's mass transit provisions or its allocation formula had more than enough votes to beat back efforts to amend the legislation. Our chances of getting a better deal ranged from zero to none.

So, in a way typical of Hoosiers, Dick Boehning started looking at alternatives. He came up with a creative idea—that we use state funds to speed interstate completion and pay ourselves back when federal dollars came through the pipeline. If we got federal approval, we could complete the original interstates in six years, not ten.

There were several ideas on where to get the funds. The final decision was to borrow them from the Arterial Road and Street Fund, used to build high-traffic local roads that were not part of the state system. Funds in this account came from the gasoline tax. Due to the time needed to plan and build these roads, expenditures lagged well behind receipts. We could draw from this fund and repay it without affecting any local projects.

Everyone agreed that this was a marvelous idea. Boehning and highway officials went to Washington and got Federal Highway Administration approval. Interstate funding is 90 percent federal, 10 percent state. The plan compressed the inflationary effect on interstate building costs to six years, so Boehning's approach saved the Federal Highway Trust Fund a substantial sum and saved Indiana precious highway dollars.

All original interstate mileage in Indiana was completed well before I left office. (Short stretches, like the Interstate 64 spur into Evansville added to the system after the original design, remained for Bob Orr to complete.) There is no way to estimate the economic impact of the accelerated interstate completion program, but it was immense.

Highways also were one of my most trying burdens. There never was enough money to do the roads that needed doing, let alone what everyone wanted done, and there never was a shortage of ideas on where to spend scarce dollars. Almost everyone thought that I could, and should, short-circuit the process to speed up an area's pet project.

A good example of this pickle was a persistent lady's visible campaign to get us to repair Posey County roads. She blamed me for their condition. After visiting the county, I agreed that its roads were in terrible shape, but I couldn't convince her that the problem rested with her commissioners, who for years had failed to use gas tax revenues sent to Posey County to maintain its roads. Similarly, she didn't agree that it would be grossly unfair to use state funds to fix Posey County roads and not do it for ninety-one other counties. (We couldn't afford the latter.) She just wanted her roads fixed.

My strong support for the 55-mile-an-hour speed limit was not especially popular. I generally oppose federal mandates, but the "double nickel" limit reduced gasoline use and reduced traffic fatalities and injuries. I tried to curtail travel as much as possible. When we had to travel, my trooper/driver went exactly 55 in zones where that was the limit. When people passed us, I held up both hands to remind them of the limit. I was incensed when state-owned cars passed us. Their drivers were saying to other Hoosiers, "Do as I say, not as I do." I took down license numbers, found out who was driving, and sent that person a letter saying that I expected a better example from state employees.

Late in my second term, reorganization of the state transportation agencies was discussed as part of a "sunset" review. With Bill Watt in the lead, assisted by Dr. William Black, an Indiana University transportation expert, we supported the creation of an Indiana Department of Transportation. The original proposal was to combine the Highway, Toll Road, Toll Bridge, and Port commissions and other transportation functions. Toll Road Commission members were the principal objectors. (We felt that this commission, with offices distant from India-napolis, needed more oversight. Bill Watt put it more bluntly, saying the commission needed "adult supervision.") State Highway Commission members objected, but their offices' physical proximity to the governor's office made it difficult for them to be as vociferous. The trucking industry objected. The Port Commission objected, later was removed from the bill, and remains independent.

The agencies' objections proved the proposal's point—that each transportation mode was planning without regard for the needs or interests of other modes or how they related to each other. The proposal was mostly structural, not earthshaking, and it passed. Bill Black became the first Department of Transportation head. We left Bob Orr, my successor, with a better way to execute and develop transportation policy.

Before this change, everyone had wanted to serve on the State Highway Commission. Some sought appointment because they thought they could speed up their communities' projects. Lobbyists and those associated with the highway industry—concrete firms, stone and gravel producers, and highway designers—supported persons they thought would be fair to their interests. I appointed individuals I knew to be honest and knowledgeable about highway needs. As our history proves, this department spends so much money that favoritism and graft sometimes rear their ugly heads. In my years as governor, I believe that Indiana's citizens were well served by the Highway Commission.

The first Indiana deep-water port on Lake Michigan was authorized while I was a legislator. Burns Harbor was in its infancy when I became governor, but it had proven its value as an economic stimulant. Its success prompted a look at Ohio River possibilities. We recommended, and the legislature authorized, the Southwind Maritime Center in Posey County and the Clark Maritime Center in Clark County. These locations soon were moving coal, ore, grain, and other commodities.

One of the most vexing transportation problems I faced was the near-collapse of the railroad industry after the Penn Central and six other eastern carriers went bankrupt. With Bill Watt's and Dr. Black's expertise, we kept working toward a solution to this convoluted problem that would preserve some kind of rail service in Indiana.

The issue lent itself to demagoguery, and there was plenty of it. A good example was the demand by Governor Milton Shapp of Pennsylvania that any solution preserve every mile of his state's railroad lines, whether or not they could generate revenues justifying their continued existence. With Bill Watt feeding me facts, we took the position that some Indiana lines could never be profitable and should be abandoned. We also made it clear that we would stand and fight for those lines that had favorable prospects.

At President Ford's direction, Transportation Secretary William Coleman called governors of the eleven states with the worst problems to Washington in June 1975. The other ten governors recommended a moratorium on reorganizing the bankrupt railroads. None wanted to abandon unprofitable lines or seemed to appreciate the fact that keeping all the lines would doom a reorganized system. (The obvious flip side was that abandoning unprofitable lines might keep the profitable ones operating.)

I told the group, "It is time that we faced reality with respect to the problems of the bankrupt railroads . . . but I am opposed to delay and am opposed to the notion that we are supposed to retain large numbers of lines that are heavy money losers. . . . We must get on with it. We must stop the accelerating deterioration of the system. We must direct our money toward rebuilding and not continue to squander it to cover operating losses."

President Ford agreed with this common-sense approach and ordered reorganization to continue. After months of wrangling, Indiana's approach became reality. Unprofitable lines were abandoned. Potentially profitable lines were incorporated into a reorganized system. As a result, Indiana and its sister states still enjoy rail service.

With Bob Orr in the lead, economic development was a major accomplishment. Bob was—and is—a master in this business. He created a highly professional Department of Commerce with aggressive business and industrial development, international trade, and tourism programs that reached into Midwestern states, other areas of the country, and other countries. As commissioner of agriculture, Bob Orr also worked well with farm groups. He understood that agriculture is one of the legs of the state's economy, and that without a strong agricultural sector, Indiana could not prosper.

I have no doubt that Bob Orr's economic development work as lieutenant governor and governor from 1973 to 1989 enabled Indiana to shuck off its "Rust Belt" image. I also feel that his hard work laid the foundation for today's vibrant Indiana economy.

Crisis is a fact of life for public officials. We had our share—blizzards, tornadoes, floods, a coal strike, the energy crisis, and a prison riot. Our efforts to deal with these situations had no lasting effect, but I see our responses to a series of major crises as another hallmark of my administration.

My most anxious period began on December 6, 1977, when coal

miners walked off the job. Our electric utilities were (and are) 97 percent dependent on coal to produce electricity, but there was no immediate problem. The utilities and large users had large stockpiles. (Commissioner of Administration Ray Sanders stockpiled large quantities
for the state, which also was a larger user.) There were threats of violence. Loading dock and truck fires were set at Rockport, and trucks
were damaged at Boonville.

Colder than normal weather soon reduced supplies to a dangerous
point. On January 17, 1978, I ordered a 10 to 15 percent cutback in
state government use of coal and electricity. Three days later, I urged
Hoosiers to voluntarily cut consumption of coal and electrical energy.
Voluntary cutbacks did little good, but I again called for them when
another cold spell hit. We had little help from the feds, who mostly
told us things we already knew and told us to do things we already were
doing. We soon were down to a ten- to twelve-day supply of coal, much
too small a cushion for comfort.

On February 14th, I did what no one wanted, calling out the National Guard to move coal and using Indiana State Police officers to
protect Guard personnel. This action was necessary to prevent school
closings, business and industrial shutdowns, and problems for hospitals and nursing homes. There were instances of attempted sabotage—
such as nails spread along routes used to truck coal—but we kept coal
moving to the generating plants and avoided general chaos and whole-
sale disruption of the state's economy.

President Carter refused to invoke the Taft-Hartley Act to force a
cooling-off period and send the miners back to work. To me, the reason
was obvious—states affected by the strike generally were pro-Demo-
crat like the unions. President Carter knew that something needed to
be done. At a Washington meeting that he called for the governors of
coal-producing states, I described what we were doing. He later took
me aside and said, "Thank God, somebody's doing something." On
March 6th, he finally invoked Taft-Hartley, but left enforcement to the
states. That and warmer weather ended the crisis. The situation was
serious, but a letter from a coal miner's wife tickled me. "Thank you for
your action," she wrote. "It's good to get my man out of the house
again."

In weather emergencies, citizens expect a governor to act, and
rightfully so. His first concern must be the safety and well-being of
those affected, and his first actions must be those that minimize death
and suffering. Rescue efforts sometimes are necessary. Only after taking care of these issues can a governor begin dealing with displaced

people, property damage, cleanup, and restoration of basic services. (We tried to keep helping even after the worst of a crisis was over by setting up offices at disaster sites and staffing them with people from state agencies to assist those needing help.)

We coped with the same kinds of weather emergencies earlier governors had faced, but we didn't get "garden variety" tornadoes and snowstorms. One of the blizzards with which we dealt was the worst in state's history. The other was the second worst in the twentieth century. The 1974 tornadoes were the worst outbreak since the 1965 Palm Sunday tornadoes. We had floods. There was even a mild earthquake. Each disaster required responses that were similar in some respects and different in others.

After a tornado, for example, roadways must be cleared of fallen trees, limbs, and hot electrical wires so that rescue vehicles can reach those needing attention, and so that utility and other vehicles can begin cleanup. Injuries are common. Illnesses and births take no holidays, so medical facilities and personnel must be made available.

Blizzards pose different problems. People stranded in vehicles on snow-clogged highways must be rescued. Food, medicines, and medical attention must be delivered to homebound persons. Seriously ill people must be transported to hospitals. If electrical power goes out, generators will be needed—and not just for hospitals and nursing homes. For example, dairy farmers need electricity to operate milking equipment and cool milk. After the blizzard of 1978, we even dropped hay to stranded cattle. Shelters must be opened, and food, blankets, cots, medicine, and other supplies and services must be made available to those staying in them. The prolonged sub-zero weather that followed the 1977 and 1978 blizzards forced us to muster every available vehicle—from private snowmobiles and pickup trucks to Guard tank retrievers—to rescue and transport people, make deliveries, and clear roads.

Every rescue effort I ever saw renewed my faith in people. Guard, Civil Defense, and State Highway personnel, local law-enforcement officers, emergency medical service technicians, road crews, and thousands of volunteers were genuine heroes, going at it until they were almost literally dropping from exhaustion. The professionals were indispensable because they knew how to organize to do things and seemed to know the right time to do the right things. Still, we wouldn't have gotten the job done without volunteers.

Our folks' "let's get on with it" attitude contrasts sharply with that of federal officials. After Indiana got a second huge snowfall atop an earlier big one, a Federal Emergency Management Administration official told me, "Now, you understand that we can only help you clear away the first snow." I couldn't believe what I heard!

After the 1977 and 1978 blizzards, I helicoptered over the worst areas. Immobilized vehicles, mostly semis, blocked miles of Interstate 65. Extreme cold had locked their brakes so tightly that tow trucks snapped chains trying to move them. Guard tanks and tank retrievers used cables to drag them off the roads.

In 1978, we stopped at the Rensselaer armory. We found it full of stranded but grateful motorists. While there, word came that a lady who was to have a baby by Caesarean section was in labor but couldn't get to the hospital. Flying our large Air National Guard helicopter, we reached her location, set down, put her on a gurney, and loaded it on the chopper. I monitored her condition as we flew her to a Lafayette hospital.

Floods also require the use of shelters and involve massive cleanup. Between 1973 and 1981, Indiana's worst floods were in southern Indiana, including a disastrous one at English in Crawford County. There also were floods in northwest Indiana and in Allen and Adams counties in northeast Indiana.

From my disaster experiences, I learned that governors need the National Guard in emergencies. At a National Governors Association (NGA) meeting, Department of Defense officials told us that they were considering reorganization of the Guard above the company level. Their plan would have deprived governors of the authority to call out the Guard in emergencies. As NGA's Public Safety Committee chair, I told them that "if there is any change in the state's ability to use the Guard in state emergencies, fifty governors will rise in arms against you." I still can't believe I said that, but my comments were popular with other governors. Defense never mentioned reorganization again.

I believe the federal government truly tries to respond to emergencies. It has policies in place to deal with such situations, but our country is so big, the federal bureaucracy is so deep, and people's expectations are so high that federal responses are too slow in coming, and implementation occurs in too cumbersome a way.

There were many other accomplishments. We built or acquired all kinds of facilities. Typical was a large addition to the State Library and Historical Building, made possible by a private gift. We helped Ivy Tech State College (then Indiana Vocational Technical College) acquire the former American United Life building at Meridian and Fall Creek, a move that gave it needed stature. The preliminary work on the new

Indiana Government Center and its adjacent garages was done during my administration. Many communities have National Guard armories that were built while I was governor. These federally financed training facilities are important in emergencies, but they also are centers of community activity.

I'm proud of many other things. For example, when I appointed V. Sue Shields of Sheridan to the Court of Appeals in mid-1978, she was the first woman named to a state court. I'm proud that minority persons served with distinction on my personal staff and elsewhere. I'm proud of my support for the open meetings and open records laws.

This short list is enough to illustrate that my administration tried to make a difference. Nothing man does is forever, but the effects of some of these initiatives lasted after I left office. Even today, Hoosiers still benefit from some of them.

✻ 14 ✻

A Defeat, a Disappointment,
and Tribulations

MY ONLY MAJOR defeat as governor involved pari-mutuel betting. To my dismay, we now have bingo, raffles, a lottery, off-track betting, and boat-based casinos.

As chair of the National Governors Association's Committee on Criminal Justice, I once invited FBI director Clarence Kelley to speak to us. In our roundtable discussion, I asked if crime increased in states with pari-mutuel. He replied, "Absolutely," and emphatically banged his fist on the table as he said it. I am proud of my three vetoes of pari-mutuel betting bills and regret that they were not enough.

I know on a personal level that Hoosiers would be better off without legalized gambling. In early 1999, a bashful former patient came to my home in tears. Earlier, she had gone with friends to the Michigan City boat to see how it looked and worked. Hooked, she kept going back, still losing, but believing she would win big at some point. She used earnings from a good job and borrowed from friends to gamble. Tired of begging her to repay loans, a former friend was suing her. Her husband, children, and parents had turned against her. When she asked me for money, I tried to give her advice. Despite her desperate situation, she disdained it and left a little angry when I refused to "rescue" her.

At the grocery store, newsstand, and filling station, I see people shelling out dollars they can't afford for lottery tickets. Although self-imposed, it's still a cruel tax on them.

My biggest disappointment involves something I learned about nearly twenty years after the fact. Although both of us were Republicans and we served together, former attorney general Ted Sendak and I never were friends. Perhaps friendship was impossible, for Mr. Sendak was an ultra-right-winger. As Lake County and First District GOP chair, he participated in a cartel that denied me nomination for governor in 1968. (Nominated that year as attorney general, he won his first term.) While governor, I knew that Mr. Sendak was unhappy with some of my decisions and intensely disliked key members of my staff. He never declared for the office, but he also wanted to be governor.

Despite our differences of opinion, our lack of closeness, and his burning political ambitions, I saw our professional relationship inside and outside the Statehouse as cordial and professional. My only real complaint was Mr. Sendak's constant desire for attention. To get it, he ranged far afield from his duties and on occasion even seemed to ignore them. Obsessed about Communism, he saw Communists lurking behind every bush.

Reasonable people would expect the state's chief lawyer to be a seeker of fact and truth. This was not true with Mr. Sendak, who assembled thin allegations and isolated facts into gigantic conspiracies. His ideology often got in the way of his objectivity. His official opinions, his opinions on legislative bills he reviewed for me, and documents he was required to review for form and legality became soapboxes that he used to express personal points of view, even when they had little to do with the issues at hand.

Mr. Sendak viewed the law narrowly. Even when a law's language made multiple interpretations possible, and when other lawyers' interpretations were as reasonable as his, he contended that only his interpretation was right, and he saw no room for reasonable people to disagree. In effect, he said the law was what he said it was.

Perhaps no one identified the nature of the problem better than Howard Circuit Court judge Robert Kinsey, a Republican and Title XX advisory board member. After Sendak rejected a $330 grant to send troubled juveniles on a "tough love" camping and canoeing trip, Judge Kinsey icily said in a public way,

> The office of Attorney General . . . is not a constitutional office, and the Attorney General was never intended to be an overlord or godfather of executive and legislative affairs. The office plays no part in our constitutional scheme of checks and balances. The Attorney General has no au-

thority to thwart or veto acts of the General Assembly or executive programs. . . . Mr. Sendak's main statutory function is to serve as the state's lawyer . . . to represent the state in lawsuits and give legal advice to the public agencies and officials. His opinions are advisory only and have no force and effect of law. With regard to state contracts, by statute he is to pass only on their form and legality. . . . [H]e has no right to assume the power of defeating state contracts because he might disagree with the subject matter or the principal of the contract. Mr. Sendak, however, continually uses the office . . . to work his will or personal biases and prejudices. The Title XX program is a good example of his inability to function objectively as lawyer for the state and its agencies. He is apparently opposed to the programs on principle or philosophy, and Title XX contracts are disapproved on veiled assertions of illegality, such as being in violation of "congressional intent."

Nearly five years after we left office, Mr. Sendak convinced a U.S. senator to vote against my confirmation as secretary of the U.S. Department of Health & Human Services. Mr. Sendak and Senator Jeff Bingaman of New Mexico served at the same time as attorneys general. Senator Bingaman's vote didn't affect my confirmation, but I wondered what was bothering Mr. Sendak so much.

In mid-1998, I first saw Mr. Sendak's 1997 book, A *Pilgrimage through the Briar Patch: 50 Years in Indiana Politics*. It starts with an account of his meeting with FBI director William Webster, at which he asked that the FBI investigate my subordinates and me. To his credit, Mr. Sendak records the fact that his presentation evoked a major ho-hum from Judge Webster. (The reason is obvious—there never was anything there. That still didn't keep Mr. Sendak—years later—from again claiming that there was.) His book left me wondering how I was so blind to his venomous hostility. Since he passed away fairly recently, and can no longer respond, it seems unfair to comment further.

In some areas of state government, there are small opportunities for progress or no opportunities at all. The constant turmoil in corrections, mental health, welfare, public safety, and regulatory functions makes a governor feel like the natives are eyeing him while bringing a cauldron of water to a boil.

In corrections, a governor can do everything right and be wrong. Advocates at one extreme want criminals to get a slap on the wrist. At the opposite end, activists would line inmates up and machine-gun them down if that were possible. Part of a governor's challenge is to find a tough, smart corrections commissioner who can find middle ground and do the job in a way that's fair to the public. Indiana's 1851 constitution emphasizes rehabilitation, but we are far from that goal. Rehabilitation requires inmates who want to change, and some genuinely do. Many more are not the least bit interested.

As I took office, the criminal justice system was responding to citizen demands that criminals be dealt with forcefully—the General Assembly with tougher laws, police with stronger enforcement, prosecutors with vigorous pursuit in court, and judges with longer sentences. The predictable result was overcrowding at correctional facilities.

My first non-legislative crisis as governor was an Indiana State Prison riot on Labor Day 1973. Demanding "better food, more recreation time and better conditions," inmates took three guards hostage. The situation was complicated by the fact that we were locked out of our own prison because new gates that would have allowed us to storm the prison had not yet been installed. To get inside, we would have had to bulldoze a section of wall.

To get the guards released, I agreed not to punish the rioters. I also agreed to allow reporters inside to witness the guards' release and give the inmates a chance to state their complaints publicly. When the riot ended after thirty-six and a half tense hours over parts of three days, we had thousands of dollars in damage, but no loss of life. Given that the riot had occurred in a maximum-security prison filled with hardened criminals, I felt fortunate about the outcome. The guards who were held as hostages and their families were overjoyed.

In the aftermath, there was lots of criticism. Typical was an Indianapolis *News* cartoon that pictured me in a rocking chair feeding cookies to a prisoner sitting on my lap. Angered by such unthinking second-guessing, I issued a statement saying I found it hard to understand why critics believed that the only way to resolve a prison disorder was to litter the cellblocks with corpses. That quieted the critics.

Russell Lash, son of legislator Don Lash, my Delta Chi brother at IU, was the prison warden. His relationship with Corrections Commissioner Robert Heyne and the Board of Corrections cooled after the riot. Ignoring my pledge to the inmates, Lash initiated punishment processes against the rioters. As much as I might have wanted to see them punished, I had given my word and had to halt the reprisals. Had Lash persisted, more disorders and danger to other prisoners and prison staff were a menacing possibility. The situation resolved itself when Oklahoma hired Lash as its corrections commissioner.

Fifteen months later, on the day after Christmas in 1974, lax security allowed "trusty" Riley Mosley Jr. to steal a weapon and escape from a prison farm. Taking refuge in a northern Indiana farm home, he held a woman and her two daughters hostage, raped and killed the mother, killed one daughter, and almost killed the other daughter.

Such happenings made me realize that the challenge had grown too large for Commissioner Heyne, a fine Christian gentleman whom I liked. The department clearly needed new leadership. I learned that Gordon Faulkner, corrections commissioner for West Virginia governor Arch Moore, was about to lose his job because Moore had lost his race for re-election. I interviewed Faulkner, liked what I saw, and hired him. A heart attack delayed his start, but he immediately took charge when he began work.

I appointed Daniel Evans Jr., the Indianapolis attorney who was co–deputy manager of my 1976 re-election campaign, as the new Board of Corrections chair. Jim Smith, the executive aide with liaison responsibility to the department, let Faulkner and Evans know that they were in charge, and that I expected improvement.

With space an increasing concern, we decided to convert Norman Beatty Hospital at Westville into a penal facility. Westville residents didn't want a prison next door. Mental health advocates didn't like the idea of a Beatty conversion because its patients would be dispersed to other mental illness hospitals, making it more difficult for families to visit.

However, the conversion made sense. The number of hospitals for the mentally ill and developmentally disabled was shrinking as the state moved toward community-based treatment. It was too expensive to operate Beatty as a mental health hospital, but the state had too much invested in Beatty to close it down and walk away. Beatty also was well suited to become a prison because it already was a maximum-security facility.

Ultimately, the General Assembly authorized the conversion. Without Beatty, now the Westville Correctional Center, pressure would have been greater on state correctional facilities, and a court-ordered mass release of criminals would have been possible.

The U.S. Department of Justice gave us fits in corrections. Even after we made major improvements and were moving ahead on more, its minions seemed bent on forcing us to make larger prison outlays than we could afford. In a response to Justice, I catalogued improvements, answered Justice's complaints and summarized my concerns this way:

> There are glaring differences between the Department's contentions and reality. The issue is rather fundamental. Is the State of Indiana violating the constitutional rights of its correction system inmates? At this point, the Justice Department has not made its case on that basis. Rather, it centers its arguments on conjecture, assumptions, subjective judgments, and just plain bad information. I hoped the Department of Justice's attitude would be far more constructive than what has been displayed thus far. Unfortunately, we

are fast approaching an impasse that will result in unnecessary court action that, in the end, will be financed by taxpayers.

I made the same argument in other forums. Attorney General Griffin Bell had earlier promised governors that Justice would resolve these matters by consultation, not in the courts. Just prior to a National Governors Association meeting, I received a Justice official's letter threatening to sue Indiana for alleged "constitutional violations" and "deprivations" involving inmates. Bell sent deputy attorney general Peter F. Flaherty to the NGA meeting. Noting Bell's earlier promise, I said that the department's threats had broken that promise, and I told Flaherty to "take that message back" to the attorney general. Justice officials continued to argue that Indiana was not in compliance with minimum facility requirements, but they never carried out their threats to go after us in the courts.

We made major improvements at the Indiana State Prison and Indiana Reformatory, built a juvenile wing at the Reception and Diagnostic Center, modernized the Indiana Women's Prison, and built new structures at the Indiana Boys' School.

These investments were necessary for many reasons. They included a tough new criminal code that replaced indeterminate sentences with precise, usually harsher terms for each type of offense. The new code also defined "good time" as a day's reduction in sentence for every day of an inmate's acceptable behavior. With that definition, a person with a forty-year sentence who behaved perfectly still would spend twenty years behind bars. Finally, the new code limited judges' discretion to suspend sentences.

The tougher criminal code increased the number of commitments to correctional institutions and the length of time that criminals spent there. Our space problems also were heightened by the state's past deferral of facility maintenance, the increasing age of the facilities, and the federal government's unceasing pressure.

We tried to ensure decent medical treatment and opportunities for education. With few physicians or nurses willing to work in prisons at the state's low salaries, medical care had declined badly. Better access to education brought us back to the Constitution's original goal of rehabilitation, but we had to balance our efforts to rehabilitate against the fact that unrepentant, mean, and dangerous people filled our prisons.

For those trying to change, our best initiative was work release. It helped soon-to-be-released inmates begin the transition to life outside the walls. Since it was easy to walk away from work release centers, identifying inmates with the best potential to benefit from it was no small task. Another daunting challenge was to find work-release shelter sites. Even if they agreed with the objectives of work release, Hoosiers didn't want a center in their community or neighborhood.

The criminal code's toughness created huge correctional system problems, but I am satisfied that it was needed. I also supported "guilty but mentally ill" legislation as a substitute for the "not guilty by reason of insanity" plea. Persons "not guilty by reason of insanity" escaped punishment. Those found "guilty but mentally ill" were committed to mental hospitals until their condition improved and they could be tried.

Clemency was a job that I did not relish, but I tried to do it conscientiously. Inmates seeking clemency did so in the hope of being released. Good behavior and educational or occupational attainments in prison were the most often cited justifications, but old age and medical problems, sometimes of a terminal nature, also were used. Lifers were most likely to seek clemency. Prisoners or former prisoners also requested pardons. A pardon restores full citizenship rights and clears— erases—a person's criminal history. Pardons are requested when the original convictions were tainted or when inmates have totally turned around their lives after a single, usually non-violent criminal act as a youth or young adult. Sitting as the Clemency Commission, the Indiana Parole Board reviewed all clemency cases and made recommendations to the governor, who had the final decision.

I did not consider clemency for murderers until they had served at least twenty years. If an inmate was old, the murder was one of passion, there was no public outcry, and the Clemency Commission was unanimous in its recommendation, I occasionally deviated from that approach. All told, I granted clemency to about two hundred inmates in eight years. I granted few pardons, and then only after seeing proof that the individual was deserving.

Clemency also involves requests to commute death sentences. The old Indiana death penalty law was held unconstitutional. I allowed a new death penalty statute to become law without my signature. No one sentenced to death under the new law exhausted their appeals before I left office. Had the situation arisen, I would have allowed an execution to proceed if a Death Row inmate had exhausted all appeals and I was convinced, after considering advice from the Clemency Commission and the Board of Corrections and carefully reviewing the case, that the inmate was guilty.

Bob Orr became the first recent governor asked to grant clemency to a Death Row inmate. After reviewing the facts of the horribly brutal murders for which Stephen Judy was convicted, he decided to allow the execution to proceed. It was the right decision.

Mental health was another area in which there was no lack of advocates. People suffering from mental illness or with developmental disabilities deserve our sympathy and help. Advocates constantly remind us of our obligation, but they often have expectations that go beyond what is practical or realistic.

Care of the mentally ill changed significantly while I was governor. Psychotropic drugs (tranquilizers) allowed us to "de-institutionalize"— send home—all but the most chronically ill patients. Earlier, many individuals committed to mental hospitals had stayed there all their lives. With the new drugs, hospitalization became a short-term process, designed to stabilize patients and return them to their communities, sometimes to group homes. Community-based systems then provided follow-up. The new drugs and new treatment methods also made it possible to return developmentally disabled persons, even profoundly retarded ones, to their families or group homes.

The populations of hospitals for the mentally ill and the developmentally disabled declined dramatically as a result of these changes. This prompted us to convert Norman Beatty Hospital into the Westville Correctional Center. Since I left office, the state has closed New Castle in Henry County and Northern Indiana at South Bend, both hospitals for the developmentally disabled, and Central State in Indianapolis, a hospital for the mentally ill. Chronically ill persons requiring long-term care in hospital settings always will be among us, but I suspect that more hospital closings are in our future.

Community-based treatment of the mentally ill and mentally retarded was and is a good idea, but it created new problems. After patients requiring only minimal care went home, only the most chronically ill or most profoundly retarded and disabled patients were left in the hospitals. We assumed that the hospital staffs had it easier with smaller populations. In fact, the job became tougher and more stressful.

"Deinstitutionalization" had an even worse outcome. Pushed into the streets, mentally ill patients failed to get follow-up treatment or stay on their medications. They became nomads, drifting from one place to the next. Tracking them was next to impossible.

Such problems are sad reminders that reactions always follow our actions. Our humanitarian impulse to normalize the lives of mentally ill or mentally retarded persons ignored the fact that some can be served only in institutions. Mental health is not a numbers game. It involves people, often the most vulnerable among us.

As the mental health law then required, Commissioner William Murray was a psychiatrist. A talented professional and loyal public servant who cared deeply about the patients in his keeping, Bill felt that patients should be in the least restrictive environment. He favored "open campuses"—grounds fully open for patients not confined in locked wards. This made security impossible, and patients walked away, sometimes with tragic consequences. After many embarrassments and lots of urging from my office, Dr. Murray consented to improvements in hospital security. Like most doctors, Bill was not a good administrator. Mental Health's management problems were so serious that I considered keeping Bill as boss and commissioner to handle medical policy and using another, essentially equal person to run the administrative end. Realizing that this would create turf problems and make things worse, I later opted to get Dr. Murray the best help and leave him as the unquestioned authority.

Public safety was another challenge. As I took office, I reappointed the popular and able Bob Konkle as Indiana State Police superintendent. Eight months later, he resigned. Typically, an Indianapolis *Star* news story claimed that "speculation has increased . . . that Konkle was tired of the continued harassment, not from the governor, but from unknown or unidentified forces possibly within the Bowen administration or close to Bowen advisors." This not-so-veiled language suggested that my executive assistant for public safety, Robert DeBard, and my administrative assistant, Jim Smith, were the real problem. If those two ever harassed Konkle, they kept it so secret that I never heard of it. Similarly, Konkle never claimed harassment or blamed DeBard, Smith, or me.

I named DeBard to chair a committee to screen candidates to succeed Konkle. I was surprised when the group recommended DeBard, a likable six-foot, eight-inch retired ISP officer with a Ph.D., but I appointed him. His appointment never worked out. While he was superintendent, there was lots of disharmony, and he seemed unable to deal with the discord; just why, I never knew. Perhaps he was not accepted because he came directly from my office and jumped over other top administrators to the superintendency.

I decided not to reappoint him as my second term began. Either Smith told DeBard of my decision or he sensed it. Being a gentleman, he resigned without being asked. I named a blue ribbon committee to help me and the State Police Board find a replacement. In one hard afternoon of interviews, we looked at about ten candidates. The group unanimously recommended and I appointed Major John Shettle of Orestes, a respected State Police veteran. He served me well and continued as superintendent under Governor Orr.

The other State Police issue of consequence involved the design and location of badly needed new posts, including a new central headquarters on Post Road off Interstate 70 on the east side of Indianapolis. I had to referee a quarrel between the State Police Building Commission, the State Office Building Commission, and the Department of Administration. I felt that experts needed to decide the design issues, and the State Police Building Commission needed to decide the locations. Both decisions had technical overtones. Each post was to have new equipment as part of a radio communication system ensuring full coverage of the state. I asked the State Police Building Commission to carefully review the building plans, and they got the message. The new facilities have been in use for years.

A hot spot was the location of a north-central Indiana post. The area had posts at South Bend and Ligonier. The South Bend post was in an area into which Michiana Regional Airport was expanding. Experts felt it should be moved south so that less signal coverage was wasted on southern Michigan. The ideal spot was twenty to thirty miles south of South Bend, a fit with Bremen. Ligonier was close to Fort Wayne, where a new post was planned. The State Police Building Commission decided to close Ligonier and relocate the South Bend post to Bremen, reducing the number of posts without affecting coverage.

I felt sorry for the Ligonier community, which liked a State Police presence. As a citizen of Bremen, I liked the decision to put a post there. As governor, I had to question commission members closely to determine whether their decision was based on the fact that Bremen was my home. They swore that this was not the case, but I suspect it played a part. (Bremen folks gave me the credit anyway. I also got equally undeserved credit when a U.S. 6 bypass was built around Bremen. The project had been on the drawing board for years, and the decision to build it was made without regard to my role as governor.)

A controversial agency was the new Indiana Occupational Safety and Health Agency (IOSHA), a program more or less foisted upon us by the feds. Indiana's occupational safety record wasn't really bad, but it needed improvement. As we implemented standards with a federal gun to our heads, industry complained about nitpicking, penalties out of proportion to violations, and increased costs of doing business. At times their complaints were valid. However, most Indiana businesses and industries want to operate in the right way. They learned that creating a safe and healthy workplace is right from a human standpoint and may be less expensive in the long run. I tried to make certain that OSHA and other state regulatory programs did not become so unreasonable and inflexible that they became the problem. I felt their purpose was not to levy fines and impose other sanctions, but to contribute to workplace safety so that Indiana's businesses and industries could grow, expand, and provide more jobs.

State employee morale was low as I took office. In the lean years prior to 1973, state workers had fallen far behind their peers in the private sector with regard to salaries and fringe benefits. We got legislative approval for reasonable annual salary increases and fringe benefit improvements. Others claiming to represent state employees saw what to us seemed reasonable as insufficient or even paltry. Those who thought state employees should be paid like hamburger flippers saw us as overly generous. We resigned ourselves to the fact that we could not satisfy everybody, and we did our best.

Early in my first term, we recognized turnover as a major problem. Some argue that turnover is not necessarily bad in government, but it was a fact that constantly hiring and training new employees was costly, and that a reduction in turnover was needed to create a more stable and expert state government workforce.

Part of our approach involved job reclassification. As state personnel director, I was fortunate to have Bob Roeder, who capably handled this project and other personnel issues. The primary goal of reclassification was to restore fairness to a system that was out of whack, and to ensure that people taking similar responsibility and doing similar work received similar compensation.

We also tested the private-sector market on our competitiveness in hiring professionals for agencies like mental health, public health, corrections, and air and water pollution abatement. Many professional positions were vacant when I took office. That was not the fault of my predecessor. We soon realized that the state personnel system did not relate to the real world, where employers offering the best salary and benefits and providing a challenging work environment get the best people. As best we could, we tried to change that. Hiring qualified professionals remained a major problem throughout my tenure. At that time, and probably now, state government was a good place to learn the ropes. Once past that, state employees could get better salaries and benefits in the private sector.

Collective bargaining was a continuing legislative issue and administrative challenge. Over the opposition of superintendents, school boards, and principals, teachers won the right to organize. I thought the time had come for teacher bargaining, but I was lukewarm to the idea.

The American Federation of State, County and Municipal Employees (AFSCME) had far less sophistication or strength, and there was less cohesiveness among other public employees on collective bargaining. This probably accounts for AFSCME's failure to get legislative authority to bargain collectively for state and local government workers.

Another issue getting our attention was individual privacy. For valid reasons, state agencies collected all kinds of personal information on Hoosiers, and they routinely collected Social Security numbers, whether needed or not. As long as this information was used for a lawfully authorized purpose, there wasn't a problem. Until recent times, citizens were protected by the fact that government kept most records on paper in file cabinets, making retrieval difficult. With computers, state agencies could use Social Security numbers to pull together data into individual dossiers, creating a potential for governmental invasion of individual privacy. Bill Ruckelshaus chaired a commission for me that looked at privacy issues in the public sector. Many of its recommendations became law.

The privacy laws forced us to look at what personal data should be kept and how to safeguard it. As part of a major forms and records management program, we redesigned data-collection instruments to bring them into the computer age and ensure that they collected only the data needed to do our job. We scheduled records so that we didn't keep routine ones forever, and we disposed of tens of thousands of tons of old records. The work opened up badly needed floor space and eliminated fire hazards. We saved money downstream by collecting less data and more quickly disposing of outdated records.

❧ 15 ❦

Folks Who Made a Difference

I WOULD BE remiss in this self-evaluation of my tenure as governor if I did not mention the key people who worked with me in state government.

My "original" set of executive aides included Ray Rizzo, Bill Watt, Bill Lloyd, Bob DeBard, Bill Ray, and Lee Ellen Ford. With one possible exception, all were doers and experts. This committed, loyal, intelligent, and practical set of people always sought to make the right things happen, not for me, or for themselves, but for Hoosiers. A lot of the credit for what was done while I was governor belongs to them.

The possible exception was Dr. Ford, an attorney and a Ph.D. She was adamantly inflexible about matters in her realm. Her fellow aides did not like her much, but they treated her with benign tolerance because they knew I expected it. I saw her as our "conscience." She resigned soon after my second term began, saying she no longer "felt welcome."

Ray Rizzo, my aide since my speaker years, moved into the governor's office with ease and assuredness. With an intellect matching his physical size (both are large), he was an idea man without equal. On my staff, he did my speechwriting and handled most of the human service agencies.

An attorney, Lloyd was the logical person to handle agencies like the Highway and Alcoholic Beverage commissions that got involved in tricky, controversial situations. He did his job with finesse and patience before returning to practice in Bloomington in 1978.

Before becoming an administrative aide to Lieutenant Governor Richard Folz, Bill Watt worked for the Associated Press in its Indianapolis bureau. My liaison with state environmental, transportation, and energy agencies, he also functioned as press secretary throughout my years as governor. Both sides of Bill's duties were critical, and his strong performance was a major contribution to my success. In 1981, Bill authored *Bowen: The Years as Governor*. After working for the federal government in Washington, D.C., he operates his own public affairs and public relations consulting firm in Indianapolis.

Jim Smith served me for eight years. Functioning under a management contract as an administrative assistant before Bob DeBard took the superintendency of the Indiana State Police, he replaced DeBard and took responsibility for public safety and criminal justice. An attorney, he was my liaison with the General Assembly in the 1980 session. (Rizzo had earlier handled that duty.) Smith served to the end of my eight years in office.

I was fortunate to have W. T. (Bill) Ray as an executive assistant for eight years. An Indianapolis realtor and insurance executive, he was patient, tolerant, and tactful, and he served effectively and efficiently in the areas of economic and human development. Because he was black, he was able to keep me informed of the black community's special needs and provide my administration with a bridge to them.

As time went on, I replaced or added executive aides. The first additions were Judy Palmer, an attorney, a long-time State Budget Agency staff member, and an expert in state budgeting and finance, and Bill Du Bois, former managing editor of the Muncie *Star*. Both came aboard at the start of my second term. Judy Palmer handled a variety of difficult issues and agencies. She later served Bob Orr as state budget director before then-president John Ryan hired her as an Indiana University vice president, a role in which she still functions.

An excellent, dependable, sound thinker, Du Bois was an expert at writing, editing, and public relations. He earlier functioned at party expense as my political man Friday at GOP state headquarters, filling multiple roles on the party staff and serving as co–deputy manager for my 1976 re-election campaign. He later served Governor Orr as an executive assistant and executive director of the State Student Assistance Commission. He now is retired after serving on Ivy Tech State College's executive staff.

Susan J. Davis replaced Bill Lloyd, coming to my staff from the attorney general's staff. Ted Sendak may have thought that I pirated Susan from him, but I had nothing to do with her application. In our interview, she said she was not happy in Sendak's office. An outstanding aide, she later served as an executive assistant to Governor Orr.

Susan married Jim Smith after I left office. Both had divorced their original mates. If they were romantically involved in my office, I never noticed. I was Jim's best man at their wedding. Susan was attractive and Jim handsome, and they made a fine-looking couple. Both later became respected lobbyists. They had only a few years of marriage before Jim suffered a brain hemorrhage while driving. He was kept on life support until brain dead. His heart was used for a transplant after his death. Susan has since remarried.

When Rizzo departed in my second term to join what was then Hook Drugs, he was replaced by Brian Bosworth, a former Foreign Service officer recruited by Rizzo as the state's first Title XX social services program director. After handling several human services agencies for me, Brian later became a public sector innovator with Lieutenant Governor John M. Mutz. Du Bois took over Rizzo's speechwriting duties.

(My speeches were prepared in advance, first by Rizzo and later by Du Bois, with Watt taking the lead on State of the State messages and helping on others. A prepared text ensured that young reporters didn't misquote me. Typed in large letters on non-glare green paper and positioned so I could read them with my trifocals, scripts also helped my confidence as a speaker. I read them and seldom ad libbed. My reliance on a script was so strong that my staff rightfully called those green sheets my "security blanket.")

A super-doer, Vi Walker, was the other truly key person on my staff. When I first came to the House, she worked part-time for me. She became my full-time secretary when I became minority leader in 1965, and she continued in that role after I became speaker and governor. Her executive secretary title belied the fact that she managed the support staff. Vi's severe arthritis led to her departure before I left office. After she left, my right-hand helpers were Mary Kay Davis, Ann King, and Sue Senff, all excellent individuals.

One of my most cherished memories is the respect my agency heads accorded me and the fact that they always tried hard to be a credit to me. I was the first governor since 1851 to face a decision on whether to keep my original appointees. Of those who wanted to continue, I reappointed all but four—Heyne, DeBard, Civil Rights Commission director T. Beatrice (Tommie) Holland, and Department of Veterans Affairs director Earl Heath. Instead of saying that the latter two were fired, I say I "released them reluctantly." That sounds better and describes my actual feelings.

A charismatic speaker, Tommie accepted so many requests that she had too little time left to direct staff. A huge case backlog accumulated. Commission members, especially chair John Garvey, felt that her enthusiasm and talent also impelled her to assume that persons against whom complaints were filed were guilty and had to prove themselves innocent rather than be proven guilty. In the end, commission members asked me not to reappoint Tommie. Furious, she sued me for $5 million. The attorney general got the suit dropped, and the situation quieted down once people heard both sides.

An Amvet, Earl Heath was a "good ol' boy" with a stubborn streak that made it hard for him to keep his department at peace with the Veterans of Foreign Wars and American Legion. After receiving repeated complaints, I replaced Heath with John Knop, a retired colonel in the U.S. Army Reserve and a former mayor of Huntington, and he served well.

I reappointed Jim Sims as Alcoholic Beverage Commission (ABC) chair against the advice of many others. Through my years as governor, he and other ABC members sat on a hot seat, ruling on liquor industry issues while dealing with very difficult people. The agency was under constant attack. Whether or not the attackers spoke the truth, the media thrived on every derogatory assault. The arena made legislators so uncomfortable that the less they had to do with it, the better they felt. Major ABC issues involved

- territorial rights for beer distributors (distributors wanted to keep exclusive territories that gave them a virtual monopoly);
- beer and wine sales by groceries and drug stores (package liquor stores wanted such sales banned);
- advertising content (to remain true to the ABC law, which defines state policy as encouraging temperance, the commission wanted to continue controlling advertising content, but those who had advertising space to sell—particularly newspapers, and specifically the Indianapolis *Star* and Indianapolis *News*—wanted outlets to have an unfettered right to advertise); and
- the proximity of outlets to schools and churches (applicants wanted the requirements of the law stretched or bent so they could get a license).

Governor Orr named Bob Skinner to replace Sims as ABC chair, but he remained under fire. About six weeks after Jim's tenure ended, in an "It's going to happen" kind of story, the Indianapolis *Star* reported that FBI agents soon would present "evidence" of "alleged bribery, extortion and conspiracy" to a federal grand jury. Federal authorities never brought an action against Jim Sims or any ABC official. All in all, Jim walked a tightrope for eight long years. My appraisal is that he did a commendable job.

Many others did stellar work. The stalwarts were Revenue Commissioner Clark, State Budget Directors Thuma and Huie, Commissioner of Administration Sanders, DNR director Cloud, Aging and Aged Commission director Maurice Endwright, Adjutant General Alfred Ahner, State Tax Board chair Carleton Phillippi, Teachers Retirement Fund director Loren Tiede, Health Commissioner William Paynter, Motor Vehicles Commissioner Ralph Van Natta, Washington liaison office director Don Newman and Education Employment Relations Board chair Victor Hoehne.

Tiede and Hoehne were friends of long standing. Tiede taught and coached at Bremen High School before joining the faculty at Lakeland College in Wisconsin. I delivered Loren and Rosemary Tiede's four children. A nurse, Rosemary worked several years in my office. Vic and I both graduated from Francesville High School, where his father was the principal and my father taught and coached basketball and baseball. Both of us attended IU in the same period. Vic had earlier been the business manager for the LaPorte and Monticello schools. Both men were well qualified and performed well.

If I were to single out "heroes of the heroes" among my agency heads, they would be Milt Mitnick, director of the Department of Civil Defense, and Larry Wallace, chair of the Public Service Commission. Both performed heroically in the 1974 tornadoes, the blizzards of 1977 and 1978, the prolonged sub-zero cold spells of 1978 and 1979, the coal miners' strike, and other energy crises, emergencies, and disasters.

Milt, who passed away shortly after I left office, was frustrated by the fact that people devalued civil defense in peacetime, but he always was ready for the next emergency.

Wallace was the least-sung hero of my administration. An Indianapolis attorney and former House member, he was a tad more liberal than most Hoosiers. He performed well as my legislative liaison in the critical 1973 and 1974 sessions. When W. W. (Dub) Hill resigned as chair of the Public Service (now Utility Regulatory) Commission, I appointed Larry to the position. He was a giant in our weather and energy crises and in his "day job" with the commission. This period was a chaotic and contentious one for utility regulators. Larry handled all the heat and controversy with aplomb and common sense.

At the Governors' Residence, Beth and I personally depended on Blanche N. West and his wife, Alvania, who were in their seventies. They were the kindest, most considerate, effective, and efficient couple I've ever seen. Officially the butler, Blanche helped inside and outside. A super cook, Alvania made the best dinner rolls.

Susie Hicks, our housekeeper, was a delightful person who worked for every governor from George Craig to me. She did everything—cooked, cleaned, did laundry and ironing, and took care of governors' children (but not ours). She drove some governors (but not me) to the Statehouse if their drivers failed to show. Open-heart surgery made her miss President Ford when he stayed at the Governor's Residence in early 1976. He gave us a pen for her, and Susie's eyes lighted up when Beth and I presented it in her hospital room.

Indiana State Police troopers were responsible for my security except when I was at the residence. They did the driving. My detail included Ken Sale and Bill Merritt, who served throughout my years as governor; Will Lows, who died of cancer not long after my second term ended; Jim Sears, the first black State Police officer and the first black to serve on a governor's security detail; Dave Vermeulen; and Charles (Chuck) Fewell. At the residence, a civilian security force directed by an ISP officer watched over us.

Anyone who knew Beth knows that everyone was a friend in her eyes, and no one could be just help. When Beth invited Alvania West to the Lodge, Alvania expected to work. On that visit, however, she was Beth's guest, and Beth did all the work.

Similarly, what we did, our troopers did. They became family. When and where we ate, they ate. If we spent the night away from the residence, they were with us. A "fixer-upper" and handyman, Ken Sale offered to do work at the Lodge. I couldn't allow that because it would be using public employees for private work. As a result, at Donnybrook, troopers watched me mow my lawn. A capable, pleasant, and dependable man, Jim Sears attended church with us on occasion. I found it interesting to watch people's expressions when a fine-looking uniformed black trooper came with us into the sanctuary.

As governor, I got threats. Part of our security detail's job was to check them out and decide if and when to step up protective measures. Threats usually turned out to be jaw flapping, but I wore a bulletproof vest at a 500 Festival parade and a Veterans' Day parade. After the fact, I was told of other situations. One involved Anthony (Tony) Kiritsis of Indianapolis, who held a mortgage company executive hostage for sixty-three hours in 1977. Supposedly, I was on his list of possible hostages. Our troopers kept Beth and me safe, and we never truly felt in danger.

The day I moved into the governor's office, Governor Whitcomb told me that the two red telephones on the desk were direct lines to an office somewhere in Washington, D.C., and would be used in a national disaster, catastrophe, or invasion. I never used the phones, and I dreaded the thought that they might ring. Once, they did. The caller was just checking to see that the connection still was good. There also was a red telephone at the residence.

✺ 16 ✺

On Being Governor

BEING GOVERNOR IS like no other job, although it has similarities to being a country doctor. Like a physician, a governor is on call twenty-four hours a day, seven days a week, asleep, awake, eating, in the shower, traveling in a car, or at a meeting. There are emergencies, so he lives with unpredictability. As earlier noted, many state government activities involve health and medical questions, areas in which I have expertise.

There the similarities end. There is nothing like being governor, not even being a member of a president's cabinet.

My days were fairly long, about twelve hours on average. A few were as long as sixteen to eighteen hours, and a few as short as seven or eight hours. There was routine on most days—staff meetings three days a week, and a huge volume of letters, rules and regulations, contracts, proclamations, and other documents that I examined and usually read and signed. Absent outside commitments, I arrived in the office at 7:45 A.M., had a quick lunch at the residence or State Office Building cafeteria, and returned to the office to stay until 6:30 P.M. (I got lots of work done from 5 to 6:30 P.M., when there were no interruptions.)

Filling vacancies on more than 100 boards and commissions was neither routine nor easy. Most boards have an odd number of members, and no more than half plus one can come from a governor's party. Members usually serve staggered terms. Residence requirements are common. If a board regulates a profession or industry, members usually must reflect its various interests. For example, appointees to the animal health board might include representatives of the dairy, hog, sheep, and poultry farming industries and veterinary medicine. Usually, one or two public members are required.

This laudable effort by the General Assembly to ensure a voice for all interests makes the appointment process so complicated that it takes a Philadelphia lawyer to figure out who can serve. (The legislature ought to simply charge a governor with appointing the best people.) Finding people who meet all the requirements and will serve for nominal "mileage and per diem" allowances takes persistence and hard work.

After settling on appointees, I called them. Thinking that their leg was being pulled when I said, "This is Governor Bowen," some said, "Sure, sure, it's the governor." Once they were convinced it was me, we had good conversations, and I had very few turndowns.

Most of my days as governor were peppered with appearances, speeches, meetings, talks to Statehouse visitors, and telephone calls. On any day, I might talk to a federal official one minute and respond to a reporter or hold a news conference the next. When the General Assembly was in session, I met regularly with my legislative team, legislators and legislative leaders, and proponents and opponents of legislation.

My days were less ordinary when the state employees' association marched on the Statehouse. My days were out of the ordinary if there were blizzards, tornadoes, and floods or a prison riot. There were fun things. I enjoyed reviewing the troops at the Indiana National Guard's summer encampment and going to Indiana State Fair events.

Traveling to and from events outside Indianapolis was time-consuming. On trips of any length, I usually took work. If long distances were involved, the weather permitted, and the event was non-political, I used a state-owned helicopter. This shortened travel time and eliminated airport drive time. Sparingly, I used the State Police plane for in-state non-political trips. (For political trips, the GOP State Committee chartered planes.)

Some of my duties were pleasant, some full of drudgery, some exciting, and some downright exasperating. I enjoyed meeting people, even if the subject was controversial. If those talking to me had open minds or were "satisfied customers," our meetings were pleasant. However, happy people are not usually the ones who show up at the door, and unhappy people don't usually have open minds.

Independent truck drivers were an example. They came to my office after creating congestion by driving their rigs around the Statehouse. Concerned about rising diesel costs, they wanted me to know that they needed higher weight limits so their rigs could carry more and they could make a living. Unfortunately, the truckers had a chip on their shoulders, and they became abusive in their language and actions. I finally banged my fist on my desk, announced that the meeting was over, and had security escort them out.

After a snowstorm, I got a phone call one day from an irate lady in the 7400 block of North Meridian Street. She said that her driveway had just been cleared when one of my snow plows came along and filled it up. "What are you going to do about it?" she asked. I said I was sorry and would have it taken care of immediately. I put on my coat, stopped at the residence to pick up a snow shovel, and went to her home. In five minutes, I cleared the drive. I knocked on her door, introduced myself, and told her what I had done. She smiled but was speechless. Smiling back, I bid her goodbye. I've always wondered how she really felt about the governor shoveling her snow.

Beth and I had a fair amount of social life related to our official roles. We also attended sports events (particularly IU football and basketball games) and political functions. If free on weekends, we usually went home to the Lodge at Donnybrook.

When we couldn't go home, we often went to the Aynes House, a rustic cabin on a beautiful Brown County State Park overlook. Reserved for the governor or those he authorizes to use it, the cabin sleeps about twelve. While staying there, we hunted mushrooms in the spring, fished in the park's lakes in the summer, and used the hiking trails. The cabin had a kitchen, so Beth could cook if she wished. If not, we went to the inn or into Nashville. The Aynes House was a quiet, peaceful place to relax. During IU's football and basketball seasons, it also was conveniently close to Bloomington.

A rustic Wyandotte Woods cabin also is reserved for the governor. Beth and I went there once with Clarence and Mildred Long. It had a curtain to convert its one sleeping room into two "bedrooms." Over the years, we've laughed a lot about the arrangement.

Beth and I had few vacations while I was governor. The most memorable took us to Cabo San Lucas on the southern tip of Mexico's Baja Peninsula with Brad and Donna Grubbs, Clarence and Mildred Long, Dick and Phyllis Boehning, Joe and Alice Kotso, and our daughter and son-in-law, Judy and David McGrew.

We played doubles in tennis, an activity from which I emerged with a deeply skinned knee that allowed me to retire from further athletic pursuits with wounded dignity. We gathered seashells and hiked to a spot, almost in its virgin state, that would be a paradise for archeologists. There we saw all kinds of ossified sea creatures and other animals. The natives said that the ocean had once covered it. I even got a haircut in Cabo San Lucas. The barbershop had a dirt floor and the barber spoke no English, but he did a pretty good job. At night, we changed to dress-up outfits and had dinner together in the hotel restaurant. A mariachi band played beautifully and even took requests.

I particularly enjoy deep-sea fishing. While there, I hooked a ten-foot, six-inch marlin weighing 110 pounds that took me forty-five minutes to land. I assumed that my fish had been given to the natives, as is the custom. About three months later, however, a package arrived at my door. Other group members had secretly "rescued" my marlin, sent it to a taxidermist, and forwarded the mounted fish to me. It now hangs on the museum wall at the Bowen Library on the Bethel College campus.

Meeting with peers—the governors of the other forty-nine states, Puerto Rico, and the trust territories—was one of the best parts of being governor. There were three groups—the National, Midwest, and Republican Governors associations. For a brief period, I was the only "governor of the governors," simultaneously chairing all three groups. Governors learned from each other in these groups. Every state is different and has unique problems, but there also is commonality. We shared information on how we addressed problems, talked about approaches that worked and didn't, and became better governors.

The year I chaired all three groups, the Midwest Governors met in Indianapolis. For most attendees, including governors' wives, the highlight was a lunch at the residence, where we were entertained by the Dimensions in Brass, directed by Jerry Frank, a Grace College music professor who later was director of music at Marion College, now Indiana Wesleyan University. A diabetic who had gone blind overnight, Jerry became a world-famous trumpet player known for his "triple-tonguing" skills. While I was secretary of the U.S. Department of Health & Human Services, Jerry played for H&HS employees in the Hubert H. Humphrey Building auditorium. His wife guided him to the podium, but he so wowed them with his music that his audience soon forgot his blindness.

I chaired the Education Commission of the States, a Denver-based educational policy and research organization created by the governors to ensure that the federal government did not take over education. I served on the executive committee of the Council of State Governments, based in Lexington, Kentucky, an organization that disseminated information of interest to its member states. I chaired the Interstate Mining Compact Commission in 1978. My participation in these groups broadened my knowledge of the issues and gave me a set of friends around the country on whom to call for advice and counsel.

I'm less sure about the federal commissions on which I served. President Gerald R. Ford appointed me to two—the Commission on Federal Paperwork and the President's Commission on Science and Technology. The paperwork commission's work was unproductive. With only a bit of tongue in cheek, I suggested that it was creating too much paperwork. That earned me a call from the commission chair, asking why I was dissatisfied. After what I had said, the fact that he had to ask says a lot about his mindset.

While I was governor, Beth and I took three overseas trips. The first was to Weisbaden, Germany, to give the commencement address for Ball State University students studying at BSU's German Center there. The trip allowed us to visit Beth's German cousins in Esebeck, the little village where her mother was born and many of her relatives still lived. Soon after our arrival, Beth's relatives—trying to be good hosts—poured me a jigger of hazelnut schnapps, a type of brandy. I took one swig and didn't think I could handle the rest of that hot, pure liquor. The man of the house asked if I would like to see his cattle. I answered "ja," and he opened the kitchen door. There they were, eight to ten cattle, in stalls. The barn, attached to the house, was neat and clean and had no cow or manure odor.

At the local cemetery, we saw the graves of Beth's grandparents. (On a recent trip to Esebeck, Beth's brother, Harry Steinmann, and his wife, Edith, couldn't find the graves. On inquiry, he learned that the Germans vacate graves that are thirty years old to prepare them for new burials.) We also visited Frankfurt, where we saw the Gutenberg Bible and the movable type and machinery with which it was printed.

Our next trip was an Eisenhower People-to-People tour on

which I was the spokesperson for forty restaurant owners, dairymen, hog and cattle farmers, slaughterhouse operators, and meat processors. In Denmark, Sweden, Switzerland, Greece, and Russia, we saw meat-processing plants, dairies, restaurants, and livestock and grain farms.

We were treated royally except in Russia. The Russians didn't mistreat us, but they were stern and cold. We took along cards with a friendly message in each language on them. In Russia, half the people read the message, smiled, and went on their way without a word. They feared they were being watched, I suppose. Our hotel in Moscow had a manager on each floor. Each time we left, we left our room key with him. When we returned, we picked up the key from him. At the U.S. Embassy, we asked if we were being followed and if our rooms were "bugged." The ambassador said, "Count on it."

We visited Red Square and the Kremlin, saw the changing of the guard, and paused at Lenin's tomb. (Yes, he was in it, looking well-preserved.) Guards were everywhere. We were not allowed to take pictures or put our hands in our pockets. I usually walk with my hands in my coat pockets, and twice I was asked to take them out.

As gifts, we brought along gum, blue jeans, and other small things. (Jeans were popular, we were told.) Our Russian guide refused to let us hand them out. A member of our group left a pair of jeans for the help in one hotel. At our next stop, miles away, our Russian escorts returned the jeans with a mild rebuke.

My favorite place on this trip was Athens, a noisy city. The Parthenon, the Acropolis, and a museum that housed 2,500-year-old artifacts excited us. To top off our stay in Greece, we visited Corinth and traversed some of the same territory as the Apostle Paul.

William Janklow (then and still governor of South Dakota) and I, accompanied by our wives, made the third trip for the National Governors Association. The Austrian Chamber of Commerce wanted to show Austria's industries to U.S. political leaders and give our counterparts an opportunity to talk with us about governmental processes. We visited Vienna, Salzburg, Innsbruck, Graz, and other Austrian cities to talk to the governors of Austria's political subdivisions. Our accommodations were luxurious, and the food was excellent.

Suffering from jet lag on arrival in Vienna, we would have preferred to go to bed. Instead, we went to a performance of *La Bohème*—in Italian. I couldn't understand a word, and I dropped off to sleep every few minutes. With my well-known sweet tooth, this trip's most memorable moment was my introduction to Sacher torte, a chocolate dessert. It was so good that I still bore friends with a description.

❧ 17 ❧

The Governor as Party Leader

MUCH EARLIER, I mentioned that a governor's major roles include that of political leader. I probably cleared the tallest political hurdle when I was elected in 1972, but politics didn't end once I walked into the governor's office.

In fact, political events started happening quickly. On February 2, 1973, GOP state chair Jim Neal resigned. I don't think I caused his resignation, and I was disappointed by it. Jim had been an astute chair. In a tough campaign, he had endured complaints from Republicans who thought I was "too liberal." Having accomplished what he was asked to do—create a climate for a 1972 victory—I think Jim felt he didn't have to tolerate it anymore and decided that it was time to get back to the Noblesville *Daily Ledger*.

Customarily, the governor gets his choice as chair. Initially, Jerry Olson of Columbus was a possibility. With the blessing of his boss, J. Irwin Miller, president and CEO of Cummins, Jerry had helped me immensely in 1972. However, Cummins frowned on his assuming the state party's reins, even on a part-time basis, and he withdrew. Bill Gee was reluctant to take the big step from Marshall County to Indianapolis. Cass County chair Don Heckard and Greene County chair Lavon Yoho were possibilities. In my 1972 campaign travels, I learned something about every county and district chair and was impressed with a young, energetic Richmond attorney, Tom Milligan. He accepted my suggestion that he replace Neal and was elected to the post by the state committee.

Our relationships were excellent. We had one huge disagreement. I supported shifting nominations for governor and U.S. senator to a direct primary. Tom wanted them to stay in the party conventions. My 1968 loss at a boss-dominated convention made me feel that all of a political party's adherents should choose its candidates, not 2,000 or so delegates. I also felt that a direct primary would be more representative, would broaden the party's base, and could not be controlled by party bosses. Tom saw the change as diminishing party authority. Both of us were right.

I worked hard to keep my political fences mended, attending many Lincoln Day meetings. Occasionally I attended state committee meetings. I made it a point not to tell them how to do their business. They never made unreasonable demands on me.

In 1976, the year I sought re-election, I spoke at twenty-four Lincoln Day dinners and attended dozens of bicentennial celebrations. Every community wanted me at their celebration. I went to as many as I could and lost lots of sleep. However, I enjoyed the events and was proud of each community's efforts to celebrate our nation's two hundredth birthday.

Public notice of my intent to stand for re-election first appeared in the Indianapolis *Star* on April 18, 1973, probably as a result of a reporter's inquiry. I never had a doubt about seeking a second term, so I saw no reason to be coy.

Disgrace in high office marked the early and mid-Seventies. Republicans were heartbroken by Vice President Spiro Agnew's felonious behavior and President Richard Nixon's inexcusable actions. Democrats genuinely abhorred what had happened, but they also were pleased to get an issue that helped them. Before Watergate, President Nixon was gaining respect for many accomplishments, his China dealings being the most dramatic example. After resigning, he lived long enough to publish works full of sound advice for national and international leaders and to regain the respect of the American people.

The only bright spot in that sorry episode was President Nixon's selection of Gerald R. Ford to replace Spiro Agnew and Mr. Ford's elevation to the presidency when Mr. Nixon resigned. Jerry Ford was exactly what his country needed in those dark times. After he became president, he asked for suggestions for vice president. Many Hoosiers suggested George Bush, then the national GOP chair. Bill Ruckelshaus and Mayor Lugar were mentioned. I suggested former secretary of defense Melvin Laird, Governor Robert Ray of Iowa and Ruckelshaus. At least two Congressmen suggested my name. The President selected former New York Governor Nelson Rockefeller. He turned out to be a good partner for Jerry Ford and a good choice for the nation.

The 1974 elections were an unmitigated disaster for Republicans —in Indiana and the nation. Nationally, the GOP lost a large number of House seats, some Senate seats, and many governorships. The Hoosier GOP lost every statewide race. Mayor Lugar lost to incumbent U.S. senator Birch Bayh. Indiana's delegation in the U.S. House went to 9-2 Democratic as four challengers upset GOP incumbents and Andy Jacobs won his rematch with William H. Hudnut, later mayor of Indianapolis. What had been a 73-37 Republican margin in the Indiana House became a 56-44 Democrat majority.

These results showed that Watergate disaffection could affect every candidate for office. As a result, I approached 1976, the year in which I had to stand for re-election, with some concern. We saw a bright spot in 1975, when the GOP gained mayors. Dick Lugar, who had lost to Birch Bayh in 1974, planned to try again in 1976 and probably was more vulnerable than I was to Watergate backlash. His integrity and the fact that he was a good thinker and problem solver were to carry him through in 1976, however.

Campaigning in the bicentennial year, I gained confidence about my prospects. I knew that my first years as governor had required decisions that displeased some voters, but reports from my "kitchen cabinet" were encouraging. By this time, the PTR program was working. People believed that I had kept my promises.

While campaigning, I did not neglect my duties as governor. (I have no idea how my opponent campaigned so much and still performed as secretary of state.) I tried to keep a normal office schedule. On travels to political or other events outside Indianapolis, I took a briefcase full of work. I am blessed with the ability to read while riding. After dark, I even used the car's interior lights to keep working.

The 1976 campaign differed substantially from 1972. Candidates for governor and U.S. senator were nominated in a primary. With no opponent, I remained governor-like until Democrats decided who my fall opponent would be.

The Democratic aspirants were Jack New, Bob Fair, and Larry Conrad. The state treasurer since 1971, New was a quiet, capable man who had been Governor Branigin's chief of staff. (His son Tom later was Governor O'Bannon's chief of staff.) Jack was not well known. Neither was Fair, an able senator and Senate leader. An excellent speaker and people-greeter, Conrad was elected secretary of state in 1970 and re-elected in 1974. His goal always was to be governor. He lost his first bid in 1972, to former governor Matthew E. Welsh.

If I had to choose the toughest opponent, it would be Conrad. If I had to pick who would have been the best governor, it would be New, with Fair a close second.

Conrad easily won the 1976 primary. State senator Thomas J. Teague of Anderson became his running mate. Conrad began the campaign with heavy baggage. In November of 1973, Indianapolis *News* political editor Ed Ziegner revealed the existence of a Conrad "master plan" to gain control of the Democratic apparatus and use it to win election as governor. Ziegner felt the "master plan" was authentic and came from Conrad's camp. Conrad called it the "most slanderous, libelous, concocted instrument . . . I have ever seen" and denied having had anything to do with it.

Conrad came back in 1974 to handily win re-election as secretary of state. However, the "master plan" continued to haunt him. Soon after Ziegner broke his stories, the *News* alleged that Conrad and his staff had made political calls on state telephones and used official state stationery for political purposes. The hubbub did not subside until Conrad repaid the state thousands of dollars for the questionable phone calls.

In the other races that might influence my re-election bid, I favored Dick Lugar over Ed Whitcomb for the U.S. Senate and Gerald R. Ford over Ronald W. Reagan for the presidency. My support of Lugar came easily and for obvious reasons. Supporting President Ford over Mr. Reagan was more difficult. Jerry Ford had brought stability and common sense to the presidency and restored the nation's faith in the office. I felt this down-to-earth man from neighboring Michigan deserved a chance to serve in his own right in the nation's highest office.

The beginning of my first term as governor overlapped the end of Mr. Reagan's as California's governor. I knew him, but not well. At two governors' conferences that he and I attended as peers, Mr. Reagan showed up only when he planned to speak. He always had a phalanx of security people around him that made it difficult even to say hello to him. Although I supported President Ford, I liked Ronald Reagan and thought he would make a splendid president. In 1980, I did all I could to help him win. When I later served in his cabinet, I found him easy to know and pleasant to be around.

In 1976, Mr. Reagan beat President Ford by a narrow 51-49 percent margin in the Indiana presidential primary. Since a public squabble over the makeup of Indiana's delegation to the national convention at Kansas City would work against everybody's interests, Hoosier Republicans allocated delegates on the basis of the primary vote—43 for Reagan and 42 for Ford, I believe. My own support for President Ford could turn off delegates committed to Reagan, whose support I needed at home, so I remained in the balcony during convention sessions at Kansas City and joined the Hoosier delegation only to announce its vote. President Ford won nomination, so I ended up in the majority.

I had no part in selecting President Ford's running mate, Senator Robert Dole of Kansas. I suggested Governors Bob Ray of Iowa and Dan Evans of Washington and former Texas governor John Connally. Bill Ruckelshaus was on President Ford's short list, and Mr. Ford himself indicates that the Hoosier came close to being his choice. Indiana delegates wore "Ruck" buttons at Kansas City. Just in case I needed it, I asked Ray Rizzo and Bill Watt, who were in Indianapolis, to draft a speech that I could use to nominate Bill or second his nomination. It was dictated to Bill Du Bois in Kansas City, who produced a final script. It wasn't needed, because President Ford chose Senator Dole the next morning.

Senator Dole looked dour and unhappy on the campaign trail, probably as a result of the severe injuries he sustained in combat in World War II. The dry wit that had delighted people as Senator Dole served in the Senate and while he was national GOP chair was there, but seemed to have a sharp edge. That turned off people who didn't know Bob Dole on a personal level or didn't understand how good a person he was (and is).

The outcome of the Ford/Dole race against former Georgia governor Jimmy Carter and Minnesota senator Walter Mondale was in doubt until election day. Watergate's shadow and the Nixon pardon hurt President Ford badly, and Carter and Mondale won a narrow victory. I've always felt that the American people were the real losers, because President Ford never got a chance to prove that he could do more than heal the nation's wounds.

The outcome of my own race was not much in doubt at any point, and not at all in doubt after Labor Day. We were too well organized, too well financed, and too well staffed. In the end, there was little that Larry Conrad or his staff could do.

I won by 309, 312 votes—a margin exceeding my 1972 record. I saw my victory as evidence that Hoosiers were satisfied with my performance. As "ticket teammates," Bob Orr and I garnered 57 percent of the major party vote, a landslide by any yardstick. I was gratified that Mayor Lugar handily won a U.S. Senate seat over incumbent R. Vance Hartke, and that Dan Quayle upset incumbent J. Edward Roush to win a seat in Congress. Republican candidates—Sendak, Dr. Negley, and Mrs. Wertzler—won the other Statehouse offices. President Ford's loss was the sole negative for Hoosier Republicans that night.

My victory meant that I would become the first governor ever to serve eight years, and the first governor since adoption of the 1851 constitution to serve consecutive four-year terms. Prior to 1851, governors' terms were only three years.

A successful campaign has three components—a good candidate, a good organization, and money. Atop my organization in 1976 were manager J. B. King and co–deputy managers Dan Evans Jr. and Bill Du Bois. They bought into a suggestion by pollster Robert Teeter for a short post-primary TV campaign to solidify my support once the choice was clear. This was a first in Indiana campaigns. Party pros thought it was too early to advertise, but Teeter was right. The early TV kept Conrad from making inroads at any point. Another first was localized advertising. Every ad had footage from the area where the commercials were aired. For example, if a spot's subject was highways, those shown in Fort Wayne included footage of roads there.

My 1976 finance chair was the very effective Jack Lanagan, an Indianapolis industrialist recruited by his neighbor Clarence Long. Jack Tuff of Elkhart did a superior job as campaign treasurer. Allison retiree Orval Lundy, husband of Mary Lundy of my governor's office staff, was a full-time volunteer and campaign "jack of all trades." The GOP State Committee's officers—Tom Milligan, Betty Rendel, Barb McClellan, and Ed Simcox—and its staff deserve major credit.

After President Ford's loss, the GOP national chair resigned. One of eight full-time state chairmen, Tom Milligan became a candidate and found himself in the political big time with former U.S. senator Bill Brock; Jim Baker, later to be White House chief of staff, treasury secretary, and secretary of state; and Bill Simon, a former treasury secretary. I supported Tom's efforts, writing letters, making phone calls and hosting a Washington reception (at party expense), because he had the skills to be a great national party leader.

I was inaugurated for the second time on January 10, 1977, with Lieutenant Governor Orr, Marilou Wertzler, and Sendak. Beth held the Bible. My father, Vernie, administered the oath of office. It was an imposing ceremony, but all of us had been there before.

Seeing that the odds were too great, Milligan withdrew from the contest for the national party chair, and Brock was elected four days after my inauguration. Tom soon resigned as state chair. Bruce Melchert, former aide to U.S. Representative Bill Hudnut and later Hudnut's deputy mayor, succeeded Milligan. This five-foot, five-inch, enthusiastic, hardworking forward thinker did a very credible job for four and a half years.

In the race for state treasurer at the 1978 GOP state convention, former treasurer and state chair John Snyder was favored over Julian Ridlen, the Logansport city judge. If asked, I didn't deny that I preferred Ridlen. He won narrowly. In the fall, Melchert packaged Ridlen, Charles Loos for auditor, Edwin Simcox for secretary of state, and Marjorie O'Laughlin for courts clerk as the "Bowen team." Luckily for my reputation as a political winner, all were elected. The GOP gained total Statehouse control by recapturing the Indiana Senate.

Aside from Ted Sendak, I worked well with other elected state officials, enjoying non-confrontational, productive relationships with those whose terms overlapped mine. Democrats included Auditor of State Mary Aikins Curry, 1970–78; Treasurer of State New, 1971–79; and Secretary of State Conrad, 1970–78. Republicans were Auditor of State Loos, 1978–82; Treasurer of State Ridlen, 1979–83; Secretary of State Simcox, 1978–86; and State School Superintendent Harold Negley, 1973–85.

After serving as governor, I planned to return to medicine or run for the U.S. Senate. Once Beth and I knew about the illness that was to take her life, the latter no longer was an option. As Beth's health declined, I also lost my zest for politics and campaigns.

Representative Dan Quayle wanted to run for the U.S. Senate, but deferred to me. This was the genesis of his clever "If Not Bowen, Then Quayle" button. On May 8, 1979, I told Statehouse reporters that I would not run, citing my age (61), my long service (almost thirty years), and my duties as governor. I mentioned Beth's illness peripherally. Dan declared, won nomination, defeated Birch Bayh, was re-elected in 1986, and, chosen in 1988 by George Bush as his running mate, was elected vice president of the United States.

I played only a small role in the 1980 campaign, so that I could spend as much time as possible with Beth. In 1979–80, I served as a member of the national GOP platform committee, chaired by former senator John Tower of Texas. (Tower is short, which usually helps me to like people, but it was hard to like the egocentric Tower.)

For Republicans, 1980 was a good year. Ronald Reagan and George

Bush were easily elected to the nation's highest offices, and Bob Orr and John Mutz easily won election as governor and lieutenant governor. Republicans won all state-level races. Dan Quayle wrested the U.S. Senate seat from Birch Bayh. Indiana's House delegation went from 7-4 Democratic to 6-5 Republican. I was pleased by John Hiler's upset of John Brademas, the long-time congressman in my district.

⚹ 18 ⚹

Last Days in Office

GOOD THINGS HAPPENED even as Beth's condition worsened. The best was an offer by Bethel College, located on a slightly rolling, beautifully wooded site in Mishawaka. Bethel had 400 students but wanted to grow, and it needed a new library to do it. President Al Buetler and the Bethel trustees who visited me in 1979 thought that raising library funds would be easier if the Bowen name were attached. They proposed including a wing in the library for a Bowen museum and suggested that I deposit my papers there.

I was flattered and intrigued, but not so confident that my name would help. Bethel's closeness to Donnybrook would mean easy access to my papers, so Beth and I quickly agreed to the offer. Bethel's folks raised the money, and the Otis R. and Elizabeth Bowen Library opened in 1984. It now is the focal point of an increasingly beautiful campus. Each time I see it, I see Beth's name on it and am pleased by this lasting tribute.

The museum is an interesting place for Indiana history buffs. It displays thousands of things—some valuable, some interesting, and some just things—accumulated during my life. The library holds records from throughout my life, but the bulk of the files are from my days as legislator, governor, and cabinet member.

The library seems to have helped Bethel grow. Under President

Norman Bridges, enrollments have more than quadrupled. A new gym was opened in 1998, a new dorm complex in 1999. A large classroom building is being built. These facilities should stimulate more growth. The college is nationally recognized for scholastic excellence, particularly in music, drama, and religion. Its basketball teams have won five national championships in its division and have been in the finals two other times.

In my last two years as governor, I still worked hard. I felt I had a "contract" with Hoosiers to serve until January 12, 1981, and I did not want anyone—especially some future historian—to believe that I had sloughed off or used Beth's illness as an excuse.

The historians have been kind. In late 1981, Tom Keating of the Indianapolis *Star* asked Corydon historian Arville Funk to select the ten best Indiana governors. He chose Oliver P. Morton (1861–67), Paul V. McNutt (1933–37), Otis Bowen (1973–81), Jonathan Jennings (1816–22), Thomas R. Marshall (1909–13), Matthew E. Welsh (1961–65), Conrad Baker (1867–73), James A. Mount (1897–1901), Henry F. Schricker (1941–45 and 1949–53), and George H. Craig (1953–57), in that order.

Two years later, Detroit *News* political writer George Weeks chose a top ten from the two thousand men and women who had served as governors of all the states in the first eighty-plus years of the twentieth century. I did not make Weeks's list, but he told Keating that I came close.

In his last Indianapolis *News* column, Ed Ziegner picked the three best governors and three best speakers he had known. I was pleased to make both lists.

Because it suggests that I did a reasonably good job as governor, this kind of recognition was gratifying.

Life was not as fast-paced in these last two years. I was a very lame "lame duck." In late 1979 and early 1980, there was a boomlet to make me a vice presidential nominee or "favorite son" candidate for president. I discouraged the idea, but it persisted into 1980.

In my final months, weeks, and days as governor, I was preoccupied with Beth's illness, which was by then at the critical stage. While still spending time in my office, I spent every possible minute with her, working in her hospital room or wherever I could grab a minute. She died in the early morning of January 1, 1981.

On January 8, 1981, I delivered my last State of the State message. Aides urged me to forgo it, correctly arguing that everyone would understand. But that's not my way. Besides, before she slipped away, Beth told me to "carry on for my sake and in my name" and to "live on and do things the same."

So one last time I went to the podium in the chamber where I had served so long. Looking out over that large crowd of legislators, state officials, justices and judges of the Indiana supreme and appellate courts, news media, and guests, I felt a sense of sadness when the realization hit me that my thirty years in public life were ending (or so I thought at the time). I had worked with those present so long, and we had seen each other so often, that it was hard to believe that our paths now would cross only rarely.

My staff and I sorted and packed documents, memorabilia, and other materials and shipped them to my new home at the Knoll or to the state archives. I recall little detail about those final days, for I was grieving deeply over the loss of Beth.

Four days later, after my last address to the General Assembly, there was one last ceremony. I sat on the platform in the Statehouse Rotunda as Robert D. Orr of Evansville became Indiana's new governor and my second term ended. I handed Governor Orr three keys, telling him that one was for the front and one for the back door. The third key, I said, had been given to me eight years earlier, and I had never needed to find out what lock it opened.

As I left office, newspaper editorialists and those who covered state government news were generous in their praise of my performance as governor. Then so grief-stricken that I hardly paid attention, I later realized in reading clippings that these journalists—who saw me up close and personal throughout my eight years as governor—gave me high marks. Because I had worked hard to make good things happen, that pleased me.

When my time as governor was over, I asked myself how I felt about public life. I concluded that I had thoroughly enjoyed my political forays, and in terms of satisfaction I ranked my eight years as governor as second only to the practice of medicine. However, Beth's death took the starch out of me. Physically and emotionally worn out, I wasn't sorry that it was January 12, 1981—my last day as governor.

❊ 19 ❊

Medical School Professor

BEFORE MY SECOND term ended, Dr. A. Alan Fischer, head of the Department of Family Medicine at the IU School of Medicine, and his associates Dr. Paul A. Williams and Dr. Thomas A. Jones proposed that I join the department. (I later became the Lester Bibler Professor of Medicine.) I knew the department's work well, having participated in the beginnings of its family medicine and family practice residency programs.

Beth and I had considered a return to medicine as an option after public life. With further political forays out, this offer was a close fit to our needs. I could be in medicine. We could live close to the IU Medical Center, a plus because of Beth's health. I never seriously considered other possibilities, and I accepted Dr. Fischer's offer almost immediately.

Beth and I then bought a condominium at the Knoll at Cold Spring Road and West 38th Street, a beautifully groomed place close to the medical center. The unit we bought had an alcove with a large window through which Beth could see the beauty outside if her hospital bed was properly placed. We hoped Beth would live past the end of my term, and that we could be together at the Knoll for a time. That did not happen, of course.

After leaving office, I lived at the Knoll, alone for the first time in nearly forty-three years. Because of Beth's death, the department postponed my starting date to February 1. My loneliness and deep sense of loss were only part of my problem. Throughout my busy life, Beth had taken care of my needs. I had minimal experience with cooking, housecleaning, or shopping. I couldn't even keep Beth's plants going—I overwatered them, and most died.

My deficiencies as a "civilian" went beyond home. For example, the interstates came back to baffle me. With a trooper/driver, I had never driven Interstate 465 or the sections of Interstates 65 and 70 that converge in the "spaghetti bowl." On leaving office, I was on my own. I knew where I was and where I wanted to get, and I found it easy to get on the interstates. Having never learned how interchanges and off ramps work, however, I had difficulty figuring out when and how to exit, particularly at the Indianapolis International Airport.

A related illustration shows how protected my life as governor was. Service station attendants once pumped gas. Stations went to self-service while I was governor, but troopers did the pumping. When I left office, I had to learn how to pump gas again.

As I dealt with the loss of my best helper, a mountain of materials from my years as governor and earlier surrounded me in my new home. I needed to sort the stuff and store it or give it away. The General Assembly rescued me by providing former governors with funds to employ a person for a short time after leaving office. Sue Senff, whom I delivered as a doctor and who was a member of my governor's staff, helped get me organized. She also sorted and prepared the materials sent to the Bowen Library.

The Department of Family Medicine had five family practice specialists with my arrival. As a professor, I taught residents planning to specialize in family medicine how to take a medical history and do a physical examination. I soon began taking my turn on call. Every fifth night and every fifth weekend, the on-call doctor responded to resident physicians when they needed help in medical emergencies involving their patients.

Having been completely out of medicine in my eight years as governor, I initially felt a need to catch up, so I shied away from treating patients or teaching aspects of medicine. I knew that I still could do a medical history and physical as well as anyone. Catching up on the rest didn't take long, and I soon was confident enough to do what needed doing.

I helped students relate their findings from gross and microscopic examination of diseased organs to patient symptoms and treatment.

Bringing in more of the clinical side to their pathology lab studies helped make the study of diseased organs interesting and more relevant to their studies. Several students also selected me as their counselor. At one-on-one meetings when they needed them, they got my advice on problems, asked my judgments on their cases, or otherwise picked my brain.

My work was important therapy in coping with Beth's death. After losing thirty pounds in the six months after she died, I told myself that I had to stop grieving. I soon married Rose Hochstetler, who had lost her first spouse. Decent work hours, less stressful work, being back in medicine, and Rose's presence allowed the painful memories to recede.

Several companies and not-for-profit organizations elected me to their boards. The Lilly Endowment board, on which I still serve, was my favorite. Being outside director for the for-profit companies was interesting, enjoyable, and financially rewarding. I also served on Senator Lugar's Commission on Federal Judicial Appointments.

I continued to speak to organizations, clubs, churches, schools, colleges, and medical groups, but I declined more invitations than I accepted.

In this period, I was involved with the Indiana Neuromuscular Research Laboratory, the Leukemia Society, the Mental Health Association of Indiana, the Indiana Division of the American Cancer Society, the Family Support Center, the American Red Cross, the Chemically Independent Children Inc.'s advisory council, the Fellowship of Christian Athletes, the Greater Indianapolis Council on Alcoholism, the U.S. Track and Field Federation Hall of Fame, the Future Farmers of America Foundation, the Indiana Chamber of Commerce, the Indiana Science Education Fund's board, and other groups.

I maintained my long-standing interest in higher education by serving as a Valparaiso University and Ancilla College trustee, on the boards of the Ivy Tech Foundation and the Woodburn Guild of the IU Alumni Association, on the Board of Visitors of the IUPUI School of Public and Environmental Affairs, and as a leader for Indiana University's Campaign for Indiana. I also was an honorary member of Anderson University's Center for Public Service and the Associated Colleges of Indiana boards and served on Vincennes University's advisory council.

My former partners asked me to consider rejoining the group practice at Bremen. I knew I would enjoy contact with patients in private practice, but I was in my mid-sixties and did not feel up to the number and irregularity of hours that a return to private practice would require. For that reason, I sent my regrets and thanks to my former partners.

For nearly five years, I remained in the Department of Family Medicine. A single telephone call changed my original expectation of staying there as long as my health allowed me to be a good teacher and counselor.

✤ 20 ✤

Secretary of Health & Human Services

ABOUT FIVE YEARS earlier, President-Elect Ronald W. Reagan had offered me an intergovernmental relations position on his White House staff. On January 9, 1981, nine days after Beth died and three days before I left the governor's office, I wrote Mr. Reagan:

> I am pleased and to a degree excited about the opportunity to serve as a member of your White House staff. I have given much thought—yes, prayerful thought—to your invitation. The type of responsibility—dealing with governors, mayors and county and township officials—is appealing. However, I feel that I could not, at this time, do justice to the position. I want your administration to succeed in every way. I'm completing 22 years of legislative and gubernatorial service at which I've tried to apply myself as diligently as possible. My dear companion of 42 years, Beth, passed away on Jan. 1st and I feel crushed. After a few months of healing, and if there be a vacancy and another opportunity to serve you and our country in some capacity, please reissue the invitation.

President Reagan soon approved my appointment to a panel making a two-year nursing and nursing education study for the Institute of Medicine and to his Advisory Committee on Federalism. These groups completed their work in late 1982. About that time, I agreed to President Reagan's request to chair the Advisory Council on Social Security, later called the "Bowen Commission." Its study of Medicare fi-

nancing issues for Health & Human Services secretary Richard
Schweicker ended in December, 1984.

Advised in late 1985 that the White House wanted suggestions for
the position of secretary of the U.S. Department of Health & Human
Services, Senator Quayle asked me to let him submit my name. When
I gave permission, Dan said he planned to push for my nomination. I
had a strong supporter in the White House—Mitch Daniels of Indianapolis, a long-time associate of Senator Lugar, who was President
Reagan's political affairs advisor. Once Dan and Mitch got my name on
the president's long list, it stayed there.

Robert H. Tuttle, White House personnel director, and his associate director, Kathie Regan, already had interviewed me in Washington. Since this meant that the president was more than casually interested, I assumed I had made the first cut.

The genesis of the president's call was the departure of H&HS Secretary Margaret Heckler. A former member of Congress from Massachusetts, she had replaced Schweiker in late 1982 after losing her
House seat to Barney Frank. She had been battling with White House
chief of staff Donald Regan over who filled high-level H&HS positions. Regan argued that it was the White House, Mrs. Heckler that it
was the secretary.

A former Army officer—a colonel, I think—Don Regan was accustomed to subordinates saying "Yes, sir" and obeying. As a congress-
woman, Mrs. Heckler was accustomed to running her own affairs and
office. Her refusal to buckle under contributed to a misplaced percep-
tion that she was disloyal to President Reagan. As the feud intensified,
Regan orchestrated a freeze on H&HS appointments that prevented
Mrs. Heckler from naming anyone to any position. Vacancies soon
threatened the agency's functioning.

Mrs. Heckler resigned on October 1, 1985, and President Reagan
named her as U.S. ambassador to Ireland. This was the point at which
Senator Quayle submitted my name.

I was not the only possibility. Nancy Reagan, Attorney General
Edwin Meese, and other Californians in the administration were said
to be supporting an assistant secretary of defense, Dr. William (Bud)
Mayer, who had served as Governor Reagan's secretary of health in
California. Don Regan initially supported his former Treasury employee, Anne Dore McLaughlin. Others mentioned were health specialist James K. Cavanaugh, who had served Presidents Nixon and Ford
in the White House; Los Angeles surgeon Tirso del Junco; Karl Bays,
CEO of the American Hospital Supply Corporation; Anne L. Arm-

strong, a former national GOP co-chair and ambassador to Great Britain; and Dr. William Walsh, who headed President-Elect Reagan's transition task force on health and was head of Project Hope.

Before President Reagan's call, I told my medical school colleagues —with some vehemence—that it was the last job I really wanted. Everyone knew that H&HS wallowed in controversy, suffered from widespread internal dissension, and was a bear to run.

I had remarried by then, and the first call came to my wife Rose, the person at the other end saying, "This is the White House calling." Thinking it a joke, Rose said, "Sure, sure, the White House is calling." Soon realizing that the call was genuine, she had it transferred. My secretary rang me, saying that President Reagan wished to speak with me.

As noted, President Reagan and I had known each other as governors. By the time he called, he was near the end of his fifth year; he had gotten things done on the domestic front, rebuilt the military, and restored U.S. prestige abroad. He was immensely popular.

Although cordial, President Reagan quickly got to the point. He wanted me to serve as secretary of the Department of Health & Human Services. If I accepted, I would need to come to Washington so that he could announce my nomination. My reservations went out the window. It's hard to say no when the president of the United States personally asks you to do something, especially after a lifetime in public service. I quickly said yes.

Before there was public knowledge that I was to be nominated, FBI agents fanned out across Indiana to see if I had skeletons in my closet. I know they interviewed people in Bremen and talked to former Indiana Democratic Party chair Gordon St. Angelo, but I have no idea who else they contacted or how many contacts they made. All I know is that Senate Finance chair Bob Packwood said at my confirmation hearing that I didn't "have a blemish nor apparently an enemy."

Rose, my children, relatives, friends, and colleagues were excited by my nomination. Physicians and medical groups were thrilled. Most major organizations supported me, but the national right-to-life group questioned my purity on abortion. Indiana's right-to-life group came to my rescue, saying that my position and performance as governor were okay.

If confirmed, and once nominated there was little doubt that I would be, I would become the sixteenth secretary and the first physician to hold the position.

The roots of H&HS are in the Federal Security Administration, created in 1939 and absorbed into the Department of Health, Education and Welfare (HEW) in 1953. H&HS was created in 1979. Within nine years, its budget—$425 billion—was the largest of any federal department, and it employed 120,000 people. The Social Security Administration then was part of H&HS. It also operated the Public Health Service, the National Institutes of Health, the Centers for Disease Control, the Food and Drug Administration, the Alcohol, Drug Abuse and Mental Health Administration, the Health Care Financing Administration, the Health Resources and Services Administration, and lesser agencies.

My prospects for a long tenure were slim. Many distinguished Americans had served in the post, but a secretary's average "life" was one and a half years. Earlier secretaries were Oveta Culp Hobby (1953–55), Marion Folsom (1955–58), Arthur Flemming (1958–61), Abraham Ribicoff (1961–62), Anthony Celebrezze (1962–65), John Gardner (1965–68), Wilbur Cohen (1968–69), Robert Finch (1969–70), Elliott Richardson (1970–73), Caspar Weinberger (1973–75), David Mathews (1976–77), Joseph Califano (1977–79), Patricia Harris (1979–81), Schweiker (1981–83), and Mrs. Heckler (1983–85).

I was to serve longer than all my predecessors—three years, a month, and six days. My successors—Louis W. Sullivan, who served all but two months of President Bush's term, and Donna Shalala, still President Clinton's H&HS secretary—were to last longer.

I flew to Washington for President Reagan's announcement of my nomination on November 7, 1985. Fog made my plane late. I met briefly with the president, Vice President Bush, and Mr. Regan. Despite what I had heard about Mr. Regan's battles with Mrs. Heckler, I liked him. The announcement was routine. Mrs. Heckler's warmth and her desire to help me understand the secretary's role also impressed me at a later lunch. She did not badmouth Mr. Regan or anyone else in our conversation, an indication of her character.

Friends and a horde of media met me on my arrival at Indianapolis International that night. The media peppered Rose with questions. Asked how she felt about being the wife of a Cabinet member, her down-to-earth response was, "What they see is what they get."

I shuttled between Indianapolis and Washington to prepare for confirmation hearings. I had long, frequent briefings on the workings of H&HS. I called on key senators and representatives. The Senate Finance Committee staff requested copies of all the speeches that I had made in the three prior years. That being impossible, I submitted a sampling.

To avoid a conflict of interest, I sold stocks and bonds that were in any way related to medicine. I didn't have many, but most were in the medical field. If I could have kept them, my net worth today would be much greater. Stocks and bonds not sold went into a blind trust to be fully controlled by a trustee while I was secretary. I also resigned from the boards on which I served. Rose and I not only had to find a place to live in the Washington area, but we also had to dispose of our condominium, pack, and move.

The Senate Finance Committee's confirmation hearing came in early December. The hearing room was such a jumble of news media, other people, cameras, recorders and cables that it caused even me a moment of panic. After remarks by Senators Lugar and Quayle and Representatives Andy Jacobs and Elwood H. (Bud) Hillis, senators asked me about abortion, tobacco, public health policy, Medicare, and other issues over the next two days.

At one point, I noted that a Medicare issue was the fact that catastrophic illnesses were depleting many elderly people's life savings. When Senator Lloyd Bentsen mentioned that he had a bill on the issue, I asked, "Senator, what is the number of that bill?" That brought laughter from committee members.

Concerned about the support of living wills by the Advisory Council on Social Security, which I chaired, Lyndon LaRouche's fringe group predicted that I would be an eighties version of Joseph Mengele, the Nazi doctor who conducted hideous experiments on Jewish people in concentration camps. That prompted Senator Daniel Patrick Moynihan to say that he had planned to ask "difficult questions," "but now that I see that Mr. LaRouche has absolutely denounced your appointment, you have my absolute support."

After the polite Senate Finance hearing, the Senate Labor and Commerce Committee held a combative, almost hostile one. While governor, I had said more than once that I wanted the federal government to keep its clumsy hands out of Indiana's affairs. Senator Edward M. (Ted) Kennedy bore down on that in an especially vicious way. Our exchange became so heated that Rose cried. Afterward, Kennedy hugged Rose, apologized, and told her he liked her name because Rose was his mother's name.

Labor and Commerce unanimously recommended my confirmation. Finance had the final decision, and its members also voted unanimously to confirm. While awaiting action by the full Senate, I returned home to continue preparations for the move to Washington.

Senator Dole presented my nomination on the floor on December

12, 1985, and Senator Quayle added support. The vote was 93-2, with North Carolina Republican Jesse Helms and New Mexico Democrat Jeff Bingaman against. The fact that Senator Helms represented a tobacco-growing state probably accounted for his vote, but I heard that my anti-abortion position was not pure enough for him. As noted, Senator Bingaman told Senator Quayle that he voted "no" because former Indiana attorney general Ted Sendak had urged him to do so.

Relaying the vote's outcome, the White House asked that I have a federal judge swear me in privately so that I could legally act. Judge Sarah Evans Barker of Mishawaka did so on a Saturday evening at the Federal Building in Indianapolis. Present were Rose, Brad and Donna Grubbs, Clarence and Mildred Long, and my minister, Rev. David Kahlenberg.

The public ceremony soon was held at the White House. Rose, my children and their spouses, and Rose's daughter were all eyes and ears as we met privately with President Reagan in the Oval Office and at the ceremony in the Roosevelt Room. Rose held the Bible as I repeated the words of the oath, given to me by Vice President Bush.

In my first days, I went from office to office in Washington, Atlanta, Baltimore, and elsewhere. Directors and employees told me it was the first time they had seen a secretary, let alone have one come to their offices. The visits went a long way toward restoring morale.

Like Secretary Heckler, I found little to like about the federal personnel system, and I soon was grousing about White House "micromanagement." I not only wanted the best, but I also wanted people whose philosophies and approaches were compatible with mine, including former associates that I knew and trusted. Understandably, the White House wanted to place individuals who had helped President Reagan in some way. I had to battle for every one of my choices.

J. B. King and Dan Evans Jr. of Indianapolis helped me interview candidates for top positions. The former dean of the IU School of Public and Environmental Affairs, Charles (Chuck) Bonser, provided advice on organizing my office.

Don Newman of Osceola was approved as undersecretary. A Mishawaka pharmacist before nearly defeating Representative John Brademas in 1972, Don directed the Indiana office in Washington for Governor Orr and me. While in Washington, he earned a law degree.

As chief of staff, I chose a career H&HS executive, Thomas R. Burke, formerly the executive director of the Advisory Council on Social Security. A conservative economist, he was a physically imposing, profane, and short-tempered man. Those who didn't know him saw him as brash and pushy, but Tom had a well-deserved reputation for getting difficult things done, and he cared about others more than he ever showed.

As executive director of the office of the secretary, I chose Kim Fuller, whom I had known since she was president of the Arizona State University chapter of Bacchus, a group trying to reduce alcohol consumption on campuses.

After folding programs that help families into the Family Support Administration, I brought in Wayne A. Stanton from the Chicago regional office as its first administrator. Wayne had earlier been state welfare director for me. I also named Bill Gee of Plymouth to head the department dealing with refugee resettlement.

The undersecretary and chief of staff are part of the secretary's staff. Assistant secretaries oversee functional areas—planning and evaluation, management and budget, legislation, and personnel administration. They and the heads of major program areas, the inspector general, general counsel, and civil rights and consumer affairs heads report through the undersecretary and chief of staff. Regional directors report to a deputy undersecretary, also part of the secretary's office.

Life in the federal government, I quickly learned, was far more frustrating and far less satisfying than being governor. A governor has authority and can lead and act. In the federal government, the president rightfully has absolute authority, but there are hundreds of other bosses. They include the White House chief of staff, the secretary of the Cabinet, the director of the White House Office of Personnel, the Office of Management and Budget (OMB), and the Domestic Policy Council (DPC). Congress had twenty-three oversight committees continuously looking at H&HS. All try to impose their will and beliefs on a secretary.

Two days after taking office, I found myself at odds with OMB over proposed cuts in funding for AIDS research, Medicare, and the National Institutes of Health. After making my displeasure public, I realized that such disagreements should remain in-house. I also learned that speech drafts went to OMB and the White House, where they usually were edited. Feeling that the administration's top people either were not intelligent enough to know the right thing to say or could not be trusted to say it, the president's staff felt impelled to guard against high-level employees' saying the wrong thing.

Federal processes often are distorted and contorted. As secretary, I had to decide what medical procedures Medicare covered. My discussions with Jim Miller, the OMB director, and Beryl Sprinkle, the president's chief economic advisor, on whether Medicare should cover heart transplants show how silly some federal officials can be.

Medicare did not pay for experimental procedures. At one time, heart transplants were experimental. By the time I became secretary, they were being done daily. I felt the time had come for Medicare to cover them. Rules were needed to govern who could do heart transplants and where. I submitted such a proposal.

The ultra-right Sprinkle carried his free-enterprise philosophy to extremes. Trying to offer opposition or a less costly substitute, he proposed what to him seemed like a free enterprise solution. "Well," he said, "if we're going to cover them, let's let just anyone do them; let them do it on the kitchen table if necessary." In support, or perhaps in an effort at oneupmanship, the equally conservative Miller added, "Okay, if we're going to cover them, let's just pay for the successful ones."

Even now, it's hard to believe that senior advisors to the president said that.

I also was disheartened because White House underlings determined when an issue was important enough to discuss with the president. These subordinates could and did block access to the Oval Office. For me, this was a huge change. As governor, I had kept the door open to department heads and regularly met with them. President Reagan's staff obviously was overly protective, but he probably never knew how rigid they were.

The president relied on Cabinet councils to study issues and make recommendations to him. Members of the National Security Council included the vice president, secretary of state, CIA director, attorney general, secretary of defense, and Joint Chiefs of Staff chair. Economic Policy Council members included the chief economic advisor and the secretaries of agriculture, commerce, transportation, interior, and treasury. Domestic Policy Council members included the secretaries of H&HS, labor, and interior, the OMB director, the attorney general, the chief economic advisor and others.

Cabinet meetings occurred when the president called them. The secretary in whose sphere a discussion topic fell sat beside President Reagan and presented the matter. I often found myself sitting next to him, inwardly quaking.

With respect to my Cabinet associates, I feel like the old man who took his dog to a show. On the way, a friend asked where they were going. "The dog show," the old man answered. The friend asked, "You don't think old Rex will win a blue ribbon, do you?" The man answered, "No, but it will give him a chance to meet some mighty fine dogs."

Well, I met some mighty fine people in Washington.

I've mentioned Don Regan. His successor as chief of staff, former U.S. Senator Howard Baker of Tennessee, also was outstanding.

George Schultz was an able, thoughtful, wise, and conscientious man, and a good choice for secretary of state. When George spoke at Cabinet meetings, all of us listened.

Caspar Weinberger and Frank Carlucci were able secretaries of defense. Weinberger was outgoing and spoke more often. Carlucci was quiet, thoughtful, and effective.

I've mentioned Miller and Sprinkle but left out their soulmate, Attorney General Edwin J. Meese. For reasons that will be mentioned later, he was not one of my favorites.

Secretary of the Interior Don Hodel was a less radical ultra-conservative than Meese, Miller, and Sprinkle, but not far behind. He was easier to like.

Richard Lyng, secretary of agriculture, was so quiet that he was hardly noticed. I liked him for his effectiveness. In roasts, he and I were portrayed as the Gallo Wine advertising duo—quiet, slow-talking, with a bumbling hayseed sort of image. (That suited us better than being caricatured as fast-talking city slickers.)

Malcolm Baldridge, the secretary of commerce, was a Westerner with a great interest in rodeos. While participating in one, he fell off a horse and was trampled to death. This was unfortunate, because Baldridge was a leveling influence within the Cabinet.

Elizabeth Dole, the secretary of transportation and the Cabinet's most attractive member, brought a thoughtful woman's viewpoint to the table. Because it was assumed that her views coincided with those of her husband, Senator Dole, she was doubly effective.

Secretary of Labor Bill Brock, a former U.S. senator and national GOP chair, brought practical political sense to Cabinet meetings. President Reagan, Secretary Brock, and I were the only ones in this group who ever ran for political office.

Sam Pierce Jr. was a likable, sincere secretary of housing and urban development who never rocked the boat.

John Herrington, the secretary of energy, dealt with difficult problems, including oil reserves and the huge super-cyclotron project in Texas.

William Bennett, secretary of education, was an "over-reformed

Democrat" who had sneaked into high-stakes Republican circles on the recommendation of ultra-conservative Republican friends. These included an uncle revered as the originator of the USS *Hope*, the ship that travels the world doing good things in medicine and politics. A big man with an opinion on almost everything, Bennett gets noticed. He found it easy to ignore me. Since he opposed my catastrophic Medicare insurance initiative, my negative feelings may be a reflection of my own sensitivity.

Being a secretary is a big deal socially as well as governmentally. Cabinet members and key White House staff can have as much social life as they can endure. Most were more active than Rose and I. By the time I got to Washington, I was nearly 68. I saw little value in socializing just for the sake of it, and I needed time at home to prepare for the next day's meetings, presentations, and speeches.

Rose and I attended events originating in my office, events to which the president invited us, and major Kennedy Center events. Our somewhat limited social life probably made it more difficult to get support for H&HS initiatives.

I do not mean to suggest that administration leaders socialized all the time. These intelligent, committed people worked hard. Some were too ideologically rigid for my tastes, and a few seemed less interested in serving than in winning the next struggle for power and prestige. For the most part, however, these were people doing their best as they saw what was best.

Attitude may be the big difference between Washington and Indianapolis or Bremen. "Potomac fever" produces the illusion that good comes only from Washington, that inside the Beltway is the only place to work, and that those who think otherwise are hicks. Back home in Indiana, people are less haughty, more likely to rate performance over flowery words, and more suspicious of slick-talking government officials.

Easily the most significant challenge while I was secretary was catastrophic health care insurance. Understanding its nature requires some minimal background.

As secretary, I was charged with minding the income security of poor, disabled, and elderly Americans. Increased longevity and current eligibility requirements meant that three generations were drawing funds from Medicare and Social Security. Only one or two generations were paying the bill. When people live longer, they need more treatment. Even then, America's aging was straining Medicare and Social Security.

Medicare and "Medigap" aside, major holes exist in health insurance coverage. In 1985, 30 million Americans couldn't afford "Medigap" policies. Neither Medicare nor "Medigap" policies protected the elderly against catastrophic illnesses. H&HS studies showed that people on Medicare had acute care costs of $2,000 or more annually. Against Social Security pensions averaging $6,000 to $7,000 annually, this was a heavy burden.

Senior citizens worry most about their health and their finances. Their biggest worry is which will run out first. As a doctor and as governor, I saw many elderly persons lose their life savings to major illnesses and have nothing left at death. This is wrong—people ought to be able to live with some sense of security and die with dignity.

I became interested in catastrophic health insurance as chair of the Advisory Council on Social Security. As secretary, I felt that we ought to strive for some form of insurance. In our internal discussions, we assumed that budget constraints meant that any proposal had to be cost-neutral, that those benefiting had to pay the cost.

A compassionate conservative, President Reagan was sympathetic. As California's governor, he proposed catastrophic health insurance in 1974. He proposed a catastrophic health insurance plan for the elderly in 1982. It went nowhere in a Democrat-controlled Congress whose members had their eyes on the 1984 elections.

When the White House asked departments to submit ideas for the 1986 State of the Union address, H&HS suggested catastrophic health insurance. Internal White House debate scaled this back to a call for H&HS to study the issue and make recommendations to the president. (Opponents usually call for a study when they can't immediately scuttle something. They always hope that the subject gets studied to death. It's reasonable to assume that some people around the president had this objective.)

In his State of the Union message on February 4, 1986, President Reagan said that he was

> directing the Secretary of Health and Human services, Dr. Otis Bowen, to report to me by year's end with recommendations on how the private sector and government can work together to address the problems of affordable insurance for those whose life savings would be threatened when catastrophic illness strikes.

The president followed up his public statement with a letter to me saying in part:

> You should look at what the private sector and the levels of government are doing to address the problems and examine current federal activities, from

tax policy that affects private health insurance to financing programs such as Medicare, Medicaid and veterans' health benefits. You should make recommendations through the Domestic Policy Council process on further steps, if any, that are warranted by the private sector, states, local government and the federal government. I have no preconceived notions about what the right answer should be. I truly appreciate your willingness to take on this major issue so early in your tenure. I look forward to receiving the plan in December of this year containing recommendations that I can study in order to determine actions that can be taken in 1987 toward lifting a great financial burden from the backs of many citizens.

The president probably chose catastrophic health insurance for his overall "Agenda for the Future" because it fit nicely with his monetary and welfare reform proposals. Health care reform also had immense public relations value.

The day after his address, President Reagan came to the Hubert Humphrey Building auditorium to welcome me and show his support. In remarks to H&HS employees, he reiterated his hope of identifying ways that government could work with the private sector to "help those who become victims of the terrible cost of catastrophic illnesses."

In a letter to me dated March 21, 1986, the president also said that my efforts "should include, but not be limited to, examining situations faced by Medicare beneficiaries as well as people of all age groupings, income and employment status."

Thus, my orders were explicit and my task was broadly defined. President Reagan asked me to do the study. He instructed me not to limit it to the elderly. He directed me to make recommendations to him through the DPC. (Several times in the debate on my eventual recommendations, I reminded DPC members that I studied catastrophic health care coverage and made recommendations at the president's request. After DPC members once tried to suggest that I had gone off the reservation on catastrophic health insurance, I even delivered that reminder in front of the president.)

I organized H&HS for the catastrophic coverage study by creating an executive advisory committee with Tom Burke as chair and senior staffers as members. I created three H&HS technical working groups to focus attention on study segments:

- the catastrophic health expenses of the general population, generally those below the age of 65, a group that had received little attention from Congress;
- the catastrophic health expenses of Medicare beneficiaries, generally those 65 and older, a group that had gotten lots of attention from Congress; and

- long-term care costs, in which the Congress had shown little interest.

I created a private-sector advisory committee, headed by Drexel Burnham Lambert vice president James Balog, a former Advisory Council on Social Security member. At public hearings in Dallas, Washington, Chicago, and Oakland, it sought input on ways the government could work with the private sector toward affordable catastrophic insurance.

For the president to get recommendations by December 15, 1986, H&HS had to send them to the DPC by September 15. The department met its deadlines, proposing a modest program with a $2,000 limit on Medicare cost-sharing for covered hospital and physician services. Coverage would be voluntary, funded by a $4.92 monthly premium. The $2,000 limit and premium would be indexed for inflation. Americans could shelter up to $1,000 a year in tax-free individual medical savings accounts (IMAs) earmarked for nursing home care. Those buying long-term care insurance would get a $100 tax credit. Employers could pre-fund health care benefits for retirees without paying taxes on the set-aside. States would be encouraged to create insurance pools to pay for catastrophic illness costs and to require employers offering health insurance to include catastrophic coverage. Self-employed persons would receive a full tax deduction for health care costs.

The Domestic Policy Council did not consider H&HS's recommendations until November 19, 1986. Meese chaired the DPC. He had to put the H&HS proposal on the council's meeting agenda for it to be considered. Meese dragged his feet magnificently, even refusing to recognize me at DPC meetings to talk about the proposal. His opposition was supported by his fellow ideologues Sprinkle and Miller, and by Hodel.

At first there was no Cabinet-level support, but Labor Secretary Bill Brock and Defense Secretary Caspar Weinberger, a former H&HS secretary, later came to my side. Their previous experiences gave them insights that the others did not have. Brock's sympathy grew out of a huge medical bill for his son's premature baby.

In the preliminaries, H&HS kept its report under wraps. Once it was before DPC, it no longer could be kept secret. The council itself was notorious for news leaks. DPC reluctantly gave me the go-ahead to release the report but stipulated that I make it clear that it was an H&HS proposal that had not been endorsed by either the DPC or the president. At a news conference, I did exactly that.

Predictably, groups like the Heritage Foundation opposed my plan on ideological and philosophical grounds. U.S. Chamber economist Richard Rahn contended that I was "shoving Medicare further along the socialist route." Representative Claude Pepper of Florida had no qualms about using demagoguery, saying the plan was "not the step of a giant, it is the step of a pygmy, a dwarf." Others felt that the proposal was doable because it was modest. The most popular negative argument was that the plan set precedent. This reminded me of this statement in *Microcosmographia Academica*, F. M. Cornford's 1970 book:

> The principle of the dangerous precedent is that you should not do anything or do an admittedly right action for fear that you or your equally timid successor should not have the courage to do right at some future time. . . . Every public action which is not customary either is wrong, or if it is right, is a dangerous precedent. It follows that nothing should be done for the first time!

H&HS's report set off one of the hottest domestic policy debates of the Reagan years. DPC discussed the report on November 19 and December 3, 12, and 15, 1986. The president was present for two of those meetings. Meese, Sprinkle, and Miller tried to derail the program and keep me from having a meaningful part in the discussion. Their tactics didn't work.

The matter never would have gone to President Reagan without the help of Ralph Bledsoe, Domestic Policy Council secretary, who took the report to Don Regan, and Alfred H. Kingon, secretary of the Cabinet. They understood the president's charge to me. When I persevered, they insisted, and Regan decided that I should have a chance to present the proposal directly to the president.

The December 15th meeting probably was my last chance to complete the climb up a very steep mountain. That day, I told the Domestic Policy Council and President Reagan that

- I would never do anything as secretary that would embarrass the president;
- I was a political and ideological conservative who wanted government out of individual lives whenever that was possible;
- I had succeeded in public life by listening to and acting on the concerns of people;
- catastrophic illness was a genuine problem that needed to be addressed;
- there was no private-sector answer, though that would be the best solution; and
- the proposed program would be self-financing.

At the meeting's end, the president promised to review the materials and make a decision. The presentation had gone well, and I was optimistic.

The opposition still was not done. On December 19th, I was summoned to a White House meeting of insurance executives, called by Meese and Sprinkle in a last-ditch effort to find a private-sector alternative. The executives blithely said they could do the job that H&HS proposed to do. However, absent a federal tax incentive, their comments made it clear that their version would carry a higher cost for less coverage.

On December 23, 1986, the Cabinet held its last meeting of the year. Catastrophic health coverage again was on the agenda. (Rose and I delayed driving home for the holidays so that I could attend.) To ensure neutrality, a secretary who was not a DPC member chaired the session. In advance, Bledsoe noted that the issue already had been considered five times.

Meese had appointed a DPC subcommittee to develop options, excluding H&HS from meaningful participation. His three-page outline offered no recommendations and needed no response. Sprinkle then proposed a voucher system allowing Medicare recipients to use federal dollars to buy private insurance coverage. I responded by tracing the complicated, zigzag route that voucher payments would follow. My chart had so many lines and arrows that it looked like the plans for a Rube Goldberg contraption. I asked the Cabinet to consider how a sick, frail, elderly person could negotiate that maze.

On December 24, 1986, President Reagan gave his blessing to our plan. After reviewing H&HS bill drafts, he endorsed catastrophic coverage for Medicare recipients—those over 65—on February 11, 1987. I was present the next day when he announced at a news conference that he was submitting legislation to Congress. In his weekly radio address, the president said that "all of us have family, friends or neighbors who have suffered devastating illnesses that threatened their financial security. For too long, older Americans in particular have faced the possibility of sickness that might not only wipe out their savings, but those of their families. Our proposal will make available catastrophic medical insurance for every American eligible for Medicare."

The introduced bills had 38 House and 16 Senate co-sponsors. My staff and I spent much of the next year preparing testimony and testifying. On July 22, the House passed a much-amended bill, 302-127. The Senate passed its version, 86-11, on October 27. The House dissented. Senate conferees were not appointed until February 2, 1988. Conferees invited me to their first meeting on March 16th, an unprecedented move. I again advocated the administration proposal, but conferees reported a compromise. On June 2, the House adopted the conference report, 328-72. On June 8, the Senate adopted it, 86-11.

President Reagan and I recognized that the bill had major flaws. Benefits were far more generous than the president and H&HS had proposed, and the financing mechanism bore no resemblance to the original plan. However, we believed that the defects could be cured, especially since the program had some phase-in periods. In the Rose Garden on July 1, 1988, President Reagan signed the bill, saying it was an "historic piece of legislation." For me, it was a special moment. I later received accolades from the president and Senator Bentsen for my work on the legislation. Given the ferocity of the opposition, it was a minor miracle that the bill ever saw the light of day.

The 1988 Medicare Catastrophic Coverage Act covered all hospital bills after patients paid for first-day coverage and capped the amount a patient would pay for first-day coverage at $560. Skilled nursing-home care was increased to 150 days with less co-payment cost per day. Mammography was covered. Respite care was increased to 80 hours, home health care to 38 days. After patients paid out-of-pocket expenses of $1,370, Medicare paid the rest of Medicare-covered physician expenses to help avert spousal impoverishment. After a $650 deductible, coverage of prescription drug costs was to start at 50 percent in 1991 and go to 60 percent in 1992 and 80 percent in 1993.

Benefits were indexed for inflation. Fees were graduated. The poor were to pay $4 monthly. Those better off—the upper 40 percent of the covered population—were to help the lower 60 percent pay the bill. The $800 maximum applied to the 5 percent of elderly Americans with incomes over $85,000 annually. The new Medicare coverage eased the need for "Medigap" insurance.

Medicare is like a patchwork quilt. After patches were sewn on the quilt for the poor, the elderly, veterans, the military, and workers, Congress kept trying to sew an ever-bigger quilt covering more Americans. In 1989 the quilt began to unravel, and the new act became an early Bush administration casualty. Perhaps the outcome was predestined. For the first time since Social Security was created, a major health care program was being financed by a surtax paid only by benefit recipients. As the bill moved along, Congress added provisions that ran up the cost and inflated the surtax. Reverting to New Deal days, Congress graduated the surtax so that the most affluent elderly paid the most. Other reasons why the new law became a casualty included:

• A campaign of misinformation and distortion by several groups. The most notable was the National Committee to Preserve Social Security and Medicare, headed by Jimmy Roosevelt. Its fear-mongering mass mailings and stories in *USA Today* and other publications about its anti-surtax efforts created the false impression that all elderly couples would pay $1,600 ($800 a person) per year. Only those with $85,000 or more in income would have paid the maximum. Since the act almost eliminated the need for "Medigap" insurance and the surtax would be far less than "Medigap" premiums, even those who did would be better off.

• The Bush administration's unwillingness to defend the program. As controversy erupted, the administration did nothing. Even after learning that surtax revenues would be $4.9 billion higher than expected, President Bush opposed cutting premiums, saying it "would be imprudent to tinker with Medicare catastrophic insurance" so soon.

• The bells and whistles that Congress added. Although these were included for compassionate reasons, they increased costs and imposed a financing mechanism that pleased no one.

• A feeling that Congress had done enough for the elderly. Representative George Miller of California voiced this view when he said that "we've spent 25 years lifting the elderly out of poverty and now we've become a nation of rich adults and poor children."

Congress should have revised the program to make it right. Canceling drug coverage alone might have been enough. Instead, members made a token effort, then threw up their hands and threw in the towel. In late 1989, a series of House and Senate votes sent the issue of modification or repeal of the act to a budget conference committee. Conferees separated the issue from budget negotiations and then recommended repeal. The House and Senate adopted the recommendation on November 22, 1989.

As the twenty-first century begins, we remain where we were in the eighties—a nation with hundreds of thousands of frail elderly people without hope as they face the possibility of catastrophic illness and escalating health care costs. Our lack of action is a damning indictment of our humanity and our political will.

As secretary, I fought other battles. One was how to attack the drug problem. I felt that our first principle should be to reduce demand by educating Americans on the risks of using drugs. I also wanted us to do a better job of treatment. When I was secretary, only one in ten addicts could be treated appropriately. Meese and friends wanted supply-side interdiction. They won, and scarce dollars went for more helicopters and boats.

With U.S. Attorney Rudolph W. (Rudy) Giuliani, later mayor of New York City, I witnessed open drug selling and buying on the streets of that great city. At the Phoenix Drug Treatment Center for youth, I personally interviewed about ten teenage users and came away with the painful knowledge that they stole from $500 to $1,000 a day to support their habit, and that their parents didn't care that they were on drugs.

At LaSalle University in Philadelphia, I suggested one night that we were losing the "War on Drugs." Immediately, the media asked if I had broken with President Reagan. Obviously, I had not. However, I differed with those who equated success with how many tons of drugs we seized and destroyed but failed to mention that new users were exceeding the number successfully treated for addiction. Meese and friends rebuked me, but President Reagan never called me on the carpet; he must have understood my point.

While I was secretary, H&HS dealt with the specter of AIDS (Acquired Immunodeficiency Syndrome), the twentieth century's version of the Black Plague, and coped with food and drug tampering after deranged people injected cyanide into fruit and over-the-counter drugs. Abortion was an ongoing debate, usually involving the circumstances under which federal funds could be used. H&HS dealt with government research using fetal tissue, homelessness, and animal rights. We dealt with all kinds of interest groups.

Within H&HS, I enjoyed my associations with many wonderful people. A favorite was Surgeon General C. Everett Koop. A bit of a character, "Chick" Koop had immense credibility with the news media. When we wanted to explore an idea or had something that we wanted to get a fair shake, Chick talked about it for us. Chick operated within the Public Health Service, but I gave him broad discretion on what he did. The result was his well-known, well-received effort to get out the facts about AIDS.

Dr. Anthony Fauci, head of the H&HS unit dealing with allergies and infectious diseases, awed me. His epidemiological and research studies on AIDS moved us far down the road in dealing with this disease, which is caused by a tricky retrovirus. He still coordinates and oversees anti-AIDS work. When we become impatient for an AIDS vaccine or cure, we need to remember that it took forty years to develop a polio vaccine and seventeen years to get one for hepatitis. HIV is far more complex than any previously known virus.

Don Newman, my undersecretary; Tom Burke, my chief of staff; and Kim Fuller, my office's executive director, deserve special mention for helping me run a large, complex agency. My hat also goes off to the

H&HS personnel, who were dedicated and hard-working down the line.

President Reagan's administration was in a wind-down mode by the time he signed the Medicare Catastrophic Coverage Act. Vice President Bush became the GOP nominee for president and selected Dan Quayle as his running mate. Both were elected. I did not seek or want a role in the Bush administration. To clear the decks for the new president, President Reagan asked Cabinet members to submit their resignations effective on inauguration day (January 20, 1989). All of us did so.

In the afternoon of January 19, 1989, President-Elect Bush's transition office ordered me to vacate my H&HS office by noon the next day. I found this order insulting for someone who had been a team player. I do not believe that Mr. Bush was responsible, and I feel he would have countermanded the order had he known of it. The blame rests, I think, with Mr. Bush's chief of staff, John Sununu, never known for his tact and well known for his arrogance. Sununu probably felt that Mr. Bush needed to make a complete break with President Reagan for political reasons. That would be understandable, but the order left the Reagan people with a bad taste in their mouths. (Ironically, years earlier I had taken part in a news conference at a Republican Governors Association meeting to publicly express support for an unknown named Sununu, who was running for governor of New Hampshire.)

A final small slight came the next day. When Rose and I found our seats for the inaugural, they were so far back and off to the side of the platform that we could not distinguish faces as President Bush took the oath of office.

However, we were not sorry when the ceremony was over. At the end of the Reagan era, I was nearly 71. Rose and I were eager for a slower, less complicated life in Bremen.

Serving in one of the nation's highest-ranking positions always was challenging and occasionally was exciting, but I cannot say much good about federal service. Through no fault of my good friend President Reagan, serving as H&HS secretary ranks only slightly ahead of being Marshall County coroner and far below being a family doctor, governor, IU Medical School professor, House speaker, or legislator.

Perhaps all that this proves is that Washington is no place for a Fulton County boy to hang his hat.

With my years of federal service at its end, Rose and I finished packing, saw our goods loaded on our moving van, and headed our car west, toward home in Bremen.

❧ 21 ❧

Beth, Rose, and Carol

I'M AN EXPERT on an experience that no one should have—watching and hurting as a dying spouse suffers terribly. I've had that awful experience twice—in my last year as governor, as I watched the life of my first wife, Beth, ebb painfully away; and eleven years later, when I lost my second wife, Rose, after equally prolonged suffering. During the days and through the nights that they suffered, I was at their sides. Death came to Beth at the University Hospital at the IU Medical Center. Rose wanted to die at home, and did, in my arms.

Others may think that seeing so much of death immunizes a doctor against it. As doctors, we fully understand death's inevitability, but our life's purpose is to defeat it. To us, death is never ordinary or routine. If the death involves a loved one, we are haunted by the possibility that something might have saved or extended that special person's life.

Someone who grew up in the Depression, served in combat in World War II, and was a small-town doctor, coroner, legislator, speaker, and Health & Human Services secretary knows about crises. None I ever faced was worse than the deaths of my first two spouses.

I've written much about my wife Beth. Without her, I would never have become a doctor. Without her unswerving help and common sense, I would never have become speaker and governor or served well in those offices.

Through nearly forty-three years of marriage, Beth always was at my side. When practice and public service kept me away too much, she held our family together. Through the stresses of a small-town medical practice and the highs and lows of public life, she held me together. Beth was a loving wife, a wonderful companion, a superb homemaker, an outstanding cook, a "super mom," an active churchwoman, and a community-minded volunteer.

Beth's German cooking is one of my special memories. Her pork loin, spare ribs, or pork chop sauerkraut dinner was one of her many specialties. Her secret, I learned, is to "wash" the kraut several times to rid it of its sour taste, add lots of brown sugar, and bake or cook it for several hours. Beth even taught me to like pickled or creamed herring.

In my 1976 gubernatorial campaign, Lewis Gregory, a GOP State Committee staffer and later a member of Governor Orr's staff and Indiana Parole Board chair, suggested that some of Beth's recipes be printed up for use in my campaign. With Beth's help, the party printed packets holding a small set of recipes. They were an instant hit. That led to a cookbook, *Beth Bowen's Favorites*, which was published by the GOP State Committee. The proceeds helped buy $2,000 worth of china for the Governor's Residence.

Beth did not speak English until she started classes at a Lutheran school at age six. She remained fluent in German, often sang songs and recited little rhymes in that language to our kids and grandkids, and conversed in German with her Amish friends.

Reared as a Lutheran, Beth remained true to her upbringing. Our family's custom was—and still is—to start meals with the German or Lutheran prayer: "Come, Lord Jesus, be Thou our guest, and let these gifts to us be blest."

Beth was a patriotic American who always stood with her hand over her heart and sang "The Star-Spangled Banner." On holidays, she always put out the American flag.

She was a secret "do-gooder" who did things for others without a thought of thanks. For several children, including a niece and nephew and three children from one family, Beth and I were godparents. We considered it an honor and took our role seriously. Beth remembered her godchildren with attention, cards, and an Easter "lamb cake." With their other challenges, the parents of one of our godchildren found it difficult to cope with a new baby's feeding and respiratory problems. Beth decided that we should take him into our home and look after him twenty-four hours a day. For a few weeks, Beth mothered the boy like he was her own. He recovered and went home. To this day, his parents remain grateful.

Beth also "mothered" young people. Our children's friends filled our home. Many sought her advice. Any kid was welcome to play at the outdoor basketball court at our home on North Center Street, but Beth kept order and enforced standards of behavior.

She went out of her way to help others. A typical example occurred while we lived in the Governor's Residence. Needing a housekeeper who also could cook, Beth advertised but got no responses. Learning of a young black woman with two children who needed a job, she contacted her. The lady confirmed her situation but told Beth she couldn't cook. Beth's wonderful smile came across her face as she said, "I'll teach you." She did exactly that, showing the lady how to cook, and taking her to major functions to teach her how to set up and serve large-scale meals.

Beth loved music, especially if it had good rhythm. Standing, sitting, or riding, when she heard her kind of music, she showed her love for it with dancing movements, using her arms and body, and humming or singing. She was an excellent dancer, too.

She designed, decorated, and furnished our Bremen home—the "Lodge," a two-story home at Donnybrook. On both floors, its rooms wrap around an imposing great room with a huge fireplace. We moved there the year I was elected governor. Its grounds still reflect Beth's gardening handiwork. She loved flowers. Because spring was special to her, her favorites were crocuses, tulips, jonquils, and other early bloomers that she could see from her windows before the grass needed mowing.

Beth loved small animals. We always had a cat or two, a puppy at times, a rabbit, a parakeet, and canaries. She saved thread and yarn and threw it in the yard for birds to use in nest building. We built a big feeding station and used 1,000 pounds of birdseed and countless ears of corn (for the squirrels) one cold winter. Beth bought books to help her identify birds and their sounds. She brought suet to Indianapolis for friends (because she got it free in Bremen) and always brought things back to Indianapolis to share with others. Blueberries were the best example.

Beth enjoyed fishing. We often fished at Donnybrook's stocked four-acre pond. A stub-tailed, notched-eared, scroungy cat stayed there. It kept close to Beth because she gave it the fish that were too small to keep. Beth insisted that the cat helped her fish. If her attention strayed from the bobber, Beth claimed, the cat would watch it for her. If there was a bite, and Beth wasn't looking, the cat pawed her.

Beth was one of the most organized persons I've ever known. For our children and, later, our grandchildren, she had an exact routine—

baths, dressing in bedclothes, snack, bedtime prayers, and lights out. She planned her days to avoid single-purpose trips and save gas and time. She packed bags of clothes, wet washcloths, and towels for every trip, even short ones to my parents' home in Leiters Ford, because one of our children might get carsick with little or no warning.

For church drives, she saved used stamps, canned food labels, soap scraps, used clothing, and newspapers. She saved used furniture, clothes, and pots and pans for an orphanage. She clipped coupons for friends. She picked up corn that had dropped off wagons en route to farm storage bins or the elevator. She even recycled greeting cards, inserting a clean sheet in the middle for her message and noting on it that the card was "recycled by Beth." After her death, I found a card that said on the front, "If all my good wishes were Easter eggs . . . " Beth had replaced the center page with a new blank page on which she wrote: "You'd be eating egg salad sandwiches the rest of your life. Happy Easter."

By choice, Beth had only a few formal dresses. After wearing one, she affixed a tag to it showing the date on which it was worn and the event. For example, her gown for the second inaugural ball (January 10, 1977) also was worn to the Indianapolis Hyatt Regency dedication (April 29, 1977), national Republican functions (October 10, 1977, and November 26, 1978), and the 500 Festival Ball (May 25, 1979), when President Ford was our guest.

With her long, narrow feet, she wore AAA width shoes. She insisted on buying shoes at Metzler's in Nappanee that I thought looked awful. I teased her about wearing granny shoes, but she said they were comfortable and that's what mattered.

Beth never let pain stop her. Once, she fell getting into the car, landing on her hands and hyper-extending her right wrist. It hurt badly and became swollen. After a couple days, she asked me to look at it. An X-ray showed a broken wrist. Her injury shows two things—how stoic Beth was, and how inconsiderate I was for not noticing her distress.

Beth collected unusual things. While Dwight D. Eisenhower was president, we took a vacation trip to Washington, D.C. On the way back, we toured the Gettysburg battlefield and visited the Eisenhower farm. We admired Ike, so Beth wanted a souvenir. Along the roadside at Ike's place, Beth jumped out of the car and went to the fence row, returning with a stone weighing about fifteen pounds. We brought it back, and it's still at the Lodge. Beth took pride in pointing out her "Eisenhower stone" to visitors.

Beth was fond of Lemans peppermint candy, made in Bremen. She kept a supply to give away and supplied my office. We first bought a couple of bags at a time, but demand eventually reached a case every other week. The Lemans liked the way we used the mints and later supplied us at no cost. Representative, later Senator, Michael K Rogers had Beth count out eight mints for him before he went home to New Castle on weekends. When he finished the fourth one, he told her, he was just about home. That left four to use on his return.

Beth and I loved mushroom hunting for exercise and for the excitement in finding good ones. When we stayed overnight or weekends at the Aynes House in Brown County State Park, we hunted there and seldom were skunked. With the Roy Hirsteins of Bremen, we once went to the vicinity of Cadillac, Mich., and found about a peck of good mushrooms.

From 1964 to 1972, when I practiced solo, Beth rightfully said that she was my janitor, bookkeeper, secretary, nurse, and driver. She used great tact with my patients, who often told me how grateful they were for her advice. For example, to the mother of a small child with a 103-degree temperature, she might say, "Dr. Bowen would advise baby aspirin, a tepid sponge bath, an alcohol rub, and a cool, plain water enema." If I was expected soon, she told the mother she would have me call. If a child needed immediate attention, and I was out of town, she suggested the hospital emergency room.

Beth's genuineness and lack of pretension came through to everyone. Even after becoming first lady, she remained what she always was—a kind, considerate, helpful person, committed to family and friends, who saw everyone as an equal.

In politics and public life, Beth was my confidante and co-strategist. She never knew a stranger. She also could spot a phony a mile off. She liked to drive. I usually started out behind the wheel, but Beth took over when I got sleepy. Her foot was a bit heavier than mine, so I called her Parnelli or A. J. When we had a driver and I napped, Beth helped the driver stay alert. At political events, Beth timed my speeches so I didn't exceed my twenty-minute limit. (Beth and I waited tables, cleared and cleaned them, folded up chairs, and swept up at those events. The symbolism of this grassroots political tradition is obvious.)

While I was in the House, Beth sat in the balcony, watching, listening, and working at a needlepoint piece. As colleagues lost buttons or tore or ripped something, Beth made repairs. She always had other emergency "tools," like spot remover.

Her needlepoint, crocheting, and crewel skills are well known. Many people treasure needlepoint pieces that she gave them. Even while ill, she did needlepoint. By Christmas of 1980, she had forty-three needlepoint scenes, enough to give one to each member and former member of her staff at the Governor's Residence and my office staff.

Earlier, she was invited to contribute needlepoint to a hanging in the U.N. Building in New York City representing all nations of the world. Beth's part represents the island of Tahiti. She did needlework everywhere—in the House balcony while I was speaker, in our car on trips while I was governor, and in the hospital or at home in her last two years.

When she became Indiana's first lady, it was no surprise to me that she acquitted herself with grace, good taste, and dignity, or that she handled her new role as if born to it.

The old Governor's Mansion at 4343 North Meridian Street had fallen into such disrepair that Governor and Mrs. Whitcomb had moved to a Riley Towers suite. Beth and I lived in the same suite, but expected to eventually move back to the old mansion. However, the General Assembly created a commission to look at other options. It recommended that the state buy the former home of C. Severin Buschmann, a beautiful brick structure on 6.25 acres of wooded land on the northwest corner of 46th and Meridian streets.

Making that house into a home was no small task. With lots of help, including that of her residence secretary, Jackie Hendricks, Beth oversaw renovations. She then decorated and furnished the home, integrating fine antiques from the older mansions. Her work created a special place, decorated in good taste. Every residence guest—presidents, world figures, celebrities, political and governmental associates, friends, and family members—complimented Beth on its simple, elegant beauty. After we moved in, the commission raised some funds, and Beth convinced organizations to donate work and materials. That way, major improvements were made at no cost or minimal cost to taxpayers.

Later first ladies continued a practice that Beth started—allowing groups to use the home's public rooms. This made the residence less of a mystery to its real owners, the people. Groups could use any one of a list of pre-approved caterers, who would supply good food and clean up. The result was a wonderful social event, also at no cost to taxpayers.

The General Assembly provided funds to operate the residence, but was not inclined to make further capital outlays. Beth and I were reluctant to ask for any. If Beth were alive, she would say that better dining facilities are needed. The commission never realized its hope of raising funds for a large dining and meeting room at the rear of the residence.

After my election as governor, Beth became incredibly involved. She co-chaired the Marion County Mental Health Association's program to provide Christmas gifts to the mentally ill and WNDE's benefit for St. Jude Children's Research Hospital. She served on the President's Committee on Child Abuse and the Education Commission of the States' Advisory Committee on Child Abuse and Neglect. She was honorary fundraising chair for the Indiana Chapter of the Cystic Fibrosis Foundation. As a Riley Memorial Hospital Association board member, she was instrumental in raising funds for Camp Riley at Martinsville, which provides camping experiences for handicapped children.

This was my Beth, my love and my lady. Early in my second term, she was diagnosed with multiple myeloma, and her health began an irreversible decline.

Even as that happened, her indomitable spirit kept asserting itself. A good example is an Indiana Republican "Tribute to the Bowen Years" on December 10, 1980, just three weeks before her death. From her hospital bed, Beth helped make arrangements. Her health was so fragile that we doubted that she could make the dinner, but Beth always got done what she set out to do. With the aid of her good friend Lelia Chernish and her nurse, Mary Moffat, she got there. As Beth's wheelchair was lifted to the platform so she could sit with me, I said, "Oh, Beth," and tears began to roll. In her typical way of being concerned more about others than about herself, she asked, "Are you all right, Otie?"

At the podium, I thanked Hoosiers for giving Beth and me the opportunity to serve Indiana. I then recited this part of "Together Still," a poem by Peggy Cameron King:

> Let me hold your hand as we go down hill.
> We've shared our strength and we share it still.
> It hasn't been easy to make the climb,
> But the way was eased with your hand in mine.
> We move more slowly, but together still.
> Let me hold your hand as we go down hill.

Our sons helped Beth to the podium. Saying she wanted to talk about the original Bowen team, she introduced our sons and daughter and thanked those present for their support through the years. There was hardly a dry eye in that huge hall, for everyone knew this was her farewell. In that Christmas season, it also was in character for Beth to ask the ambulance driver to make a small detour around Monument

Circle "so I can see the beautiful lights." The driver did as asked, of course.

The day of the tribute, Jack Colwell of the South Bend *Tribune* wrote, "It is nice to know that a political marriage can work and that decent people can get ahead in politics and remain decent." We were, he said, "the same Doc and Beth Bowen who moved into the Governor's Residence eight years ago." Noting that "good fortune is not now with Beth," Jack suggested that Christmas cards be sent to her. Before they stopped coming, she received between 2,500 and 3,000 cards. We opened a few each day until she became too sick. After her death, I opened the rest, but did not finish until February 8th.

In her last month, Beth laboriously wrote out lists—birthdays and anniversaries and names, addresses, and telephone numbers that she thought I would need. On a daily basis, she proved that she could do more from a hospital bed than most people can when up and about.

In her final days, Beth told our children, "Take care of Dad. It'll be hard on him. We were so close. He'll be so lonely." Her advice to me was to "carry on for my sake and in my name. Live on and do things just the same."

On December 24th, Beth's doctors allowed her to go to our condominium for a family Christmas. Although close to death's door, she still was giving. After checking to see who was working at University Hospital, she selected flowers for the nurses, attendants, and others from the scores of bouquets and planters sent by well-wishers.

Our daughter, Judy McGrew, and her husband, Dave, could not be present, but the others came to the Knoll on Christmas Eve. The residence staff brought us a Christmas dinner. We had our family exchange. Beth wanted each boy to have one of my cowboy hats and an antique light globe from 304 North Center Street, where our children grew up. (Judy already had one of the globes.) The boys drew straws to determine who got what. Our youngest son, Rob, had been elected the previous month as a Marshall County Court judge, and my wife wanted to see him be sworn in. The next morning, with Beth holding the family Bible, I administered the oath of office.

We stayed at the condominium until Beth returned to the hospital on Saturday, December 27. Her condition quickly worsened, and I called our children back. Beth was semi-conscious when Judy arrived from the West Coast, but we feel that she recognized all her children. Her last words were, "Just keep touching me."

At 2:50 A.M. on New Year's Day, 1981, she was gone.

Tributes to Beth came from President Ford and President-Elect

Reagan, many governors, members of Congress, state officials, legislators, judges, mayors, business leaders, college and university presidents, and many other dignitaries.

On Friday, January 2, we had public calling hours at the Governor's Residence. More than 800 persons came by to pay their respects. About 175 family, friends, and government colleagues then attended a private memorial service there. Escorted by Indiana State Police officers, a hearse took Beth's casket to Bremen, where we had public calling at Mishler Funeral Home the next day. Nearly 2,500 persons paid their respects there.

About 650 persons attended her funeral at St. Paul's Lutheran Church. An honor guard of 24 state police and conservation officers lined the sanctuary. Rev. Raymond Metejka of Lawrenceburg, former pastor of St. Paul's, and Rev. David Kahlenberg, pastor of Pleasant View Lutheran Church in Indianapolis, conducted the service.

Attendees included Governor James Thompson of Illinois and his wife, Jayne; Billie Ray, wife of Governor Robert Ray of Iowa; U.S. senators Lugar and Bayh; Bayh's son, Evan, later to be Indiana's governor and a U.S. senator; Senator-Elect Quayle; Governor-Elect Orr; Lieutenant Governor-Elect Mutz; House Speaker J. Roberts Dailey; IU basketball coach Bob Knight; former governor Whitcomb; Indiana University chancellor Herman B. Wells; and many other dignitaries.

The honor guard stood at attention in parallel rows as Beth's casket was taken from the church to a waiting hearse. On the way to Bremen Cemetery, the funeral procession passed the fire station, where Bremen Fire Department members stood at attention. A sign over their quarters said, "Beth, we will miss you." At the cemetery on that severely cold winter day, Revs. Matejka and Kahlenberg conducted graveside rites.

As a doctor, I knew that multiple myeloma had made Beth's death inevitable, but accepting her passing was exceedingly difficult. Indescribable grief, heartache, and loneliness became the dreadful substitutes for her missing presence. Many people tried to help me in this period, but Beth had been such an important part of my life that there was little that anyone could do. Dr. Walter Daly, dean of the IU School of Medicine, later told me that the main causes of severe stress are a death in the family, especially the loss of a mate; a change of job; and a change of living location. In an eight-day span, I had experienced all three.

Nearly two months after Beth's death, I received a letter from Rose Hochstetler of Bremen, whose husband had died of a massive heart attack on July 24, 1980. She asked if we could talk at some point about why her doctor had not allowed her to see her husband as he lay dying. I wrote back that I would stop by when in Bremen.

Born at Plymouth on August 13, 1923, Rose was the daughter of Lem and Bertha Crothers. Reared at LaPaz in northern Marshall County, she graduated from high school in 1941 and the next year married Merland Hochstetler, a graduate of Bremen High School and South Bend College of Commerce. They had four children—Alton, Danny, Mrs. Jack (Cynthia) Garner, and Mrs. Richard (Donell) Housel. I delivered three of Rose's children. Rose and her daughter Cindy came to the funeral home during calling hours for Beth to offer their condolences. Seeing that Rose still was grieving, I offered her my sympathies.

In Bremen the Saturday before Easter, I drove by Rose's home. There were several cars there, so I didn't stop. In Bremen the next Saturday (May 2, 1981), I drove by her home. She did not appear to have company, so I stopped. She answered the door in blue jeans. Her first words—"Oh my goodness, I was expecting someone else"—made it obvious that she was shocked to see me. (I had made no advance arrangements.) Rose was expecting her insurance man. I remained in the living room while Rose talked with him.

I told her that I couldn't understand why she was kept from the hospital room while her husband was dying. An antiques dealer, Rose showed me her beautiful old lamps, plates, and furniture. Having been exposed to a beautiful lady, albeit an old friend and patient, I decided I wanted to see her again. After a speech in Elkhart, I returned to Bremen and surprised her with a call about 8:30 P.M. I told her I'd like to drop out and talk to her again. When I arrived, she was working at a card table on property assessment figures, because she was a deputy to her sister, the township trustee and assessor.

The loss of our first spouses had devastated us both. Our aching hearts and loneliness led to a wonderful relationship. I started coming home every weekend that I could, seeing Rose each time. We kept our developing relationship to ourselves. On our first "night out," we went to Win Schulers at St. Joseph, Michigan, but we couldn't get seated, so we had our first dinner at the Navajo Inn. Between weekends, we called each other so frequently that I sent her money because I knew she couldn't afford the phone tolls we were running up.

Soon we were talking about a future together. I proposed at the L&K Restaurant at Plymouth. At our age, we decided, it made no sense to wait. We wanted as many years together as possible. We sought counsel from my minister, Rev. Kahlenberg. He advised us to marry as soon as we were comfortable with the idea.

The evening before our wedding, we had dinner at the Columbia Club for thirty-five people, including our families. That night, I stayed with my friends Brad and Donna Grubbs, and Rose stayed at the Knoll with my daughter, Judy McGrew, and her husband, Dave. Brad and I teased Rose mercilessly about a bachelor's party that night. Until I leveled with her, because one can't fib to a new bride, Rose wasn't certain that there was no party.

With our children—her four and my four—standing up with us, we were married on September 25, 1981, at Pleasant View Lutheran Church in a ceremony extensively covered by the news media. Governor Orr, Lieutenant Governor Mutz, and scores of other state officials and former colleagues attended. Rose was scared to death, but you wouldn't have known it.

After a brunch, we drove to the Munster home of my friend Joe Kotso, who had arranged for a limousine to take us to Chicago for a honeymoon weekend at the Continental Hotel. (Until then, Rose had never stayed in a hotel.) Champagne was waiting in our room. At dinner, strolling violinists played requests. Rose was so excited—and tired—that she ate only a few bites of the specially prepared dinner. That so concerned the maitre d' that he became worried about whether the food had been prepared correctly.

The next morning, we walked in the Loop. Rose was apprehensive when we went to the top of the Sears Tower, but she tolerated it well. In mid-afternoon, our limousine took us back to Munster. We drove to Donnybrook, and the next morning to Indianapolis. We lived at the Knoll, and I taught at the School of Medicine for the next four-plus years.

During her first marriage, Rose rarely got to bed before midnight or 1 A.M. For years, she fed and milked fifty-six cows day and night, climbing into the silo to fork down feed. Chemicals used to clean and sterilize the milking equipment cracked the skin on her hands and made them sore. For a South Bend chicken and egg route, she butchered chickens and carried crates of eggs up and down the steps of the basement, where she stored and graded them. She hoed weeds from the corn and bean fields in the hot summer.

Rose was a meticulous housekeeper. She wanted every piece of clothing cleaned and pressed. (She even ironed her babies' cloth diapers.) I teased her that I was lucky to get out of my work clothes before they went in the machine. She washed dishes before they went in the dishwasher. She wouldn't keep leftovers beyond a second day.

Rose loved many things—cleanliness, neatness, courteousness, promptness, flowers, birds, squirrels, gospel music, potpourri, scented lotions, good-smelling decorative soaps, perfumes, jewelry, the magazines *Victoria* and *Bon Appétit*, mail-order catalogs, and beautiful but not truly expensive clothes. Shy and quiet, she disliked impoliteness, vulgarity, or being "out front." Proud of her daughters, who were only eighteen months apart, she sewed lookalike clothes for them and for herself. She still found time to be an antiques dealer, teach ceramics, serve as an assistant township assessor, and be a 4-H leader, a Sunday school superintendent, and a wonderful mother.

Rose had never had an opportunity to do things. She had rarely been outside the Bremen area or attended any kind of event. She had been to the Indiana State Fair once. She had never flown, never been on a long trip, never seen a live theater performance. As a result, our first years of marriage were filled with new experiences for her.

As onlookers, we attended President Reagan's second inauguration in 1985. It was memorable because the temperature was a bone-chilling 10 to 15 degrees below zero. A fire alarm went off about 10:30 P.M. at our Holiday Inn, midway between the Capitol and the White House. Rose and I pulled clothes over our pajamas. Guests who didn't do the same had a rough time in the cold. It turned out to be a false alarm.

Inauguration Day was so cold that President Reagan canceled the parade. We watched the ceremony, held in the Capitol Rotunda, on TV. A friend, WISH-TV co-anchor Mike Ahern, was unprepared for the weather. I loaned him an extra pair of long underwear.

Rose saw her first play at Beef & Boards, an Indianapolis dinner theater, and liked it so much that we bought season tickets. We saw Indianapolis Symphony performances, attended Indiana Repertory Theater plays, and went to the circus at Market Square Arena.

After becoming H&HS secretary, I got Kennedy Center tickets, and we used the president's box. It had eight seats in the center of the balcony, a private sitting room, a restroom, and a pantry stocked with soft drinks and wine. Our favorite play was the musical version of Victor Hugo's *Les Misérables*, which we saw twice. The sets were imposing. The play was long, but it was the most powerful I ever saw.

We took in the Indiana State Fair, going to country and western shows, watching 4-H auctions, attending 4-H dinners, visiting the senior citizens building, seeing exhibits, and watching horse- and tractor-pulling contests and horse racing. (Later we were invited back to the Fairgrounds to have my handprint and name enshrined in concrete in front of the Coliseum as a "State Fair legend.")

Sports are one of my passions, so Rose quickly got initiated into athletics. We saw Michael Jordan hit the winning basket against

Georgetown in the 1982 NCAA finals at the New Orleans Superdome. Dorothy and Bob Osborn of Culver stayed at our hotel and we toured the city together. (Bourbon Street shocked my innocent Rose.) While we were there, the Indiana high school basketball finals were in progress. I called my mother at Leiters Ford to see how Plymouth was doing. "It's in the second overtime now," she said. Calling back, I learned that Plymouth had won the title. That launched the college and NBA career of Scott Skiles, the tourney hero.

Rose enjoyed her first 500-Mile Race in 1982, when Gordon Johncock barely beat Rick Mears. We were across from the pits, five or six rows up, a great vantage point.

We saw lots more basketball, including most IU home games. While I was at Purdue University to help dedicate a building authorized while I was governor, I also spoke to students, and we attended a gala honoring Purdue's music greats, including Purdue Glee Club singers. (One was Ken Knowles, who sang at Beth's funeral, at Rose's and my wedding, and later, sadly, at Rose's funeral.) We stayed for the next day's IU-Purdue basketball game. We were surrounded by noisy Purdue students and supporters when we found our seats near the top at the end of the gym. I tell my Purdue friends that I'm for the Boilermakers every game except one, but I own too many bricks on the IU campus not to cheer for the Hoosiers. That day, I think, my Purdue friends still were trying to deliver a message.

We saw the U.S. Olympic basketball team's game at the Hoosier Dome, attended by 67,000 people, the largest crowd ever to watch an indoor basketball game. Bob Knight coached the team, composed of pro and college players, including Steve Alford. At a pre-game reception, Coach Knight gave Rose a T-shirt on which was printed "USA, World's Largest Basketball Game, July 9, 1984, Hoosier Dome, Indianapolis, Indiana."

Rose enjoyed doing things for kids, especially my grandchildren. At Bremen, we dressed up for Halloween, although we lived out of town and expected only Rob and Patty's children and two or three others. When we met those little trick-or-treaters at the door, the surprised and half-scared look in their eyes was a treat. One year we dressed as a clown and a witch, another as a hobo and a flapper.

Our lives changed dramatically on November 5, 1985, when President Reagan asked me to serve as H&HS secretary. Two days later, I stood at the president's side as he announced my nomination. By mid-December, the U.S. Senate had confirmed me. We soon moved into a beautiful first-floor condominium at Porto Vecchio on the Potomac at the southern edge of old Alexandria, Virginia. (Our furniture did not arrive until December 22nd, so we actually stayed the first few days with Don and Mary Newman.)

My bashful Rose first learned about the demands of public life in our high-profile marriage. When I arrived home after President Reagan had announced my nomination and was greeted by a swarm of media, she learned a bit more. The thought of becoming part of Washington society scared her, but she had a natural graciousness and handled herself well at formal White House dinners and many Health & Human Services functions.

Rose appeared with me at confirmation hearings. With my four children and one of her daughters, she was there on December 20, 1985, when I was sworn in at the White House.

She was pleased with our condominium, which had twenty-four-hour security, inside parking, a doorman, and limousine service for the residents. To and from work, it was about twenty minutes in moderate traffic and an hour to an hour and a half in heavy traffic. Our condo had two bedrooms, a living-dining room, two bathrooms, basement storage space, and an outside balcony on two sides. A driver and security man picked me up each morning in a black Lincoln. (I paid taxes on this Cabinet "perk.") Rose could go with me anytime. If I was not in the car, drivers could take her only to official functions. Rose was a favorite of the drivers, who told me she "was just plain nice" and "not a bit snooty."

Barbara Bush once invited Rose to a luncheon at the vice president's home. Always on time or early (neither of which is common in Washington), Rose was the first to arrive, and she had to summon up her courage to ring the doorbell. Mrs. Bush invited her in and showed her around, even taking her upstairs to see Barbara's huge needlepoint rug. The luncheon was pleasant and enjoyable, Rose said, all the more so because she got to feed crumbs under the table to Millie, the famous Bush dog. She and Mrs. Bush became good friends. (Within the administration, Rose became famous for quipping that she was the only Cabinet officer's wife who had ever milked a cow.)

Via TV, we saw Indiana University win the NCAA basketball championship in 1987. President Reagan then invited the Hoosiers to the White House. Because I was an IU graduate and Coach Knight's friend, the president included me in his private meeting with team members, President John Ryan, Athletic Director Ralph Floyd, and Bob Knight. In the Rose Garden, the president and Knight spoke briefly. Rose watched from the front row, probably amused by the sight of her five-foot, six-and-a-half-inch husband among those young giants. She earlier had been in the welcoming party at Washington National Airport and later was the hostess for an H&HS reception for the Hoosiers.

Rose never enjoyed flying, but she became reasonably good at it. Cabinet members and their wives once were invited to welcome President and Mrs. Reagan back from a successful meeting with Mikhail Gorbachev. We were to fly from the Pentagon on a military helicopter to Andrews Air Force Base outside Washington. This huge "bird" dwarfed all the choppers in which I had flown as governor. Rose eyed it suspiciously. There was a reason for her concern—she could get carsick riding in the back seat.

On takeoff, the pilot made dizzying moves around obstacles. Even when the helicopter was high enough to go more or less straight, its tail swayed back and forth with a "whip cracker" effect. On arrival at Andrews, Rose was dizzy and a bit nauseous. Barbara Bush greeted us at the reception room, offering Rose a cookie and a soft drink. Rose paled and sat down. With Mrs. Bush's help and sympathy, Rose recovered, and both of us were able to join in greeting President and Mrs. Reagan when Air Force One landed. However, I called my office and had them send a driver and car to take us home.

Rose and I traveled extensively while I was in the Cabinet. We visited Puerto Rico. We were in Hawaii three times. We saw China, Japan, Hong Kong, and India. We were in Paris, Vienna, and London. We visited Germany, Austria, Luxembourg, Lichtenstein, and Switzerland. We saw the Taj Mahal in India and walked on the Great Wall of China. We stayed at the New Delhi home of the U.S. ambassador to India, had breakfast at the Tokyo home of the U.S. ambassador to Japan, lunch at the home of the U.S. ambassador to Hong Kong, and dinner at the Beijing home of the U.S. ambassador to China. We stayed at the U.S. ambassador's home in Paris and attended a formal dinner at Versailles Palace. While I was in meetings, Rose went to a Christian Dior fashion show.

She handled all the pomp and ceremony with grace and graciousness.

Fourteen months after my federal service ended, we returned to Washington to unveil my official portrait at H&HS's huge Hubert Humphrey Building. (Secretaries' portraits hang permanently in each federal agency's principal Washington buildings.)

We sat on a platform with Vice President Quayle, Secretary Louis Sullivan, Mrs. Sullivan, and the artist, Everett Raymond Kintsler of

New York City. (Kintsler previously had painted my official portrait as governor.) Rose told Dan that she had kidded me about coming back to Washington for my hanging. The vice president asked, "You really didn't say that, did you?" Rose relished repeating the story and the line I used that day about life's three stages (youth, middle age, and "gee, you're looking good").

We hoped for many years of retirement after coming home to Bremen. We soon learned that it was not to be.

On April 17, 1991, Rose had chest distress. She usually had her annual chest X-rays and mammograms at the IU Medical Center, so we went there. The X-rays showed a change in a spot on the upper lobe of a lung and revealed that her heart shadow was one and a half times normal size. (First detected in 1984, the spot had been diagnosed as histoplasmosis. Regular X-rays since then had shown no change.)

At the South Bend Clinic two days later, an echocardiogram showed pericardial fluid. A bone scan and needle biopsy of the lung were done. The biopsy revealed cancer. A lobectomy and lymph gland biopsy confirmed the diagnosis. Rose's chances of living were virtually zero. I warned her children to expect the worst.

Rose suffered terribly from the lobectomy. Over the last three weeks of her life, we had to use pain medications and oxygen continuously.

On December 12th, we went to Nappanee to get a portrait taken. (In that picture, her face shows pain, but she looks beautiful.) She wanted me to get a new suit for Christmas, so we went to Plymouth. She walked with me about a half-block to a clothing store and helped me choose a suit, tie, and socks. We went for a Christmas Eve dinner at my son Rob's home in Bremen, but she got sick and couldn't eat, and I had to take her home.

Our minister, Rev. Roger Rohde, came often with his wife, who sang Rose's most beloved songs to her, including her favorite, "We'll Say Good Night Here, but Good Morning Up There." We took Holy Communion often, the last time on Wednesday, January 15th. The day before she died, Rev. Rohde and his wife, Rose's four children, and I were with Rose. Struggling for breath and full of pain medications, she did not respond to questions. We decided to recite the Lord's Prayer. To our astonishment, Rose recited—very audibly—every word of that comforting Scripture with us.

Through her illness, Rose asked me to "keep holding my hand until I'm gone." She loved life and wanted to live. Over and over, she said, "I'm not afraid to die, but I can't bear the thought of leaving you alone."

She said these things as she suffered dreadful pain, panted for breath, and was dry, feverish, and thirsty. Near the end, while we were alone, I'm sure I heard her whisper, "I'm ready."

At 7:20 A.M. on January 21, 1992, her suffering ended.

Her funeral was held three days later, at St. Paul's Lutheran Church. Many people later said that they had never seen a more meaningful service. Rev. Rohde's sermon was superb. The eulogy by Rev. David Kahlenberg, who had married us slightly more than ten years earlier, was remarkable for its description of Rose as a person. A song by Mrs. Rohde and three songs by Ken Knowles, ending with "The Lord's Prayer," were unforgettable. It was cold and snowing as the funeral procession made the short trip to the Bremen Cemetery. For me, the graveside ceremony was almost unbearable.

The desolate and sad period after Rose's death perhaps was equaled by only two other periods in my life—when I was away for three years in World War II and did not see Beth or my son Rick until he was nearly two years old, and when Beth died. Caring for Rose had consumed almost every minute for months. Suddenly she was gone, and what had filled my days and nights and occupied my mind no longer was required.

Few men are fortunate to have two wonderful wives. The Lord has been especially good to me, allowing me to find Carol Lynn (Hahn) Flosenzier Mikesell as my third wife. One of my patients in Bremen, she was the daughter of Ernest S. and Mary Jane (Carl) Hahn and a Bremen High School graduate. By her first husband, Richard A. Flosenzier, she had two children, Vance Flosenzier and Mrs. Ronald (Mindy L. Flosenzier) Welty.

Carol was rather non-political, but a $25-per-person fundraiser I hosted for Kent Adams of Bremen, a Senate candidate, brought us together. Mrs. Adams's sister, Sue Charlton, was selling fundraiser tickets because Kent's district included the Warsaw area. Sue knew that Carol, a vice president and trust officer at First National Bank at Warsaw, had been born and raised at Bremen, and that I had delivered her two children. She asked Carol to buy a ticket, and Carol decided to attend.

I had not seen Carol for thirty years, but I immediately recognized her as the somewhat bashful but attractive lady who had been my patient. I also recalled that I had taken care of her when a bleeding peptic ulcer required thirteen blood transfusions.

Eight months after Rose's death, I was leading a lonesome life. At the fundraiser, I learned that Carol also was alone. For weeks, I pondered calling her. Finally, on a Saturday night, I did. Before letting her talk, I apologized and said I knew nothing of her situation but would like to invite her to dinner. She said she was unattached. Responding to my invitation to have dinner, she said, "I think I'd like that."

We made arrangements for the next Saturday and went to Francisco's in Fort Wayne. We had lots of conversation about long-ago events and thirty years of catching up to do. It was such an enjoyable evening that we forgot that it was rainy and chilly outside on that October night. I asked Carol if I could call again. She said yes. Our relationship quickly developed beyond friendship, and soon we were discussing marriage.

When our plans became public, I was criticized for planning to remarry. The criticism bothered me, but I felt that no one could rightly criticize until they had suffered through losses and loneliness like I had endured. Remarriage in no way belittled my first two wives or our wonderful lives together. I sought advice from my old friend, Rev. David Kahlenberg, pastor of Pleasant View Lutheran Church in Indianapolis. He said that I should consider remarriage to be a tribute to Beth and Rose, because my marriages to them had been so satisfying that living without a mate was unbearable.

Carol fills my days with loving companionship, laughter, and joy. We say we rescued each other from loneliness. As much as I appreciated and loved Beth and Rose and thanked God for the special privilege of being their husband, I cherish my present marriage. Carol and I are grateful that our children heartily endorsed our marriage.

In a ceremony attended by immediate family, Rev. Kahlenberg married Carol and me on February 5, 1993, in front of the huge fireplace in the Lodge's great room. My son Rob was best man, and Carol's daughter Mindy was bridesmaid. A former patient, Louella Jensen, provided the music on our electric organ, and a recording of "The Lord's Prayer" by my old friend Ken Knowles provided an appropriate ending to the ceremony.

About fourteen months after our marriage, Carol resigned her bank position and retired.

We share many interests. We love sports, especially basketball, and attend IU home basketball and football games and Bremen High School athletic events. We watch as grandsons Chris and Andrew play soccer, basketball, and baseball, and as granddaughter Betsy plays soccer and T-ball. We enjoy reading. Before retiring, we play gin rummy, keeping a running score. I usually win a little more than I lose, but Carol is a good sport. She knits and crochets, especially while riding in the car. Outdoor activities—gardening, raising flowers, lawn care, and bicycling with Betsy—are her main love.

Being retired, I think, has made me a better husband to Carol than I was able to be for Beth and Rose. I have more time to work at being a good husband, do enjoyable things together with Carol, and travel. Since Carol also is retired, it works both ways.

I've been blessed with three grandchildren and two great-grand-children since retiring. At last count, this made sixteen grandchildren and two great-grandchildren between us. We keep a card file so we can keep track of birthdays and anniversaries.

I've tried to reduce the number of meetings, talks, and appearances, and I've succeeded about as much as I could expect. I still participate in community activities and remain on the periphery of politics, occa-sionally advising candidates and would-be candidates.

Carol and I take a big traveling vacation a year and several mini-ones. We have been to Singapore (to visit my daughter and her fam-ily), Alaska, and Switzerland. We took a Baltic and North Sea journey. In 1998, we sailed from Vienna on the Danube River to its mouth, ending up in Istanbul. (All were beautiful, but I've seen enough tem-ples, mosques, and cathedrals to last me a while.) On the Danube trip, we visited Belgrade and traveled under and over the bridges blown up in the Kosovo situation.

In January and early February of 1999, we motored through Colo-rado, Arizona, New Mexico, and Texas, staying off the interstates and traveling on back roads. We spent each night in a different town, saw beautiful places, visited museums, and traipsed down trails. There is so much to see there that we took a second trip west in the fall of 1999, going through Wisconsin and Minnesota to South Dakota, Wyoming, Idaho, and Montana.

With children and grandchildren in Wisconsin, Massachusetts, Kentucky, Alabama, Pennsylvania, North Carolina, California, and Indiana, we have many other places to visit.

Retirement has been a satisfying phase of my life, but so was every phase, except for Beth's and Rose's deaths. Retirement offers many small rewards—you don't have to shave or wear a necktie every day. I still threaten to use my neckties to tie up my tomato plants. It's great not to have to set the alarm every night, and to finally have time to read some of the huge number of books I've accumulated.

I've had several surgeries in my life. I had an appendectomy as a high school junior, two surgeries while I was practicing, and two painful but not major surgeries as governor. One of the latter was a tonsillectomy. I was the oldest person on whom my surgeon had ever performed that surgery. Two years ago, I had a kidney removed after doctors found early-stage cancer. I am fully recovered, with no ill effects.

My days as a retiree are about as busy as those I had in public life, but I'm outdoors a lot now, mowing, sawing up limbs and fallen trees for fireplace wood, planting and tending a garden, and running back and forth for groceries, mail, and gas. With our special "zero turn" mowers, mowing our five acres is not an overwhelming job. I get on my 60-inch mower and Carol gets on her 42-inch one, and we chase each other around the yard.

We have about 250 trees and bushes. I planted nearly all of them over 27 years. The 75 varieties include a raintree, plum leaf beech, hemlock, lily of the valley, bald cypress, mountain ash, dawn redwood, persimmon, marine locust, magnolia, flowering crabs, pears, firs, dogwoods, and redbuds. In late April and early May, the yard is a big bouquet. I have 25 black walnut trees for the squirrels, friends who like black walnuts, and me. (I thought everyone liked black walnuts, but it's not so.) We plant lots of flowers. We put in a big garden, for exercise and for the joy of planting and tending it, and to allow us to supply friends and neighbors from it. Rabbits, coons, groundhogs, and deer are our biggest problem, but they have to eat, too.

I sporadically play the organ and piano. Occasionally I dabble in the kitchen. Carol encourages my kitchen forays and is very tolerant of my mistakes.

Except for news and sports, we don't watch TV—too many programs are little more than sexual trash and violence.

I'm grateful to my God for granting me a long life and a keener sense of relationship with and dependence upon Him. Having survived the removal of that cancerous kidney, and having recuperated from the loss of two wonderful mates from cancer, I'm especially grateful to my Maker for allowing me to otherwise enjoy life as a retiree.

❧ 22 ❧

Presidents and People I've Known

IT'S BEEN MY good fortune to know and work with or for several presidents.

My encounters with President Richard M. Nixon were in a governmental context—a governor interacting with a president, usually at a governors' meeting. I mentioned my first meeting with him—a campaign "photo op" visit to the White House.

President Gerald R. Ford, who ranks at the top of my list of presidents for his thoughtfulness, common sense, and courage, was and is a good friend. A sports enthusiast, President Ford wanted to see the 500-Mile Race. Beth and I invited him to stay at the Governor's Residence.

Through no fault of the president, getting ready for his visit was an ordeal. His security detail strung lights all over the grounds, inspected and searched the residence, and even questioned Alvania West, our cook, who was already overwhelmed by the prospect of preparing breakfast and dinner for the president.

Because Jerry Ford is a tall man—about six feet, four inches—his advance people and his personal valet insisted that the bed in which he was to sleep was too short. So we hustled to get an oversized bed.

Upon arrival, the president asked if I could find a barber. At the neighborhood shop I used, my barber was a lady, and I suggested her. A Secret Service check showed that she had been cited once for some minor thing. Before they would let me ask her to cut President Ford's hair, I had to vouch for her. She was overwhelmed by the prospect of coming to the Governor's Residence, let alone giving the president a haircut, but she did a good job.

President Ford ate his breakfast with Beth, our sons and daughter and their spouses, and me. Someone supplied us with a half-dozen 500-Mile Race jackets. We wore them as President Ford posed for pictures with us and with Alvania and her husband, Blanche.

We obtained Gasoline Alley and pit passes so that the president could be there as the drivers and their crews made final race preparations. At the time, A. J. Foyt was "king" of the track. He let President Ford sit in his vehicle, and it was a tight fit because of Mr. Ford's size. (A. J. is one of my heroes. A week earlier, he had taken Beth and me for a ride around the track in his personal car, a convertible, at speeds between 80 and 100 miles and hour, coming within inches of the wall coming out of every turn. What an experience!)

I've mentioned the meeting at which President Jimmy Carter complimented me on Indiana's actions in the coal strike. My relationship with President Carter was unusual and interesting. At one point in his term, I was the National Governors Association chair. This led to many contacts, and I became President Carter's "token Republican." I don't mean that in a derogatory way, but I usually was the only Republican in the meetings to which he invited me. President Carter always was friendly and a gentleman.

While NGA chair, I was invited to Camp David for Mr. Carter's much-publicized "economic summit." This came at a time of raging inflation and high interest rates. We flew to Camp David and returned to Washington on the president's special helicopter. Once again, I was outnumbered politically. Little business was conducted, but I had a chance to become better acquainted with President Carter, his wife, Rosalyn, their daughter, Amy, and the other governors. In the dining room, I sat at President Carter's table, with Amy on my left and Rosalyn on my right. New York governor Hugh Carey and Georgia governor George Busbee and I occupied one of the three-bedroom cottages at Camp David. The president and his family used a larger one.

I've mentioned many meetings with President Reagan. I admired him immensely and found it exhilarating to sit by him at Cabinet meetings. On one occasion, I was called to his White House living room to report on our studies on drugs. Nancy Reagan and the official photographer were the only ones there. The meeting lasted about five minutes.

It was difficult to know Nancy Reagan well. I have no reason to think, however, that she needed to know me or believe that she intended to give the impression that she was difficult to know. It was just the way she was.

I was with President George Bush a few times, none of them substantive. As vice president, Mr. Bush accepted my invitation to lunch following a concert in the Hubert H. Humphrey Building's auditorium by the Dimensions in Brass, a musical group from Marion College, now Indiana Wesleyan University.

I first became acquainted with President Bill Clinton while he was governor of Arkansas. My impressions were that he was a very bright young man who had an opinion on every subject and expressed every one of them. The way he courted the national media made it obvious that he was angling for higher office. When Chelsea was born, Beth made her a little outfit and sent it to the Clintons. I don't believe they ever acknowledged its receipt. When I was H&HS secretary, Bill Clinton was the National Governors Association chair. The entire agenda for one of the NGA's Washington meetings focused almost exclusively on welfare and Medicaid. As a result, Governor Clinton came to my office on several occasions. We even flew together in a small plane to Detroit for a meeting.

It's unfortunate that President Clinton could not control his amorous activities. In my opinion, he is a master politician. Had he had more self-control, he could have been more effective and would be remembered for more uplifting achievements.

I became well acquainted with Midwestern governors. The two I admired most were Robert Ray of Iowa and William Milliken of Michigan, both Republicans. Our philosophy and approach to governing were quite similar. Another Midwestern governor, the colorful James Rhodes of Ohio, a Republican, came from a different mold. He spoke out on almost everything, sometimes using language that his colleagues considered inappropriate. However, he was effective, and one couldn't help but like and admire him for telling it like he thought it was.

Perhaps the least liked of the many governors with whom I served was Jerry Brown of California, a Democrat. At our meetings, he positioned himself so that the news media would notice him, and he attended only those sessions at which he had the opportunity to be the center of attention. I don't recall a substantive conversation with him.

A highlight of my tenure as governor came after a Republican Governors Association conference at Austin, Texas, at which former secretary of state Henry Kissinger had wowed that audience of somewhat hardened politicians. Beth and I got to ride back to Indianapolis in a small private plane with Mr. Kissinger. He was not particularly talkative, but he responded to our questions. His deep, accented voice sounded the same to me sitting beside him as it did in a news conference or other event.

I could mention many other politicians and celebrities, but there is a time to quit throwing around names, and this is it.

There is one other person, not in politics, with whom I have been identified for years. Our relationship developed out of my love for basketball, the fact that my Dad was a coach and I was raised with a basketball in my hand, and the fact that I am an Indiana University alumnus.

My association with Bob Knight goes back many years. In my opinion, he is one of the most misunderstood persons ever to coach a major college basketball program. Coach Knight is two different individuals. One side of him shows when he's coaching, the other when he's off the basketball floor. In practice and at games, he's intense. That may be a fault, but who can fault his success? It's his way.

My only suggestion—if he were to ask me—would be that he avoid using so many four-letter words. However, I haven't been asked and don't expect to be. If I butted in, his response probably would be that I should stick to delivering babies and political endeavors and leave the coaching to him. Such a response would be right on target.

I like and admire Bob Knight, not only for being a master coach but also for his numerous philanthropic acts. I could mention many, but he prefers anonymity.

❧ 23 ❧

Final Thoughts

At this point in my life, it's appropriate to ask myself what I have really accomplished, whether my effort to become a doctor was worthwhile, and whether submitting myself to the rigors of politics and public service was worth it.

Looking at where I've been, the people I've met, and the things I've done, I have absolutely no regrets. It's been a wonderful life and a great ride.

I've been permitted to serve in two noble professions—the practice of medicine and the world of politics and governmental service. My experiences and satisfactions in both fields make it easy for me to urge those with similar interests to pursue them vigorously.

At a time when I am in my eighties, the world is full of uncertainty, but it has always been so. None of us can know where another Iraq or Kosovo festers, or how it may affect our lives and those of our children, our grandchildren, and more distant generations.

Our nation and our state still have major problems. Drug use and crime, which are related, and the pollution of our virtues and values, symbolized by rampant pornography and violence on television, remain challenges. With such unsolved problems at home, we still foolishly persist in trying to police the world.

Rather than dwelling on negatives, I prefer to argue that they are outnumbered by the positives. We are on the verge of solving some of the world's biggest headaches—the causes and cures for cancer and AIDS, for example. With the use of tobacco products likely to decline dramatically, and with better knowledge of the importance of a good diet and healthy environment to personal health, I expect future generations to live longer.

I am pleased to have made a small contribution to a better life and future for Hoosiers and Americans. Persons my age supposedly find it difficult to be positive about the future, but that's not true for me. I have faith in the inherent wisdom of Hoosiers and Americans, and I believe that today's leaders and those who will emerge tomorrow will make the right decisions for their times and circumstances.

My fondest hope is that the Good Lord gives me a few years of the new millennium so that I may see wonders yet to unfold and experience the bright future that lies just ahead.

Index